ALEXANDER VON HUMBOLDT

How the Most Famous Scientist of the Romantic Age
Found the Soul of Nature

MAREN MEINHARDT

Published in Great Britain under the title *A Longing for Wide and Unknown Things* by C. Hurst & Co. (Publishers) Ltd.

Published in North America in 2019 by

BlueBridge

An imprint of
United Tribes Media Inc.
Katonah, New York

www.bluebridgebooks.com

ISBN: 9781629190198

Library of Congress Control Number: 2019948096

Jacket design by Cynthia Dunne
Cover art: Friedrich Georg Weitsch, Portrait of Alexander von Humboldt
(1806). Photo Credit: akg-images
Text design by Cynthia Dunne

Printed in the United States of America

10 9 8 7 6 5 4 3 2 1

For Iona and Mary

Contents

The young Humboldt

The chateau at Tegel

The interior of the crater of Pico del Teide, Tenerife

Passionflower (Passiflora ligularis)

Golden-backed uakari, Cacajao melanocephalus (Cacajao monkey, Simia melanocephala)

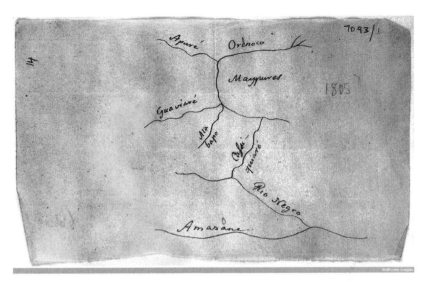

Sketch of the Orinoco basin: Orinoco-Casiquiare-Amazon River-System,
drawn by Humboldt in 1799

The rope bridge near Penipe

Inti-Guaicu, the 'Sun Rock'

A raft on the Guayas river

The house Humboldt thought of as the highest habitation in the world,
on the slopes of the Antisana

An engraving of Cotopaxi based on a drawing by Humboldt

Cross section through South America based on the Chimborazo

'Evening lectures with King Frederick William IV of Prussia', with
Alexander von Humboldt, Friedrich Karl von Savigny, Prince William
(the future emperor)

Introduction

In August 1804, on his return from his great journey to the Americas, Alexander von Humboldt was very much the hero of the hour. After five years of travelling, his coffers were full of the scientific treasures of the New World, and regular bulletins about his progress, published in the papers, had ensured that his exploits had not gone unappreciated by the public. The thirty-four-year-old Humboldt—tanned, confident, and gifted with social ease—had, everybody knew, climbed the highest mountain in the world, the Chimborazo in the Andes. He had walked in untouched forests, spoken to the people who lived there, and discovered a secret natural canal, the Casiquiare, that linked the great water-systems of the Amazon and the Orinoco. He would have returned to Europe some months earlier had not Thomas Jefferson, president of the United States, personally asked to make his acquaintance and to profit from his advice.

Alexander von Humboldt was the most celebrated scientist of the nineteenth century. Jefferson called Humboldt 'one of the greatest ornaments of the age.'[1] Charles Darwin took a copy of Humboldt's account of his travels in South America along on his voyage on the *Beagle* and declared, 'my whole course of life is due to having read & reread as a youth his *Personal Narrative*.'[2] Edgar Allan Poe dedicated a poem to Humboldt, Lord Byron mocked him in one of his, and the great German poet Goethe invoked him in a novel.[3]

An astonishing number of places and things have been named after Humboldt, more, in fact, than after any other human being. Just a small selection includes an ocean current, three counties (in California, Iowa, and Nevada), several universities, an oak, a penguin, a squid, an asteroid, and a crater on the moon.

And yet, the fabric of Humboldt's life does not settle easily into a narrative defined by superlative achievements and public honours. Here, after all, is a man who recoiled in dread when told that a statue was to be erected in his honour. What is more, many of the claims made for him don't quite hold up when pressed into the framework of a heroic narrative.

The Chimborazo, of course, turned out not to be the highest mountain in the world at all. And while Humboldt had probably climbed to a greater height than anybody before him, he did not reach the summit, but had to turn back at around 5,600 metres. The existence of the Casiquiare canal had not only been known to local people, but also to the Académie française, thanks to reports from the explorer Charles-Marie de La Condamine, who had described it in 1745. The claim that is sometimes made for Humboldt—that he anticipated the discovery of the theory of evolution—distorts his vision, and sells short its distinctiveness. While Darwin did cite Humboldt's account of his travels as a personal inspiration, Humboldt's interest in unity in nature was in the tradition of Goethe's search for an underlying synthetic plan, a project fundamentally different from Darwin's theory of evolution by natural selection.[4] (An eventual encounter between the two men in 1842 failed to reveal much common ground: Darwin reported later that he could not remember anything particular about their conversation, except that Humboldt had been 'very cheerful and talked much.'[5])

If we change the focus and turn to presenting a man whose contradictions and ambiguous achievements are a function of his time, then a more nuanced, as well as a truer and more interesting picture emerges. Humboldt's life was deeply in tune with the most significant and ambitious themes of early German Romanticism. It was an exceptional life, lived in no less exceptional times.

German Romanticism was a heady movement. The Enlightenment had brought about a weakening of religious and societal restrictions on a scale that had not been seen before. At the same time, the

Romantic focus on the individual placed a new value on feeling, legitimising the pursuit of personal needs and desires. With established ways of living often deeply unsatisfying, German Romantics discovered the thrill of living differently. There were new and often daring experimental set-ups, aimed at fashioning ways of life that better chimed with people's ideas of themselves than those prescribed for them by a still restrictive social order. In Berlin, salons sprang up, enthusiastically attended by the young Humboldt, where different segments of society mixed. People entertained the idea of trying out triangular arrangements, as did Humboldt's friend and mentor Georg Forster, who lived—for a while—with his wife, Therese, and her lover. Women rebelled against the idea that they had to persevere with unsuitable and often loveless marriages, and, if they found the economic means of escaping them, they did at times. Caroline Schelling (née Michaelis) and Dorothea Schlegel (née Mendelssohn)—both women of letters and part of Humboldt's circle—divorced their husbands, remarried, and discovered that societal disapproval was something they were able to live with.

Real life, of course, had a way of paling in comparison with an unachieved ideal. It was therefore in the nature of the project of finding new and better forms of living that the goal should never be quite reached, but should remain in the realm of the absolute. The unfulfilled was programmatic. The Blue Flower, the mysterious, ethereal symbol of German Romanticism, is so vaguely defined as to be forever elusive, and generally there is a preference for the absolute over the tangible.

Alexander von Humboldt was deeply committed to the Romantic project, both in his science and in the bold way that he chose to live his life.

The person who had introduced the motif of the Blue Flower was Friedrich von Hardenberg, who wrote under his better-known pen name, Novalis. Like Humboldt, he was a mining inspector, and, also like him, an alumnus of Germany's foremost mining academy.

A number of Romanticism's leading figures worked in mining or wrote about it, and the connection left a mark on the thinking of the time. Going inside the earth became a metaphor for turning inside, towards the self and its dark depths, in the search for personal enlightenment and truth.

The turn to the interior also meant that the most objective criterion was, eventually, found in the most subjective one: what Humboldt's own senses told him. From his mining days onwards, Humboldt began to look at his own body as his most reliable and most decisive instrument. He conducted galvanic experiments on himself until the pain became so overwhelming that he had to stop; he tested the amount of dangerous mine gas that his newly-developed miner's safety lamp could take before going out—and almost extinguished himself in the process, having to be dragged out of a mine by his feet, unconscious. An ascent of the volcano Pichincha, near Quito, had to be abandoned when Humboldt came to the point of fainting. On the banks of the Orinoco, he contemplated the idea that the essence of a natural phenomenon could be grasped in its truest form through an emotional response. For this, it was necessary to go beyond the purely quantitative, the mere collecting of data, and gain what he called a 'total impression.'[6] This thought finds echoes in some of the ideas of the Romantic philosopher Friedrich Schelling, Humboldt's acquaintance and sometime collaborator. If nature was an independent entity with agency of its own, and constructed on similar lines as the self, then its phenomena could be understood by intuition—a process that would merge nature and self, the objective and the subjective.

Once a limit had been established, be it that of one's own body, experience, or tradition, the Romantic impulse was to go beyond it—to widen the scope, and to open the view to the infinite. There was a predilection for the unfinished and incomplete, matched by an instinctive aversion to anything that was predictable and clearly delineated.

At the point of having secured a career that was destined to make him one of the most powerful men in the Prussian state administration, Alexander von Humboldt threw it away for an idea of almost spectacular vagueness—something that amounted, at that stage, to little more than an ill-defined yearning to travel. Indeed, Humboldt freely admitted that he 'would have sailed to the remotest South Seas even if it hadn't fulfilled any scientific purpose whatever.'[7]

On the Chimborazo, a crevasse forced him to turn around, but, in better weather, a different route might have been tried. However, when conditions improved the next day, Humboldt declined to try again. He did not seem to see this as a failure, and after his journey he kept having himself painted against the Chimborazo as a background. He preferred for his favourite mountain to be winking in the distance rather than to have it underfoot.

When he came to evaluate and write up the results of his journey, many of the volumes he planned were never completed. This was not for lack of time—he died in his ninetieth year. Most importantly, Humboldt failed to finish what was meant to be the synthesis of all his scientific achievements, his great work: *Cosmos* (*Kosmos*). The missing section was to deal with human beings; he intended it to be the culmination of *Cosmos*, and it would have completed his project. Leaving a fragment was perhaps a more satisfying way to hint at a greater whole, just beyond grasp.

The great hope of Romantic science is not just to understand nature as an object. There is an idea that nature, elevated into a subject, should in turn affect a transformation in the observer. Goethe hinted at this most pithily when he wrote, with Humboldt in mind, that 'no one can walk beneath palm trees with impunity.'[8]

Humboldt achieved this ambition—he was transformed by his experience of nature. In the Americas, he encountered a world that was defined almost in opposition to all he had known, and in it, more truly found his own self. He returned to Europe at peace with the person he was. His last decades found him in a domestic arrangement that was unusual, slightly mysterious, frowned on by his brother's family—but, it seems, wholly agreeable to him.

Although Alexander von Humboldt kept many of the exact circumstances of his life to himself, the signs are that he succeeded in going beyond the boundaries of ordinary life, and discovered the possibility of a more benign, and a more generous, dispensation.

'A Citizen of the World'

❧ ⚘ ❧

The crossing from Havana to Philadelphia was perilous. On the evening of May 6, 1804, the sun, a pallid disk, grotesquely swollen, had sunk into the sea behind bottle green clouds—'a sight I will never forget,' Humboldt recalled later, who thought it was a portent of disaster.[1] He was right—the next morning brought a heavy storm, one that would rage for six days. The rain came down so fast that it was more like a sort of dense, icy fog: 'drops fell like snow. It was impossible to turn the face to the wind.'[2] Everybody was wet to the skin, water sloshed down the cabin stairs, and cooking pots, with the meals half-cooked, could be seen floating out of the galley. The sight of circling sharks did nothing to help the general mood. The sailors seemed to have little confidence about their prospects—they kept asking for more brandy, following the logic that, if one was to be drowned, one might as well drown one's sorrows first.

Three days into this, on the morning of May 9, things got so bad that Humboldt believed that all was lost. He felt strangely exhilarated. His life, he reflected, had been full and happy. After a journey that had exceeded all that he had been hoping and wishing for, perhaps it was only fair that he should now pay the price.[3]

But he also reproached himself. He had explored the interior of South America, faced countless dangers, and yet emerged unscathed. Was he now, so close to the finishing line, to go down together with all the treasures he had gathered, his notes and his plant specimens,

many of them of species new to science? What was more, his decision to travel to the United States, he was quite aware, had been 'in
no way necessary.'[4]

After his time in South America—from July 1799 to early 1803—
Humboldt had spent a year in Mexico, and then sailed on to Cuba,
to pick up some of his collections that he had stored there earlier.
While he was preparing them for shipping to Europe, the American
consul in Havana, Vincent F. Gray, approached him and invited him
to visit the United States, and to meet President Jefferson.

There was no shortage of reasons why it would have been expedient to decline and return to Europe without further delay, and com-
pelling ones, too: while Humboldt couldn't have predicted how close
to disaster the passage from Havana to the United States would
come, he did know that, with the approaching hurricane season, it
would not be without risk. And after all these years of travelling, and
having pushed at the borders of physical endurance, he was weary,
and wanted to be home. Also, there was a concern that, with his
active research completed, his findings might lose their immediacy,
or be overtaken. Now was the time to present the fruits of his journey
to the scientific world back home. 'I think of nothing but of preserv-
ing and publishing my manuscripts,' Humboldt had written. 'How I
long to be in Paris!'[5]

And yet, when the chance presented itself to visit the United
States, Humboldt grasped at it without hesitation.

An idea of his motivation can be glimpsed in the letter he wrote
to Jefferson: 'In spite of my intense desire to be back in Paris [. . .],
I could not resist the moral interest to see the United States and to
enjoy the comforting aspect of a people who appreciate the precious
gift of freedom.'[6]

The notion of freedom had always held a place of special, almost
sacred importance in the firmament of Humboldt's ideals. He took
great pride in the fact that, on passing through Paris in the run-up
to the first anniversary of the French Revolution, he had helped cart
some sand to the Temple of Liberty with his own hands. Conversely,

having witnessed on his travels the suffering of indigenous people subjugated by colonists and the church, he had been confirmed in his belief that lack of freedom and autonomy was one of the most insidious causes of human misery.

The United States, on the other hand, was the first nation in the Americas that had successfully liberated itself from the yoke of colonial rule. While France, where Napoleon was preparing to have himself crowned as emperor, had strayed far from the ideals of the Revolution, it seemed to have fallen to the United States to show that there could be another model. After all, the man he had been invited to meet, Thomas Jefferson, had drafted the Declaration of Independence, with its ringing emphasis on equality and freedom. Both these lofty notions, of course, might have suffered some qualification due to the fact that Jefferson himself was a slaveholder. However, Humboldt seems to have opted for leaving such thorny questions aside for the moment.

The storm did not sink the ship, and on May 19, Humboldt had the chance to form his first impression of the United States from the sea. Compared to the lush tropical coastlines he had become used to, the vegetation seemed sparse—like strokes of pen on paper. It was magnificent in a different way though: travelling up the Delaware River, Humboldt admired 'its banks adorned with villages, the majestic stream covered with ships.'[7]

In Philadelphia, Humboldt encountered an enthusiastic welcome. He was inducted into the American Philosophical Society, the scholarly institution founded by Benjamin Franklin, whose members also included Alexander Hamilton, James Madison, John Adams, Thomas Paine, Benjamin Rush, and of course Jefferson—who, as president of the society, personally signed Humboldt's membership certificate.

The visit to Washington was, if anything, even more successful: Humboldt was received by Jefferson in the White House (then still known as 'the President's House'), and the two men soon fell into an easy familiarity. He had a standing invitation to come to the President's House whenever he liked, and once, when making an unannounced appearance, found Jefferson sitting on the floor of the drawing room with his grandchildren clambering over him. The president is reported to have risen, shaken Humboldt's hand, and told his visitor, 'You have found me playing the fool, Baron, but I am sure to you I need make no apology.'[8]

Hostesses went to great lengths to outdo each other when catering for the star guest. One of them, Anna Maria Brodeau Thornton, had noted down her efforts: she ordered fish, strawberries, vegetables, peppers, bacon, half a gallon of Madeira, and a half dozen claret.[9] Humboldt, in turn, didn't disappoint. We have a taste of the impression he made from Dolley Madison, who reported, 'We have lately had a great treat in the company of a charming Prussian Baron von Humboldt. All the ladies say they are in love with him [. . .]. He had with him a train of philosophers, who, though clever and entertaining, did not compare with the Baron.'[10] Another hostess, Margaret Bayard Smith, was ready to claim Humboldt for her own country. He was 'a charming man,' she pronounced, whose 'enlightened mind has already made him an American, and we are not without hopes, that after having scratched his curiosity with travel he will spend the remainder of his days in the United States.'[11]

Humboldt returned the compliment: the days he had spent in Washington, he wrote to James Madison, were 'the most delightful of his life.'

But Mrs. Smith recognised that Humboldt's vision went beyond any nation, even the United States. 'He was most truly a citizen of the world & wherever he went he felt himself perfectly at home,' she wrote. More importantly, she added, 'in all climes, he recognized man as his brother.'[12]

2

The View from Tegel

By the summer of 1769, Captain Cook had arrived in Tahiti, sent there to observe the transit of Venus across the Sun. In the Northern Hemisphere, the comet Messier cut a thick, luminous swathe across the night sky. On the northwestern fringes of Berlin, in the small chateau at Tegel, Alexander von Humboldt was born on September 14, following his brother, Wilhelm, by a distance of two years.[1]

A few days later, in the grounds at Tegel, the guests attending Alexander's christening were rather stellar themselves. Prince Heinrich of Prussia (a younger brother of King Frederick the Great) came to witness the event, as did Duke Ferdinand of Brunswick and the Prussian crown prince, Friedrich Wilhelm, with the latter two being appointed godfathers. This picture-book entry into a charmed world was, of course, not all it seemed. Many years later, when Humboldt had moved away and built his own life, distance afforded him a clearer view of some of the thornier aspects of his upbringing.

This is the family estate as described by Humboldt in 1792 to his friend Carl Freiesleben:

> Tegel is not a village as such, but a hunting lodge, built by the Great Elector [Frederick William of Brandenburg] and completely trans-formed by my father. It is by a lake, about a mile and a half in length and dotted with prettily cultivated islands. Small hills covered in

vineyards, which here we call mountains, large plantations of exotic trees, a house surrounded by meadows, and striking views of the pictur-esque banks of the lake—all these things conspire to make Tegel one of the loveliest places in the area. Add to this the leisurely and comfortable way of living in our house, and you will be all the more surprised when I tell you that this place, whenever I return to it, makes me feel wistful. [. . .] Here in Tegel I have spent the greater part of this unhappy life, among people who loved me and wished me well, and yet with whom I had not one sentiment in common—under severe constraint, in the privations of solitude, and in conditions that forced me into constant dissemblance and sacrifice.[2]

Alexander's father died when he was nine years old. In the 1740s, the young Alexander Georg von Humboldt had fought in the wars of the Austrian succession under Frederick the Great. Frederick, in a flagrant and spectacular violation of earlier Prussian assurances, invaded the Austrian Duchy of Silesia, which was wealthy and con-veniently situated just south of the Prussian possessions. In the Seven Years' War (1756–63) that followed—Austria's ultimately unsuccess-ful attempt to regain Silesia—Major von Humboldt served as an adjutant to the duke of Brunswick, whose life he helped save in the Battle of Krefeld. Humboldt was wounded in 1761, retired from the army, and was subsequently offered a position at the Prussian court. In 1765 he became chamberlain to the crown princess, Elisabeth of Brunswick. However, his life gained in complication when Elisabeth's husband, Crown Prince Friedrich Wilhelm (the future king Friedrich Wilhelm II), acquired a mistress. In the subsequent royal separation, the major had to steer a delicate course, and, while he managed to remain on good terms with both parties, he nonethe-less found himself out of a job.

He had not been the first in the family to serve in the Prussian army; his own father, Hans Paul von Humboldt—Alexander's grandfather—had fought in the wars of the Spanish succession under Prince Eugene of Savoy. Hans Paul lost a foot in battle, but by way of compensation was elevated to the minor nobility by his king,

Friedrich Wilhelm I of Prussia, known as the 'Soldier King.' The major's destiny, by contrast, was less dramatic: while he lost his position, his discretion won him connections at court, evidenced in perks such as the presence of royal princes at his sons' christenings.

Some years after his retirement from active service, in 1766, the major married a young army widow, Marie Elisabeth Freifrau von Holwede (née Colomb). She was only twenty-five years old; the major was forty-six. Marie Elisabeth brought a son, Heinrich von Holwede, into her second marriage, as well as a number of possessions. Among these was the Berlin townhouse at Jägerstraße 22; a country estate at Ringenwalde, northeast of Berlin; and the lease of the small chateau and surrounding lands at Tegel. The Humboldts rented out the country estate and took their main quarters in town, but spent whatever time they could, mainly the summers and weekends, in Tegel.

Tegel immediately took the major's fancy, and he did his best to turn the place into a family home. Trying to make of it 'what could be done by art,' he landscaped the grounds, created walks in the English style, and transformed the estate into a place where he entertained the friends from his army life.[3] Crown Prince Friedrich Wilhelm kept up the acquaintance and called by occasionally, and Goethe, during his only visit to Berlin, in 1778, found the time to drop in at Tegel to pay a visit. The major was, it seems, a well-liked, sociable man who knew how to live well: his friend, the geographer Anton Friedrich Büsching, described him as 'a man of understanding and taste, esteemed and respected by people from all walks of life. He was friendly, charitable and generous.'[4] The terms of the Tegel lease obliged the major to plant 100,000 mulberry trees— Frederick the Great had been possessed by the notion of initiating the production of home-grown, Prussian silk. However, the young trees the major bought failed to thrive in the cold climate and sandy Prussian soil, and, by the time Alexander arrived in the world, silk cultivation at Tegel had been abandoned for some years.

Warmth and nurture were also lacking at Tegel in other ways. When he looked back on the first eighteen years of his life, it appeared to Alexander as though he had been 'penned in by the sparse sandy nature' of the place.[5] When in later life he imagined setting up home somewhere—a fantasy he frequently indulged in— he always imagined places that were emphatically not like Tegel. A reason for all this was likely the difference between his mother's character and his own. Frau von Humboldt was generally perceived as a less genial presence than her husband. She had a reputation as a practical and sensible woman with a strong sense of duty, concerned with propriety, and placing great importance on the tight running of her household. The Romantic writer Caroline de la Motte Fouqué described her as 'pale, with finely drawn features, which on no occasion betrayed emotion.'[6] She was not fond of society, and disliked entertaining at home. In fact, after the scandalous affair that preceded the royal couple's separation, she was not entirely disappointed when her husband resigned his position at court.

3

An Endless Horizon

❧❧

In 1777, when Alexander was eight years old and Wilhelm ten, Christian Kunth made his entry into their lives as their tutor. He himself was barely twenty. Kunth was not the first tutor the brothers encountered. But he was the one who stayed: his grave is in the park at Tegel, on a little hill just out of sight of the family grave, under some trees he had planted himself.

Before Kunth, the resident tutor in the Humboldt household was Joachim Heinrich Campe, who had been employed for the boys' older half-brother, Heinrich von Holwede. Campe also made a start on the three-year-old Wilhelm's reading, and stayed until 1773, when he left to become a military chaplain. The next tutor, Johann Koblanck, left little impression except that he was strict and taught Alexander to read and write. He resigned after two years, also for a career as a military chaplain. At this point, in 1775, Frau von Humboldt persuaded Campe to return.

Campe, during the time he spent with Alexander and Wilhelm, was already working on the book that would make his name: *Robinson the Younger*, Campe's adaptation, for children, of Daniel Defoe's *Robinson Crusoe*. He was on friendly terms with the group of Enlightenment poets around Gotthold Ephraim Lessing and Matthias Claudius, and, influenced by Enlightenment thought, nursed a pet project of renovating the German language to make it more accessible to all, by replacing foreign words with German versions. Several of the words he introduced did take root in the German language and survive today, such as *Wust*, an alternative to *Chaos*, and *Hochschule*, instead of *Universität*. Some more partisan suggestions, however, such as the replacement of 'soldier' with the unwieldy *Menschenschlachter* (butcher of men), failed to catch on. Inspired by Rousseau, Campe taught geography by letting the boys handle maps, which may well have left an early impression in Alexander's mind—much later he wrote that, for a child, 'the form of countries, and of seas and lakes, as delineated in maps; the desire to behold southern stars, invisible in our hemisphere [. . .] may all implant in the mind the first impulse to travel into distant countries.'[1]

While it is tempting to look to Campe's adaptation of *Robinson Crusoe* as an influence on Alexander's later travels, a straightforward debt seems not so likely. Campe's version has a didactic slant that largely spoils the inspirational effect he was aiming for. In a book conceived, as the subtitle promises, 'for the pleasant and useful enter-tainment of children,' Campe's adherence to educational ideas gleaned from Rousseau necessitated substantial alterations to the original. So, in Campe's version, Crusoe is robbed even of the few tools left to him (no tobacco pipe, not even a knife), the better to present man in his 'natural' state. *Robinson the Younger* was published in 1779, and, the following year, Alexander received his own copy from the author as a Christmas present. He appears to have failed to thank Campe in person; Wilhelm, in a letter to their old tutor, took it upon himself to pass on Alexander's thanks and reported, politely, that his brother had been reading it 'quite avidly.'[2]

After Campe's second departure, Johann Clüsener, who would later pursue a career in local government, took over. According to Wilhelm, Clüsener 'wasn't much concerned whether or not I learned anything,' and in 1777 Christian Kunth arrived to take his place. Kunth was the teacher who left the deepest impression. As a grown man, Wilhelm wrote (in a letter to his bride, Caroline von Dacheröden), 'Oh Lina, what that name stirs up in me whenever I hear it, you cannot imagine. It brings back scenes, the memory of which will always upset me.'[3]

Gottlob Johann Christian Kunth was a pastor's son. His father had died only a few months before his appearance in the Humboldt household, and so he had been obliged to abandon his law degree and look for employment. Modest, serious, and without any apparent desire to push himself forward, he slotted into the household with remarkable ease and quickly developed loyalty and attachment to it. As a teacher, he was committed and took no short cuts: his history lessons were of the sort that made Wilhelm quip that 'one should wish to be Adam, when history was still quite short.' Given the narrow age gap, Kunth's position was often closer to that of an older brother than an authoritarian teacher. This lack of distance, together with Kunth's integration into the Humboldt family, sometimes crossed over into an uncomfortable intensity. Kunth flew into rages, telling his young charges that they would never amount to anything, and took their mother's side against them as a matter of course.

At this time, Major Humboldt still maintained many of his friendships from his court days and was proud that the crown prince honoured him with the occasional visit at Tegel. Such company eased the atmosphere and lifted the often oppressive focus on education and discipline. Goethe's visit took place in May of 1778. He was accompanying Karl August, duke of Saxe-Weimar-Eisenach, his friend and patron, on a diplomatic mission. The two took a detour to stop for lunch in Tegel, and, as Goethe recalled later, they spent 'a happy day,' before, in the evening, continuing to Potsdam.[4] It is probable that Alexander and Wilhelm (then eight and ten) were around to meet the distinguished visitor, though there is no record to confirm this.

Nearby, in the woods surrounding the house at Tegel, was a gamekeeper's cottage that was said to be haunted. This haunting was worked into an exchange in the Walpurgis Night scene of Goethe's drama *Faust*. Here, the forces of reason confront a group of ghostly creatures, without success:

> Away with you! We're all enlightened now!
> The pack of devils by no rules is daunted:
> We are so clever, and yet is Tegel haunted.[5]

(The speaker of these lines is a character called the 'Proktophantasmist'—introduced into the drama with the express purpose of mocking the Enlightenment writer Friedrich Nicolai.[6] The latter had given offence by publishing a parody of Goethe's *The Sorrows of Young Werther* [*Die Leiden des jungen Werthers*, 1774]. In Nicolai's *The Joys of Young Werther*, the lovers, guided by reason, escape their tragic fates and go on to live out their days in happiness.[7])

Fun and foolery came to an abrupt halt in Tegel with the catastrophe of 1779: the major's death, at only fifty-nine years of age. Natural tendencies of character hardened into more formal positions as the household struggled to establish an even keel. Frau von Humboldt, widowed for a second time, grasped the household reins more tightly. She found reliable and welcome support in Kunth, who soon took over so much of the day-to-day running of the estate that, as he reported later, 'hardly fifty thalers were gained or spent that didn't pass through my hands.'[8]

Frau von Humboldt set about capably organising the best education for her sons that good advice and sufficient money could secure. Kunth's job changed from teaching the boys himself to overseeing a programme of education. Specialist tutors, mostly associated with the Berlin Enlightenment, were engaged for different subjects. Johann Jakob Engel, a previous tutor to the crown prince, taught the Humboldt brothers philosophy, and the mathematician Ernst Ferdinand Klein lectured on what was known as 'natural law' (based on the idea that humans were by birth equipped with certain unalienable rights). The army chaplain Josias Löffler looked after their Latin, and Ernst Gottfried Fischer, a strong critic of Goethe's colour theory, their mathematics. Fischer was obliged to supplement his income through tutoring—an activity he seems largely to have resented, though, in the case of Alexander and Wilhelm, apparently a bit less so. He later recollected that 'in the first few years I was fortunate enough not to have to expend my strength on dull and stupid pupils. The instruction of such youths as Wilhelm and Alexander von Humboldt, and Joseph Mendelssohn, cannot be classed among those uninteresting labours to which duty and necessity so often reduce a man of learning.'[9]

In response to their father's passing, Frau von Humboldt now dedicated herself wholly to her sons' education, even mortgaging her country estate so as to afford the cost. Yet to step into the void, by spending more time with the boys herself, seems to have been more than she was capable of doing, and her sons clearly craved more warmth than it was in her nature to provide. In writing to Caroline von Dacheröden, Wilhelm gives an idea of the relationship: 'I'm spending the whole afternoon with my mother. You can imagine the emptiness.'[10]

Friends of the family missed the balance the major had supplied to his wife's more severe nature. Caroline de la Motte Fouqué, a family friend who still visited Tegel, perceived an outward lack of affection in someone who was at heart a steadfast and loyal character:

His [the major's] easy, lively talk used to make a charming contrast to the quiet measure and calm of his wife. Who, I assure you, looks today as she did yesterday, and will do tomorrow. The headdress just like ten years ago if not longer, always straight, firm and modest [. . .] She puts up with having [. . .] the old aunt around her all the time; there is always the old dog, Belcastel, spread out on the sofa, snoring; no dissent, no domestic upheaval will upset her calm. You can swear on it that, just as you leave the family today, so you will find them again, both inward and outward, in a year and a day.[11]

While the sons found it hard to adjust to the new situation at home, Kunth became deeply devoted to the woman who had given him a substitute family. Perhaps he was best placed to appreciate her sense of duty and lack of concern for herself. He noted, with some approval, how, in spite of several proposals of marriage, she withdrew from social life and instead focused her attention on the boys' development. 'To me,' he wrote, 'whom she regarded as the instrument to fulfil this most important wish of hers, she was more than a mother'—his own self-denial echoing, in a quieter key, that of the woman he praised. Kunth remained in Frau von Humboldt's service until her death and, even after that, continued to devote himself to Wilhelm and Alexander's affairs. It was only when duty was well and truly discharged that he allowed himself a life of his own, and was married, finally, at the age of fifty.[12]

Under Kunth's supervision, Wilhelm thrived, especially in the ancient languages, but there were concerns about Alexander. Doubts were voiced whether he would ever achieve even average educational standards. He was often ill, suffering particularly from headaches. It cannot have helped that lessons were mainly tailored to Wilhelm's needs, with Alexander expected to tag along. Sometimes his tuition consisted merely of Wilhelm passing on his own lessons to his younger brother. At any rate, Alexander reports that it was not until 'much later in my boyhood that all of a sudden the light in my head got switched on.'[13]

For the sons of the nobility, career decisions typically involved choosing between the military and the civil or court service, the higher posts of which were traditionally their preserve. Alexander and Wilhelm's elder half-brother, Heinrich, had already become an officer, but for her younger sons Frau von Humboldt was more ambitious. In Wilhelm's case, this was straightforward: since he excelled in most things, a career in state administration, by way of studying law, was the obvious choice.

Alexander, however, had no discernible talents or desires that could be channelled into a profitable career. Nor did his own ideas on the matter seem any less cloudy. There was, however, an interest in art: even before he had any formal lessons, Alexander produced drawings of heads and landscapes. His mother, though not openly encouraging of such pursuits, did keep one of his drawings on her bedroom wall; another drawing, modelled on a painting by Goethe's friend the Swiss painter Angelica Kauffman, was included in the first art exhibition of the Berlin Academy in 1786.

An early interest in nature is also recorded. While it can't have been unusual for a boy his age to hunt for beetles and butterflies, Alexander did arrange his finds into small, neatly labelled collections. This interest attracted enough notice for the family to refer to him as 'the little apothecary.'[14] The first time he was exposed to botany proper, however, nobody was struck by any presentiment of greatness. The family doctor, Ernst Ludwig Heim—'old Heim'—was an amateur botanist who had travelled widely in Europe and was a friend of Joseph Banks.[15] Of a visit to Tegel, he reports (tactfully neglecting to mention Alexander), 'Rode to Tegel and lunched with Frau Major von Humboldt; then explained to the young Humboldts the twenty-four classes of Linnaeus's system of plants, which the elder grasped easily and right away remembered the names.'[16] Alexander, for his part, remembers the experience equally for its failure to awaken his interest in the subject:

> [. . .] one day, he took the trouble to describe the Linnaean classification to my brother. He, who even then knew Greek, learned the names by heart; I glued *Lichen parietinus* and *Hypna* on paper, and a few days later all our enthusiasm for botany was gone again.[17]

When asked about his own plans for the future, Alexander tended to reply that he wanted to be a soldier. At a time when Captain Cook's voyages were fresh in people's minds, it certainly wasn't entirely fanciful to imagine oneself, as an army officer, sent alongside the scientists on a voyage of exploration. But the lack of definition in his plans seemed to be almost essential to their nature: 'From my early youth,' he wrote later,

> a longing lived in me to be able to travel to faraway countries little visited by Europeans. This yearning is characteristic of a time in one's life

when it lies before us like an endless horizon, where nothing is more attractive to us than strong emotions and imaginings of physical danger. Having grown up in a country that stands in no direct contact with the colonies of both Indies, [. . .] I felt my passion for the sea and long sea journeys become more and more powerful. Things that we only know from the vivid descriptions of travellers have a special attraction for us; shapes, rendered hazy through distance, prove themselves irresistible to the imagination.[18]

Frau von Humboldt was certainly not minded to send her problematic child off for adventures in exotic countries. What beckoned for Alexander was something quite different: the study of the cameral sciences. Cameralism can be broadly defined as the management of estates as well as of states. It first appeared as a university discipline in its own right in Germany in the late 1720s, with chairs being established in Frankfurt (Oder) and Halle. To the untrained eye, it appeared an artless jumble of assorted natural sciences, such as forestry, chemistry, and mineralogy, together with some state administration. The name derives from the German *Kammer*—the chamber of commerce of a principality. These chambers needed funds, and it was the job of the cameralists to supply them.

What this choice really showed, however, was just how low Frau von Humboldt's expectations were of her youngest son. Cameralism was known as an easy option for the less promising sons of the aristocracy. It as good as guaranteed a position in the Prussian civil service while being academically undemanding, to the point that 'a student of cameralism' had become a byword for a slow student. By 1813, the discipline's reputation had suffered so much that the Prussian authorities felt they had to issue a decree to 'warn students from the unhappy misconception that the study of cameralism required less strenuous use of the intellectual facilities than that of theology, medicine or law.'[19]

4

The Discovery of Warmer Climes

~·~ ✦ ~·~

I n the autumn of 1787, both Alexander and Wilhelm left an already
cold Berlin to move even further east, to Frankfurt on the river
Oder. Berlin did not yet have a university, and Frankfurt-on-the-
Oder was the nearest option. (It was in 1809 that Wilhelm von
Humboldt proposed the founding of a university in Berlin. It would
eventually become the Humboldt-Universität, named in honour of
both brothers.) In November, Alexander wrote an upbeat letter from
Frankfurt, announcing that it was quite possible to adapt oneself to
anything, even to 'the icy banks of the Oder,' if one but availed oneself of a little philosophy.[1] Mostly, though, Alexander's communica-
tions still reverberated with the memory of the summer he had just
spent in Berlin, and bore constant, slightly plaintive requests to the
effect that the friends he had made there should not forget him:
'Please remember me to the dear *Hofrat* [privy councillor], his excellent wife, the Veit, the Levi[n] [. . .] and anyone at all you run into
who still remembers me.'[2]

The recipient of these pleas was Ephraim Beer, a medical student
who lodged at the house of Markus and Henriette Herz—the *Hofrat*
and wife in question. (The others mentioned were Dorothea Veit,
daughter of Moses Mendelssohn, and Rahel Levin.) Letters to Beer
were a conduit that led directly into the close circle of friends that
constituted Henriette's salon, and, of course, to Henriette herself.

Henriette Herz was the daughter of Benjamin de Lemos, the director of the hospital of the Jewish community in Berlin. Famed for her exceptional beauty, the story goes that already as a child she attracted so much male attention on her way to and from school that her parents felt it necessary to remove her from the private girls' institution she attended. From then on she was educated at home, and, when she was twelve years old, her parents offered her the choice of two suitors. She picked Markus Herz, a philosopher and a physician at her father's hospital. When they married, Henriette was fifteen years old; her husband was thirty-two.

Herz had studied at Königsberg, where he had been a student of Immanuel Kant, of whom he eventually became a friend and some-time collaborator. Now, in Berlin, he acted as Kant's unofficial representative, and was often the first port of call for students sent there by the philosopher. Once he and Henriette were married, Markus began inviting friends and colleagues to an informal lecture series in their home, designed to keep up with scientific advances. Among them were David Friedländer (son-in-law of the banker Daniel Itzig), who would later become Alexander and Wilhelm's banker, and Christian Dohm, Alexander's teacher in 1785/86 and author of the essay 'Concerning the Amelioration of the Civil Status of the Jews' (1781). Both men had been students of the philosopher Moses Mendelssohn, and, together with Markus Herz, they were at the core of the Haskalah, or Jewish Enlightenment, in Berlin.

With science and philosophy taking place in one room, Henriette Herz had begun to gather her own friends, a group of younger men and women, in the adjoining one, to discuss novels and poetry. 'My husband looked upon the goings-on of my little society with a smile, though without ever interfering,' she later wrote in her memoirs.[3] Their house in Spandauer Straße developed into a double salon, and for a time became the most sought-after destination in Berlin, its fame eclipsed only when the salon held by Henriette's friend Rahel Levin came into its own.

Salon culture in Berlin was a relatively new phenomenon, and one very specific to its time and place. Jews in Prussia were still subject to severe restrictions—full civil rights would not be extended to them until 1871. Mendelssohn, Berlin's leading intellectual, was jeered when he attended one of Kant's lectures, and his application to become a member of the Academy of Sciences foundered on anti-Jewish prejudice (as did Markus Herz's application later).[4] Overall, though, and only within a generation, the situation for Jews in Germany had improved steadily, with greater access to further education and the professions; thus it seemed not unreasonable to imagine that, in line with the ideals of the Enlightenment, equality irrespective of ethnicity or religion was almost within reach.

In these strange, semi-liberated circumstances, it was Jewish women who felt the dilemma of their situation most keenly. Often brought up in households that prized culture and education, they tended to find, on the cusp of adulthood, that for them free thinking was not meant to spill over into material and personal freedom. Instead, they were expected to keep to the domestic sphere, and could only watch as their brothers and male friends took off to pursue the new possibilities opening up to them. Rahel Levin lived vicariously through male acquaintances, urging her friend David Veit to have fun on a journey—'do enjoy yourself, because you're also doing it on my behalf'—and protesting, in a more general vein: 'is a woman, then, to be blamed for being human, too?'[5] Similarly, Mendelssohn's granddaughter Fanny Mendelssohn, who had started out with as much musical promise as her younger brother Felix, was left waving him off as he was taken to Jena to meet Goethe.

The salon, then, was a rather ingenious way around this dilemma: if women weren't to venture out into the world, they would instead bring the world into their homes. Writers, diplomats, artists, and philosophers, as well as aristocrats bored by courtly protocol, were soon to be found sitting on sofas in Jewish homes, being served tea and entertained by witty, unrestrained conversation not available elsewhere. For this purpose, Rahel Levin used the attic room of her family home at Jägerstraße 54, just a stone's throw from the Humboldt family's town house, Jägerstraße 22. It was to Rahel's house that the Prussian crown prince Louis Ferdinand came to see his mistress, the actress Pauline Wiesel. And it was the death of the same Louis Ferdinand—during the twin battles of Jena and Auerstedt in 1806, between Napoleonic and Prussian forces—that signalled the end of salon culture, as the French occupation strengthened nationalistic and restrictive tendencies. Nevertheless, for the short period during which it flowered, the salon transcended its makeshift origins and became an experiment in living. It was the sort of arrangement that was alien to everything Alexander had known from his upbringing. He urgently wanted to be part of it, and seems to have felt immediately at home.

Under the tutelage of Henriette Herz, Alexander learned a little Hebrew, which he then deployed like a private code to signal his belonging. He also asked David Friedländer if he might be included in some of the prayers. His letters to Henriette from Tegel tended to be signed and dated from 'Tedium Towers.' This was done in Hebrew script for, as Henriette explained, 'it wouldn't do for a young nobleman to confess that a better time might be had in the company of Jewish ladies than at the home of his ancestors.'[6] But there was more to it than this. A way of living which, viewed from Tegel, would have looked mysterious and alien, for him spelled possibility and promise. And becoming integrated into such a culture offered the prospect of transformation, of being not quite who he was. The cloak of the unknown, shimmering and colourful, always seemed enticing to him.

A letter from Alexander, on the occasion of Henriette's twenty-fifth birthday, shows a young man keen to impress two women more mature and more sophisticated than himself. 'Even though I was just a few years older than him, I was a woman, a married one at that, and thus his senior by some distance,' is how Henriette put it.[7] Alexander's letter is a little sketch, an imagined dialogue between Henriette Herz and Dorothea Veit, which begins with the women complaining about the lack of communication from their friend Alexander—until there is a knock at the door:

D. V.: A letter!

H. H.: Give it to me, my dear! (looks at letter) If I didn't know how lazy Humboldt is, I'd swear this was his hand. (opens it) It is from him!

D. V.: Well! Let's hear it.

H. H.: If only the writing weren't so small and so crabbed.

Having read Alexander's effusive assertions of loyalty and devotion, Henriette folds the letter up again, sighing,

Good Humboldt! If he'd heard us talk just then . . .

D. V.: I didn't say anything bad about him.

H. H.: And I, even less.[8]

Dorothea Veit was Moses Mendelssohn's oldest daughter and Henriette's childhood friend. Her original first name was Brendel, and she was married to one of her father's protégés, the banker and merchant Simon Veit. The marriage was not happy, and in Henriette's salon Dorothea encountered the poet and critic Friedrich Schlegel. Confronted with the familiar conflict between intellectual freedom and constraining tradition, Dorothea chose an uncompromising path. She divorced Veit in 1799, and married Schlegel a few years later. Her move from the marital home to be with a gentile who, moreover, was eight years her junior, meant sacrificing a comfortable lifestyle as well as her reputation. Her position wasn't helped by Schlegel's novel *Lucinde* (1799), a veiled and exalted evocation of their relationship, which scandalised polite society and embarrassed their friends.

Even though Rahel Levin's salon was just across the street from the Humboldts, it was to the house in Spandauer Straße, a short walk away, that Alexander and Wilhelm were taken by their tutor Kunth, who was a friend of Markus Herz. The lectures there were an excellent opportunity to introduce his charges into intellectual company. There were satisfyingly tangible results, too: a scientific demonstration at the Herzes' resulted, for example, in the installation of a lightning rod at Tegel. (The device had been invented by Benjamin Franklin a few decades earlier, and the one at Tegel was one of the first in Berlin.) Soon, though, Alexander drifted over to Henriette's side of the salon. There, the company was younger, women were part of the group, and evenings tended to be rounded off with dinner and dancing.

Alexander taught Henriette the steps of a fashionable new dance, the *Menuet à la Reine*.[9] The better-looking of the two brothers, he began to make an impression in society. We owe Caroline de la Motte Fouqué for a description of him at this time: 'he wears two long iron watch chains, dances, makes conversation in his mother's drawing room, and all in all is beginning to come into his own. He so reminds me of his father.'[10]

Henriette gradually formalised her circle into a group known as the *Tugendbund* (League of Virtue), which stipulated that its members live according to non-conventional, idealistic rules. There were to be no secrets between members, who were united in a high-minded, quasi-mystical sort of love, unintelligible to the uninitiated. Potential members were scouted and carefully vetted (though Wilhelm von Humboldt at one time found himself reprimanded for over-recruiting women), and encouraged to write to each other. At different times, the Tugendbund included the writer Caroline von Wolzogen (she would later become Friedrich Schiller's sister-in-law); Caroline von Dacheröden (Wilhelm's future wife); the novelist Jean Paul; and Therese Heyne, the daughter of the Göttingen classicist Christian Gottlob Heyne. (Therese would marry, and then leave, the botanist Georg Forster.)

However, once Wilhelm and Caroline von Dacheröden had formed their own rather closer and more conventional alliance (they had first met in the summer of 1788 and become engaged in late 1789), Henriette Herz's rules began to seem unappealingly prescriptive and a lot less congenial to the two of them. The Tugendbund disintegrated eventually but left behind a close weave of friendships and relationships of various gradations and intensities, one to which Alexander would feel bound for the rest of his life.

A degree from Frankfurt-on-the-Oder was not the most prestigious, but it had the advantage of not placing undue demands on students who sought it. The university was popular with the sons of the Prussian aristocracy and landowners, mainly for the reliability with which it turned out graduates. Alexander, writing to Ephraim Beer, explained how it worked. In spite of a small overall student population (between 220 and 230, by Alexander's estimation), Frankfurt's university, the Alma Mater Viadrina, still turned out an astonishingly high number of medical graduates. 'Everyone flocks to Frankfurt for their doctorates,' he wrote. It was, he continued,

> the supervisor's job not only to write, but also, in effect, to defend the dissertation. The respondents, who usually cannot string more than six words together in Latin, generally act as though the objections of the examiner didn't concern them in any way [. . .]. But since it's quite possible to be a good doctor without speaking any Latin, there may well often be able men among these newly created doctors.[11]

Wilhelm concurred: 'If you know someone who'd like to become a doctor and hasn't learned anything, just send him here,' he wrote to Beer. He added that he had attended a doctoral examination in which the candidate had not uttered a single word.[12]

The facilities of the university were not particularly impressive. The library was open only on Wednesday and Saturday afternoons, so that most students did not trouble to use it at all. As for the teaching of the subject Alexander was supposed to be studying, the cameral sciences, the economist Leopold Krug complained that students

> learn to draw plans for a brandy-distillery, a tar-kiln and a flour mill, they learn the number of threads in the warp and woof of linen and silk, they learn how to make cheese and smelt iron, and how to destroy

caterpillars and insect pests; but of the principles of political economy they have not the faintest conception.[13]

'Philosophy, the queen of the sciences,' Alexander concluded, 'hasn't exactly established her temple here.'[14]

Frau von Humboldt, it was clear, had not chosen Frankfurt-on-the-Oder for its academic distinction. Wilhelm had been a particular worry. In Berlin, he had fallen in with the rakish Friedrich Gentz and Gustav Brinckmann, young diplomats who were part of both Henriette's and Rahel's circles. In their company, he had been frequenting establishments such as the Vauxhall, a bordello led by a Madame Schuwitz. Everything there, he explained with almost touching simplicity, was 'so lovely that one completely forgets in what sort of house one is.' Frau von Humboldt put a stop to all that: there would now be a day's journey, by coach, between her sons and such distractions in Berlin. She was able to recommend them to the special care of their old Latin tutor Josias Löffler, who, by a stroke of luck, had moved to Frankfurt, where he now taught theology and church history. Even better, it had also been possible to arrange for Alexander and Wilhelm, as well as Kunth, to lodge with Löffler.

Under Kunth's guidance, the brothers attended private lectures. Wilhelm, who had a clearer conception of his future career, wasn't going to be side-tracked by the attractions Frankfurt had to offer; Alexander, on the other hand, was open to new experiences, and to new people. Wilhelm wrote to a friend: 'Lately, there has been yet another comedy, and tonight there's been a ball. My brother has been to both, I, to neither.'[15]

As Alexander sat writing a letter to David Friedländer one evening, a few days before Christmas 1787, Kunth—as Alexander reported in the letter—stood behind his chair, supervising his progress and urging him to write faster. The curbs on their freedom were not welcome: Alexander was counting the days until he would be back in Berlin. The sojourn in Frankfurt, he wrote to Friedländer, was 'bearable only if one looked on it as a necessary evil.'[16]

To his friend Beer, Alexander had written that 'If it weren't for the pleasures of the friendly (though only male) company which we enjoy here so fully, Frankfurt for us would truly be a miserable place.' Among the 'friendly company,' one person stood out: Wilhelm Gabriel Wegener, a young student of theology, and one of Löffler's students. Before long, he and Alexander had sworn eternal friendship and, from then on, Alexander spent his time in Frankfurt almost exclusively in Wegener's company. In Wegener's recollections—from a distance of many years, and the modest elevation of his position as a parish priest—his wonder at this friendship, so unexpected, shines through undimmed:

> What was most important to me there was the company of Alexander von Humboldt, who went on to become so famous, and who, together with his brother Wilhelm, lodged with Löffler and already then was very knowledgeable. The elder Humboldt was too cold and too hard-working ever to look for friendship; he was only interesting to me as I learned so much from talking to him [. . .]. The younger one, Alexander, attached himself to me with a friendliness and a warmth that nobody had shown me before.[17]

Alexander, for his part, wrote impassioned letters to his friend: 'God! How can one love each other so much and yet be so far apart,' and 'I am burning with desire to embrace you again, my dear, my best Wegener.'[18] This sort of sentiment, against the background of Romanticism and the cult of friendship, does not necessarily constitute proof of a physical relationship. On the other hand, if such a relationship had existed between the two young men, how else might it have presented itself in their letters and memoirs? For Alexander, the feeling ran deep, at least for a while. 'May this open confession of my heart convince you of the love with which I will remember you, my dear, warmest and closest friend, until the end of my days,' he wrote in May 1788.[19] After Frankfurt, he continued to write to Wegener for another two years or so, before the correspondence petered out. But still in 1790, from Hamburg, Alexander wrote to him that 'my heart is glad whenever I think of you.'[20]

At Easter 1788, at the end of their first academic year, both Alexander and Wilhelm returned to Tegel, where it was agreed that they need not go back to Frankfurt. Wilhelm had made enough progress in his law studies to be thought ready for the next step, to continue to the much more prestigious university at Göttingen. Alexander, meanwhile, was going to have another year at home, doing private studies, before following his brother.

In Alexander's subject, too, Göttingen was a natural destination: it was the home of Johann Beckmann, the leading authority on cameralism, whose *Basics of German Agriculture* (1769) was widely used as an introduction to the subject. Beckmann also had a background in botany, having studied with Linnaeus in Uppsala. In Frankfurt, Alexander had begun to familiarise himself with the basics of botany by collecting whatever plant life there was available in and around the city in mid-winter. He did this with the assistance of a freshly published guide to the plants of Berlin, which he had stumbled on by accident: the *Florae Berolinensis* (1787) by Karl Ludwig Willdenow.

Back in Berlin, his copy of Willdenow's book in hand, Alexander continued these pursuits in the Botanical Garden and the Tiergarten, the huge sprawling park that had been enclosed under Frederick the Great. He was mostly after cryptogams: mosses, lichens, sponges, and ferns. These are plants that reproduce asexually—that is, by spores rather than through the sexual parts normally found in a flower. Cryptogamic botany had only recently taken off and become a fashionable area of study. It was probably no accident that it should have done so in the Romantic era. Plant life, being so fundamentally different from animal life, held a particular fascination for the Romantic imagination, and cryptogams, stranger still and less knowable, presented themselves as a worthwhile object of study.[21]

Since Willdenow worked at the Botanical Garden—he would become its curator in 1810—Alexander thought he would try and meet him. Reflecting on the formative events of his early life from some distance in time and place—in 1801, at Santa Fé de Bogotá—Humboldt wondered: 'What consequences did this visit have for the rest of my life! Would I, without it, be writing these lines in the kingdom of New Grenada? In Willdenow, I found a young person who at that time infinitely harmonised with my being.'[22] Karl Ludwig Willdenow, a student of the botanist Reinhold Forster (the father of Georg Forster), was Alexander's senior by only four years, but had already made his name with the publication of the *Florae Berolinensis*. Apart from the descriptive element, his particular interest was the distribution and migration of plants in different countries and under different climates. This idea of ordering plants according to geography, a novel idea to Humboldt, introduced a comparative aspect to botany that lifted it beyond a merely quantitative science.

The two young men went botanising together. Now that he had Willdenow's guidance, botany began to make sense to Humboldt, and drew the two of them together in friendship. This time, it was the blade of a rice plant that appealed to Humboldt's imagination, glinting with the promise of warmer climes, and of adventure. He wrote of the time spent with Willdenow:

> He gave me a blade of *Oryza sativa* [a rice plant] as a present, which Thunberg [Carl Peter Thunberg, the Swedish naturalist and disciple of Linnaeus] had brought back from Japan. In the botanical garden, I saw palm trees for the first time, and a boundless desire awakened in me to see what was grown in distant places. Three weeks, and I was an enthusiastic botanist. Willdenow at that time was considering a journey outside Europe. To accompany him was the wish that occupied me day and night. I familiarised myself with the florae of both Indies, bought the apothecaries out of tree barks and looked with infinite pleasure at the blade of rice in my herbarium.[23]

There was talk of a co-authored book on the powers of plants, and the more involved Humboldt got, the stronger he felt about the importance of botany, noting with indignation: 'Would you believe it that, among all the 145,000 people in Berlin, you can hardly count four who practise this branch of the natural sciences, even as a hobby.'[24]

In spite of the new friendship, Wegener was still on his mind. He had written four letters to him, but had only had one back: 'my friendship,' he wrote, in what purported to be mock-complaint, 'stands to yours in a relation of 4 to 1.' But if Alexander did feel that his friend wasn't returning his feelings in equal measure, he managed, for the time being, to idealise the friendship to a level where it was immune to reality:

> I am too much convinced of the strength of your principles, of the straightness of your [. . .] so affectionate character, that I could ever sincerely entertain the thought that I was forgotten by you, my brother. And even if you remained silent for years, I should suspect the strangest concatenation of circumstances rather than the breaking of a friendship.[25]

Alexander took an interest in the progress of Wegener's studies and his dissertation, trying to help his friend by sending a detailed discussion on the refutation of miracles and asking for a finished copy: 'I am looking forward with longing to reading a copy, of which I ask you to send me one once the little volume is printed.'[26] Still, the meeting with Willdenow and their ramblings through the flora of Berlin had changed him. He later acknowledged the time he had spent under Willdenow's guidance as one of the guiding influences on his life, one of the 'impressions arising from apparently accidental circumstances' that have 'so powerful an effect on the youthful mind as to determine the whole direction of a man's career through life.' These, he recalled later, also included 'Georg Forster's delineations of the South Sea islands; the pictures by Hodges, which represented the shores of the Ganges, and which I first saw at the house of Warren Hastings, in London; and a colossal dragon-tree in an old tower of the Botanical Garden in Berlin.'[27]

5

'First Step into the World'

⸙

'I do love those people who get a little hot around the heart,' Alexander confessed in February 1789.[1] He had a tendency to favour emotion over reason; or, at least, he was gaining confidence in his conviction, dimly felt at first, that intuition was the thing that mattered, with reason following behind, shoring up its advances. He began to sense that this was not the defect in his character that others, such as his brother, Wilhelm, suspected, but instead was at the core of his intellectual being. If it wasn't quite Keats's 'O for a life of Sensations rather than of Thoughts!' there was still an instinctive wariness of his brother's more analytical way of thinking, and 'the knack that logical reasoning has to kill off the spirit and the imagination.'[2]

He tried to put all this into words in a letter to Wegener, reflecting on a topic he liked to expound on—their friendship. 'Real friendship,' he explained,

> like love, emerges out of obscure feelings. It is only once a liking has taken hold that reason comes in to make adjustments. Sure, where the latter shows the former the way, you will walk more safely. But emotion is too free a thing to be subjected to the rules of strict logic.[3]

At Easter 1789, in time for the summer semester, Alexander followed his brother to the University of Göttingen, which had an excellent reputation. Frau von Humboldt had arranged his itinerary to take maximum advantage of the educational opportunities that presented themselves en route. So Alexander, escorted by Kunth, travelled to Göttingen in a journey that lasted three and a half weeks. At about the halfway mark, at Schönebeck near Magdeburg, they dropped in on Carl von La Roche, a regular at Henriette Herz's salon and a founding member of the Tugendbund. In him, Alexander thought, 'nature has happened, for once, to combine a beautiful soul with a pleasing and handsome appearance.'[4] Carl was the younger brother of Maximiliane von La Roche, who had been admired by Goethe; her 'blackest eyes' famously became a feature of Lotte, Werther's unattainable love in *The Sorrows of Young Werther*.[5] The real Maximiliane, however, had gone on to marry not Goethe but the successful Frankfurt businessman Peter Anton Brentano, and to have twelve children with him—among them Clemens Brentano, the Romantic poet, and the writer Bettina von Arnim. Bettina, as a young woman, discovered Goethe's love letters to her mother in the attic, and created something of a cult around her mother's relationship with the famous poet—which Goethe initially found charming, until Bettina's increasingly demanding and difficult behaviour led him to distance himself from the 'vexatious horse-fly.'[6]

Carl von La Roche, meanwhile, only three years older than Alexander, was already employed as a superintendent of mines. When he had left Berlin the year before, Henriette had issued him with instructions to try and recruit new members for the Tugendbund. As the mining circles he moved in at Schönebeck did not yield many promising candidates, Carl resorted to signing up Caroline von Dacheröden, whom he was in love with. If he worried that the young woman from provincial Erfurt might feel out of place corresponding with the sophisticated Berlin crowd, his concerns were unnecessary: at about the time Carl was showing Alexander around the Schönebeck salt mines, Caroline was already involved in the association. Indeed, she was arranging a meeting with another member of the Tugendbund—Alexander's brother, Wilhelm. On April 9, 1789, a breathless letter from Caroline left Erfurt in the direction of Göttingen: 'Think that I'll be in Lauchstädt for a few weeks [. . .]. I hope you'll contrive to join us there, even if it's just for a week.'[7] Wilhelm and Caroline became engaged in December that year.

Just outside Schönebeck was the settlement of Gnadau, home to a small colony of Herrnhut brethren. This pietist section of the Moravian Church, which emphasised deep personal religious experience, exerted considerable appeal at the time, particularly in the literary world. Through Henriette Herz's circle, Alexander was already acquainted with one Herrnhuter, the 'true genius, true oddball' Karl Philip Moritz, inter alia professor of art and linguistics, and the author of *Anton Reiser*.[8] This strongly autobiographical novel narrates the life of an ineffectual dreamer who—rather in the manner of Goethe's Wilhelm Meister—seeks refuge from reality in the theatre; but, not being a naturally gifted actor, he fails at life even when it's at one remove. Moritz had also published an account of his travels through England, which included a dramatic description of the caves of Derbyshire, which Alexander was to visit a few years after him. Goethe, too, was interested in the Herrnhut brethren—and indeed it was in *Wilhelm Meister* that he almost spelled out the extent of their influence on him. The 'Confessions of a Beautiful Soul' episode, which forms the hub of the novel, is based on the thinly disguised autobiographical writings of Goethe's friend, the Herrnhut canoness Susanna von Klettenberg. The philosopher Friedrich Schleiermacher, a member of Henriette's circle, had been brought up among Herrnhuters, as had Novalis, in whose poems the mark of Herrnhut-inspired mystical spirituality can still be discerned.[9]

When Alexander visited Gnadau, however, he appears to have been less struck by the spiritual aspect of the little model town than by its practical good sense. Göttingen, he reported later, for all its reputation as a famous seat of learning, did not even have a lightning rod installed on the roof of its university library; while Gnadau—no more, after all, than 'a colony of superstitious dreamers'—had 'five of them, notwithstanding the fact the town consisted of just twenty-odd houses.'[10] There was even, he observed, a rod on top of the church.

The university town of Helmstedt was the next stop. While it boasted 'many excellent people,' he found the place otherwise unattractive and dirty: 'one wouldn't want to be buried there.'[11] Further on, at Brunswick, Alexander stayed with his old teacher Campe and was introduced at the ducal court of Karl Wilhelm Ferdinand of Brunswick. The duke was married to an English princess, Augusta, granddaughter of George II. Never quite at home in her adoptive country, she had moved to a palace south of Brunswick, and named it 'Richmond.' Alexander reported that 'the crown prince is quite simple; the second and third in line completely stupid.' Indeed, the second son—another George—tended to be sent out of the way, to a nearby stud-farm, during official visits.[12]

But Göttingen! 'My academic life begins afresh,' Alexander wrote, as he finally saw the back of Kunth, who was returning to Berlin, having deposited Alexander in the rooms he would share with Wilhelm. 'My situation is utterly changed. I'm ready for my first step into the world, unguided and a free agent.'[13]

Göttingen was indeed a different world after the provincialism of Frankfurt-on-the-Oder. The university's star was in the ascendant and, by the time Alexander arrived, its reputation had eclipsed that of older universities such as Leipzig and Halle. A main factor in its flourishing was its close ties to England. Göttingen belonged to the Duchy of Brunswick, which was the ancestral seat of the Hanoverians. They had ascended to the English throne in 1714 with King George I, after Queen Anne, the last of the Stuart line, had died without any surviving offspring. George I's successor, George II, consolidated the ties between England and Brunswick when he founded Göttingen's university in 1734, named after him the Georgia Augusta. The current king of England, George III, kept up the connection by sending two of his fifteen children to Göttingen, where Alexander encountered them in his ethics course. One of them, Ernest Augustus, the future duke of Cumberland and king of

Hanover, later became notorious as a particularly vigorous champion of illiberal opinions, campaigning against the Irish Catholic Relief Bill and opposing the Reform Act of 1832. On his return to Germany as king of Hanover, he persisted in his apparent quest for unpopularity, most spectacularly in the case of the 'Göttingen Seven,' where he dismissed seven distinguished university professors from their posts—Jacob and Wilhelm Grimm among them—for failing to renew their oaths of allegiance to him.

While England had a tradition of mounting major research expeditions, and had the resources to do so, the academic interpretation of their findings was often left to others. Spectacular examples of this were the voyages of Captain Cook to the Pacific Ocean between the late 1760s and 1779. Göttingen, already established in the English orbit, was ideally placed to work on Cook's discoveries, and many specimens from his journeys ended up with Johann Friedrich Blumenbach, Alexander's professor in anatomy and anthropology. The academic connections were reinforced by personal ones. Blumenbach was related by marriage to the botanist Georg Forster, who (together with his father, Reinhold Forster) had accompanied Captain Cook on his second voyage. Georg Forster's wife, Therese, was the daughter of Blumenbach's colleague Christian Gottlob Heyne, while Blumenbach himself was married to a sister of Heyne's wife.

Blumenbach had an interest in the comparison and categorisation of humankind (it was he who coined the word 'Caucasian'). In another connection to Britain, he was in constant correspondence with Joseph Banks, who, as botanist on Cook's first voyage and now president of the Royal Society in London, had amassed a wide variety of human skulls. Those he made available generously, and quite a few of them found their way to Göttingen.

Blumenbach's most influential and original contribution, and one which still occupied him during Alexander's time in Göttingen, was his theory of a *Bildungstrieb* (formative drive). During a stay in the countryside, Blumenbach had observed a green polyp in a millpond, and had decided, in the spirit of research, to cut off some of its tentacles.[14] Instead of the wounds simply healing over, Blumenbach was surprised to see that the polyp slowly re-grew the severed limbs. On the strength of his finding, he decided that there must be an as-yet-unknown force at play, one that propels living organisms to develop their form, to defend it, and to restore it should it become damaged. He initially published his theory in the magazine *Göttingisches Magazin der Wissenschaften und Litteratur*, which was edited by Georg Forster and Georg Christoph Lichtenberg, in 1780 and 1781.[15]

Lichtenberg, Alexander's professor of physics, experimented with electricity and enjoyed his reputation as the man whom Goethe, Alessandro Volta, and William Herschel had travelled to Göttingen especially to see. His lectures as well as his scientific practice advocated the use of experiments, which at the time was relatively rare. Some years before, in 1777, he had built a huge electricity-generating device, called an electrophorus. It consisted of two plates six feet in diameter, one of them metal, the other resin, and it could be electrically charged by rubbing the resin plate. In experiments, Lichtenberg investigated the ways the energy gathered on the metal plate discharged. A light dusting of metal powder on the discharging surface created lightning trees, delicate fern-like structures that can also be observed on the skin of people struck by lightning, and which are still known as Lichtenberg figures.

Christian Gottlob Heyne, co-publisher of the *Göttingisches Magazin* and the man who had originally hired Blumenbach, was one of the university's brightest stars: Goethe had once hoped to study classical philology with him but, at the insistence of his father, had turned to law (and Leipzig) instead. Heyne was a classical historian. His presentation, according to Humboldt, was 'bumpy and stuttering,' but he thought him 'beyond question the brightest mind and in some areas the most erudite.'[16] Heyne was also director of the Societät der Wissenschaften (Society of Sciences), which had been set up with a particular purpose: to take advantage of the newly fashionable economic sciences and the many fee-paying students willing to invest in a fast track to a post in state administration. It was as part of this financially astute initiative that the celebrated economist Johann Beckmann had come to teach at Göttingen. Heyne's contribution to this enterprise was to lend a classical veneer to the study of economics.[17] In Alexander's case, this produced a curious hybrid of an essay (now lost), in which he attempted to prove that the weaving loom of the ancient Greeks and Romans was identical to the one brought to France by the Saracens and that was still in use at the time. 'It [the essay] is so learned,' he wrote to Wegener, 'it makes me quite sick [. . .]. Heyne is very pleased with it.'[18]

Alexander did not join in the traditional student pursuits, notably the duelling fraternities that so appalled the poet Heinrich Heine when he came to Göttingen thirty years later ('they move about in hordes, distinguished by colours of hats and pipe tassels, [. . .] forever knocking each other about, not greatly evolved, as far as morals and habits are concerned, from the times of the Barbarian invasions').[19] Instead, he wrote long letters to Wegener and sought out the people who interested him. Johann David Michaelis, theologian and orientalist, who—together with Heyne, Blumenbach, and Lichtenberg—was responsible for Göttingen's stellar reputation, had mostly retired from teaching, but Humboldt engineered an invitation to his house, where he found 'the atmosphere [. . .] free and open.'[20] There was also the presence of Michaelis's three daughters, who exerted an attraction sufficient, at least, to get him teased by his brother and Caroline: 'the talk in Göttingen, apparently, is that he is in love with Mademoiselle Michaelis.'[21]

The particular Mademoiselle must have been Caroline Böhmer, Michaelis's eldest daughter. Her husband, Johann Böhmer, had died the previous year, and she was now, at twenty-five, once again living in her parents' house. While she went on to cut a swathe through German Romanticism, Alexander, in his letters, mentioned her only in passing: Michaelis, he wrote, 'has several highly educated daughters, one of whom fancies herself quite the scholar.'[22] Caroline

Böhmer, in any case, had quite enough to be getting on with. Entangled with both the scholar August Wilhelm Schlegel and Georg Tatter, the tutor of the English princes, she went on, in 1792, to join Georg and Therese Forster in Mainz (which had become a bastion of support for the ideals of the French Revolution on German soil). Caroline had close links to both husband and wife. Therese was a childhood friend and a fellow former '*Universitätsmamsell*'—one of the academically gifted daughters of Göttingen professors who, being women, were unable to enrol at the university themselves, and were generally expected to marry one of their father's more promising students. But Caroline had known Georg independently, too: freshly returned from his journey with Cook, he had visited Göttingen and made Caroline the present of a fine piece of fabric from Tahiti, which she had fashioned into a shepherdess costume for herself.[23] In Mainz, she had an affair with a nineteen-year-old French lieutenant and became pregnant. When the German army re-conquered the city, revolutionaries in Mainz were arrested, and Caroline ended up imprisoned in the fortress of Königstein (in the Taunus hills nearby)—all the while with her daughter, Auguste (born 1785), by her side. She spent her confinement under the care and supervision of Friedrich Schlegel (August Wilhelm's younger brother), who fell hopelessly in love with her. She was eventually freed, thanks to the intercession of her half-brother and of her rejected suitor August Wilhelm Schlegel. Probably as a result of August Wilhelm's devotion, in 1796 Caroline married him after all—though she would later leave him for the philosopher Friedrich Schelling, her junior by eleven years. With the exception of Friedrich Schiller (the dramatist, poet, and philosopher), who loathed her, she seems to have divided opinion neatly along gender lines; Dorothea Veit Schlegel, married to Friedrich Schlegel, thought her 'coquettish and low.'

In September 1789, just after the beginning of the French Revolution, Humboldt took advantage of the break between university semesters to set off on a short trip along the river Rhine, accompanied by a young Dutch botanist, Jan van Geuns. While the ostensible objective of the expedition was to examine unusual basalt formations in a cave near the Rhine, Humboldt was keen to finally make the acquaintance of the famous Georg Forster, now employed as librarian at the University of Mainz.

Georg Forster had been one of the heroes of Humboldt's childhood. At eighteen, he had circumnavigated the globe on Captain Cook's ship *Resolution*, together with his father, Reinhold Forster, who was the botanist on this second voyage (1772–75) of Cook. The botanist on Cook's first voyage (1768–71) had been the celebrated Joseph Banks, and it was generally expected that he would continue the association. However, Banks's requirements had risen along with his fame, and, when the extensive accommodation he demanded for himself and his retinue threatened to render the *Resolution* unseaworthy, the Admiralty revoked his appointment. A replacement was needed quickly, and was found in the German botanist Forster, who took his son Georg along as his assistant.

Georg Forster published an account of his adventures, *A Voyage Round the World*, written in lively, evocative prose and illustrated with colour plates of his own drawings of the flora and fauna of the South Seas—seals, penguins, and birds of paradise. It became a publishing sensation, capturing the imagination of the German public, and earning the admiration even of Goethe.[24]

Alexander and van Geuns travelled through the mountains of the Bergstraße to Heidelberg and Mannheim. They spent three days in the 'magnificent' botanical gardens in Mannheim, famous for containing 'the treasures of both Indies.'[25] Only a few years later, in 1795, the gardens sustained heavy damage in the French bombardment of Mannheim, and they were subsequently closed.

Armed with letters of recommendation—one from Heyne to his son-in-law Georg Forster, and one from Lichtenberg—Alexander and van Geuns arrived at Mainz, where Forster welcomed them into his house. Forster was thirty-five years old at the time, and

Alexander twenty. There is no description of their meeting, but the visitors stayed for eight days, and Humboldt and Forster kept in touch afterwards.

To reach the basalt cave at Unkel, near Bonn, which had 'the most curious [formations] in Germany,' they took a boat down the river Rhine.[26] Humboldt made what he thought an exciting and original discovery: 'right in the middle of the densest rock,' there were enclosures of water.[27] The timing for such a finding was perfect, since the origin of basalt was at the heart of one of the big debates dominating natural history at the time: that between the Neptunists and the Plutonists.

The Neptunists maintained that all geological phenomena had come about through the agency of water. Most rocks, therefore, could be seen as sediment, left over from the receding waters of a great ocean that had covered a primeval earth. This theory had been propounded by Abraham Gottlob Werner, Germany's reigning authority on geology at that time and professor at the mining academy at Freiberg. Neptunism was very much the conservative, establishment position, and could even draw on the biblical flood for support. Goethe, too, found Neptunism congenial; he preferred, in life as in his scientific thinking, the idea of gradual change over the violence occasioned by revolutions and explosions. On the other side were the Plutonists. James Hutton, in Edinburgh, had pioneered the theory of a dynamic earth, in which the surface of the earth was shaped by interlocking forces of heat and pressure.[28] In Germany, the Plutonist charge was led by Werner's former student Johann Voigt, who argued that most rock formations were the result of volcanic activity. Basalt emerged as one of the deciding battlegrounds: many of the spectacular formations that so fascinated the Romantics—Fingal's Cave on the Hebrides, the Giant's Causeway in Ireland—looked as though they were of volcanic origin, but were located in or near water.[29]

With the scientific findings of his journey, Humboldt approached Campe, his former tutor and now proprietor of an educational publishing house—and, at Easter 1790, his first book, *Mineralogical Observations on some Basalts of the Rhine* (*Mineralogische Beobachtungen über einige Basalte am Rhein*) was published, with a dedication to Forster. In it, Humboldt came down on the side of the Neptunists. He graciously acknowledged the contributions of the Plutonists, but drew attention to the existence of some faked artefacts of supposedly volcanic origin that were doing the rounds. Key to his argument was his discovery of some tiny cracks in the Unkel cave's basalt columns, in which he discovered 'pure water'—an observation that could be neatly enlisted in service of the Neptunists' argument. By favouring the Neptunists, Humboldt also managed to avoid alienating Werner, which seemed a sensible course of action since Humboldt was looking at Werner's mining academy as a promising way of pursuing natural history without going openly against his mother's wishes.

While Humboldt admired Forster, who had lived the sort of life that he himself craved, Forster's situation was not as enviable as it seemed from the outside. His employment in Mainz at the university library had soon revealed itself to be thankless, and unglamorous at that. The place was in disarray, and the funds that Forster had at his disposal were entirely insufficient to fix this—and, even if he could have done so, leaving a well-ordered library was not how he envisaged his professional legacy. His private life was unlikely to provide much comfort: Ludwig Huber, a twenty-five-year-old writer and friend of both Georg and Therese, had taken the step of moving in with the couple, something in which Forster had acquiesced with a curious passivity.

It was in these bleak circumstances, in the spring of 1790, that Forster decided that a change was needed. There was potential business in England: since Forster's means were modest, if the Royal Society supported him financially, he might be able to publish a work on botany. And his recent guest, Humboldt, must have presented himself as the ideal candidate for a travel companion to England.

Indeed, Alexander accepted the invitation by the older man with enthusiasm: 'I am about to leave Göttingen, perhaps for good, and don't feel any the worse for it,' he announced to Campe on March 17, 1790. 'Tomorrow I'll be on my way to Mainz and to Forster—to travel to *London* with him. [. . .] I'm very cheerful—if confused.'[30]

Joseph Banks, by now president of the Royal Society, was not amenable to Forster's proposal, however. He had not been impressed by the attempts of Forster senior, his old usurper, to capitalise on his trip on the *Resolution* with some hastily compiled botanical publications. Nor did malicious remarks about the English court, which Reinhold had published in the polemical journal *Tableau d'Angleterre*, help his son's reception in London.

Forster had to fall back on the hospitality of a relative, a preacher at the German chapel at St. James. Humboldt went to find his own accommodation, and was soon established in congenial rooms in the house of a German wig-maker in Plumtree Street, in Bloomsbury. There, the walls were decorated with copper plates recovered from a ship of the East India Company that had sunk in a storm. Humboldt, as he remembered later, looked at them as at emblems of another life, giving substance to his vague desire to 'transport myself from an everyday, common existence into a magical world.'[31]

While Forster laboured joylessly and unsuccessfully to establish favourable relations with Banks, Humboldt, being young and unencumbered by previous history, and bearing letters of introduction from Banks's friend Johann Friedrich Blumenbach, found himself invited by the great man. Perhaps his social ease and self-confidence reminded Banks of his own younger self. At any rate, Humboldt was inducted into the most interesting and illustrious scientific company of the day. He met John Webber, the draughtsman on Cook's third voyage (1776–79), who had witnessed Cook's death; the cartographer Alexander Dalrymple; Henry Cavendish, who had revealed the chemical composition of water; and the German-born astronomer William Herschel, who nine years previously had discovered the planet Uranus.

Banks's invitation also provided Humboldt with the chance to meet and converse with the protagonist of England's most recent seafaring drama and hero of the popular imagination: William Bligh, whom Alexander frequently ran into at Banks's house, had just published his *Narrative of the Mutiny on Board His Majesty's Ship Bounty*. Alexander, in his letters home, got rather caught up in the romance of the story: 'The *Bounty* was sent to collect breadfruit trees in the South Seas and take them to the West Indies. Never did a benevolent intention look to be accomplished more happily.'[32] He appears to have overlooked the less happy motive underpinning the enterprise: the breadfruit was intended as a cheap source of food for enslaved Africans in the Caribbean, thus bolstering a practice he would later come to condemn vehemently.

In England's unfamiliar environment, Alexander appeared to flourish more naturally than he had at home; certainly, he seemed more comfortable. Travelling to Bath and on to Bristol by coach, before heading north for the Peak District and the Derbyshire caves, Forster wrote to his wife, Therese:

> Once Humboldt has gone to bed, I cannot get him out again; [. . .] Breakfast is the only means by which it can be done. Nobody sleeps as readily, easily and much as he can while sitting in a carriage; but when he is awake, he notices more than one who doesn't sleep at all.[33]

On the journey back south, they visited Stratford, admired Blenheim, and passed through Oxford, where they were shown through the Botanic Garden by the botanist John Sibthorp, a correspondent of Blumenbach. On June 28, about an hour after sunset, Forster and Humboldt were walking along the beach at Dover, 'Shakespeare's cliff tall and eerie' at their backs. As Forster contemplated the towers of Dover castle dissolving into the twilight, he was disturbed by a cry: it was Alexander, who, easily susceptible to all phenomena of nature, had been struck by the full moon rising over Calais in a blaze of light.[34]

Perhaps what Humboldt remembered most of his journey to England, he later wrote, were his walks. When he returned to London from the hills of Highgate and Hampstead, his eye would be drawn to notices displayed along the way, advertising for ships' crews. Their words were like a siren's call to him; they asked, or so he recalled, for 'young men wanting to seek their fortune outside Europe, to report for jobs as sailors or clerks. The ship is ready to sail for Bengal.' There was another world, exotic and full of promise, and tantalisingly within reach.

Humboldt and Forster left England at the end of June and reached Paris in time for the celebrations of the first anniversary of the French Revolution. The exultant atmosphere and the general rush of excitement could not fail to leave a deep mark on one so impressionable. Alexander later wrote that 'the sight of the Parisians, their National Assembly, their yet unfinished Temple of Liberty, to which I myself have carted some sand, still stands before my soul like an apparition in a dream.'[35] But Forster's leave was over, and Alexander had promised Therese to always stay by Forster's side, so they left before the festivities had properly begun, and returned to Mainz together.

Alexander stayed on in Mainz for what remained of July, living in Forster's household and exploring the surrounding countryside. In nearby Frankfurt am Main, he had the satisfaction of finding definite proof for what he had long suspected: that a lot of the stone samples that were sitting in mineral cabinets all over Europe, purporting to be of volcanic origin, were in fact carefully manufactured artefacts. In Frankfurt's Sachsenhausen district, he got talking to a stone mason, who freely admitted to having glazed 'whole crate loads' of porous stones in a brick oven, and sold them on to 'believing as well as unbelieving volcanists, as lavas, Icelandic glass and so on,' serving the high demand that existed for such objects.[36]

In Forster's house, the atmosphere was increasingly strained. It had become obvious that Therese's infatuation with Ludwig Huber had turned into a full-blown affair. Therese Forster herself wrote down a disturbing vignette from that time:

> I remember a fine story in Mainz, where Forster, Huber and Alexander Humboldt had been out drinking. On their return, in order to demonstrate their sobriety to me, they all came into my bedroom, where Forster couldn't endure being for long, and went to his study. Just then, the Hanoverian envoy Steinberg announced himself: I've never been more embarrassed. Huber was bubbling over with high spirits, Alexander laughed like a calf and kept walking around Steinberg in circles, and I poured tea and trembled like a sinner. Afterwards I often found myself laughing at this funny scene.[37]

Whatever it was that happened in Therese's bedroom, it clearly was more than Forster was able to bear. But, characteristically, he refused to make a scene, and preferred to walk away.

On July 26, 1790, Alexander said goodbye to Forster—and would not see him again. Forster would be dead in less than four years. He had long been disillusioned with the repressive atmosphere in the electorate of Mainz with its absolutist ruler. And his domestic circumstances made matters worse. Forster considered tolerating the situation for the sake of his marriage, but privately admitted to feeling 'like a plant that has been touched by frost and will never recover.'[38]

Many of Mainz's citizens, trapped within a reactionary German regime, had been looking with some yearning at the events unfolding over the border in France. In October 1792, French Revolutionary troops took Mainz in their conquest of the German possessions to the left of the Rhine (which France regarded as inside her natural borders). Therese fled, but her friend Caroline Böhmer stayed behind with Forster, who threw himself into political activity, helping to establish the Revolutionary Mainz Republic and to form a provisional government under the French. A few months later, Forster was in Paris to help negotiate the integration of the Mainz Republic into the French state, when, in his absence, Mainz was recaptured by Prussian and Austrian troops (July 1793). Regarded as a traitor to his own country, Forster was forced to stay in Paris, where he had to watch the disintegration of the Revolution. Impoverished and ill, he died there early in 1794, at the age of thirty-nine, in circumstances that have never been clearly established.

Goethe had watched events from the outside, and even though his sympathies did not lie with the revolutionaries, he was upset at the news. 'So poor Forster did end up paying with his life for his errors,' he commented, when he heard. 'I felt very sorry for him.'[39] Many years later, when Humboldt was writing *Cosmos* and knew he was nearing the end of his own life, he returned to the memory of his 'celebrated teacher and friend.' 'Gifted with a delicate aesthetic feeling,' Humboldt wrote about Forster,

> he kept within himself the vivid impressions that Tahiti and the other, in those days happier, islands of the South Seas had left on his imagination (just as, more recently, they did to Charles Darwin) [. . .]. Everything that can give truth, individuality and vibrancy to the description of an exotic nature can be found in his work.[40]

Humboldt himself was not altogether happy during this period. His brother, writing to his fiancée, Caroline, noticed this:

> The poor boy is not content. He is dissatisfied with himself, and this frame of mind is worsened by some sort of hypochondria brought about by his stay in Göttingen and by studying too hard. He writes to me that he has lost more than half of his old cheerfulness. He adds that he knows a way to restore it: to see the two of us together and to live with us.[41]

Whether living with his brother and future sister-in-law would really have improved Humboldt's spirits is questionable, but it was obvious that Wilhelm's new relationship brought into sharper relief the fact that something was lacking in Alexander's own life. Rather than emulating them, however, he seemed to seek proximity to the people he loved. He had come up with a similar scheme before, and one equally unrealistic, when he had projected a vision of the future to Wegener: 'We will live together, be sad and happy together.'[42]

Is it simply that he was attracted only to men, and that marriage to a woman was of no interest to him? Did his expressions of affection for Wegener reveal his real inclinations—which in any case he would have been unable to openly follow, or declare? Or was there a deeper motive, less focused still?

Like Forster, Humboldt did not dismiss out of hand the possibility of living in an arrangement involving a third person. Perhaps, also like Forster—the 'noble, sensitive, and ever-hopeful spirit,' as he called him—he was looking for something else, something beyond the bounds of the known and the everyday.[43] Could it be that the 'longing for wide and unknown things'—this aimless, but increasingly undeniable, feeling that he had first identified in London—was not confined to the geographical realm, but rather permeated his whole personality?[44]

For the moment, he had written to Wegener, 'I won't be swept away by strong passions. Serious concerns and, most of all, the study of nature will keep me away from sensuality.'[45] It is unclear whom he was attempting to convince. But perhaps this was a reassuring, if temporary, resolution for Humboldt, who seems to have been incapable of discerning the point of deep water if he wasn't, sooner or later, going to step right into it.

6

Hamburg, an Interlude

~~❦~~

A fter the heady time in England, the prospect of picking up his old life where he had left it was not appealing. It is clear that he felt the stay to have been decisive for him. His sojourn, he explained, with perhaps a touch of melodrama, had 'put me at odds [. . .] with the world of my fatherland and a return to Berlin, which loomed above me, dark and oppressive, like the clouds of an approaching thunderstorm.'[1]

The bad weather he foresaw—his impending absorption into the state administration in the Prussian capital—was to be preceded by a minor cloud, in the form of the Büsch Academy of Commerce in Hamburg. This institution, led by Johann Georg Büsch and Christoph Daniel Ebeling, was primarily a finishing school for young merchants, but was also used by fledgling state administrators to gain an insight into the mechanics of trade.

Alexander, as usual, went along with what his mother and Kunth had planned for him, but, again as usual, not without making some preparations for schemes of his own. So, in July 1790, while still in Mainz, he sent a brief missive to Abraham Gottlob Werner, freighted with flattery. Werner, he said, had done 'for mineralogy what Linnaeus did for botany.' The enclosed copy of Alexander's *Mineralogical Observations* was accompanied by a little note that explained how he had 'found nothing that would have needed extinct volcanoes as a prerequisite; whereas everywhere I saw evidence for the neptunic origin of basalt.' In fact, 'your idea of a layer of basalt that stretched across the earth's surface never appeared more obvious and apparent to me than when I observed horizontal layers on the highest peaks at Linz and Unkel.' His letter concluded with an expression of hope that he might one day be lucky enough to be counted among Werner's students.[2] This done, he left Mainz the very next day, stopping at Göttingen just long enough to drop in on his brother, before travelling further north, to spend the next several months in Hamburg.

Werner wasn't the only one to receive a copy of the *Mineralogical Observations*. In fact, Alexander used the book like a calling card (subscribing early on to the notion that 'shouting is part of the writer's craft'), and, as a result, his reputation preceded him.[3] 'The *Hamburger Correspondent*,' Alexander wrote, with a humility that was not entirely consistent with the fact that he himself had sent the review copy to the magazine, and enlisted the support of the director of the Büsch Academy, 'carries some outrageous praise of the book. [. . .] Büsch (whose Institute is on the decline) wishes to shout it from the rooftops what learned folk are flocking to him from far and wide.'[4]

'I live here not cheerfully, but content,' he wrote to Wegener in an early letter sent from Hamburg. And indeed Humboldt's circumstances were far from unpleasant: his room overlooked a garden, and there were no disturbances other than the bell that was rung for lunch and dinner. But it seems that after Göttingen and England, life felt a bit dull. 'As a student at Professor Büsch's merchants' academy,' he went on, 'I see nothing but numbers and accounting books before me and must forget my plants and stones.'[5] This, it has to be said, was not strictly true: when some specimens of the striking red sedimentary rock from the island of Heligoland caught his eye, and he coveted some for himself, he found a way to arrange the 'very stormy sea journey of forty-five miles' to the small archipelago, where he stayed for eight days.[6]

The academy's social life did not make up for its lack of academic distinction. 'It is not as though there were no cultivated men among the merchants here,' Alexander wrote, 'but this very culture covers them with a sort of a veneer, rendering them all alike, and rather boring, so that one would frequently wish them back into their crude state.'[7] Students tended to keep company with those of their own social backgrounds, in a way that seemed comically backwards and provincial to Humboldt. 'I move in all circles,' he wrote, 'bourgeois as well as academic.'[8] The only person from his Hamburg days with whom he subsequently kept in touch seems to have been his Scottish fellow student Archibald Maclean, and it was to him that he later explained how much he had been unable to be himself during his time in Hamburg: he had been popular and liked, yet at the same time, he was very much not in his own natural habitat. With his fellow students, he wrote to Maclean, it had been 'only by dissimulation' that he had been able 'to repay the often unwelcome affection they directed at me.'[9]

'I am, alas, destined for a career that distracts me terribly from my studies,' Humboldt wrote in a letter to his friend the botanist Paul Usteri. This left open the question of what exactly he regarded as his real studies—beyond the desire to avoid being shoehorned into a conventional career. 'My unfortunate situation [. . .] always forces me to want what I can't do, and to do what I don't like.'[10] But even if he wasn't quite able to put his finger on what it was that he did want to do, he felt its importance with a passion: 'there is some drive within me,' he wrote, 'an urgent yearning, to the point that I often fear that I'm about to lose what little reason I have.'[11]

A trip to Heligoland was all very well, but there were other interesting possibilities for an aspiring civil servant. Werner's mining academy in Freiberg was still on his mind. So just before Christmas, Humboldt wrote to Werner again. A Freiberg degree took three years, but, since he would be tied down in Hamburg until April 1791 and was expected to start his employment the following September, he asked if he could come to stay for six months instead. Even six months was more time than he really had: as he himself admitted, his visit was unlikely to extend beyond a few months over the summer. Meanwhile, he continued to hedge his bets, careful to keep his connections well tended. While Werner had been an early recipient of the *Mineralogical Observations*, now a second volley of copies issued from Hamburg in all directions: one went to Baron Heinitz, head of the Prussian mining department in Berlin; another to Heinitz's protégé Dietrich Ludwig Gustav Karsten, freshly elevated to the position of assessor of mines; Georg Forster's father, Reinhold, received a copy; as did Humboldt's former professor Georg Lichtenberg in Göttingen. A further copy made its way north to Uppsala, where the naturalist Carl Peter Thunberg taught—the man who had brought the blade of rice, *Oryza sativa*, back from Japan.

The copy that went to Joseph Banks, Humboldt's most illustrious contact in London, was accompanied by a letter that made rather ambitious claims for the basalt cave at Unkel: 'C'est le Giants-Causeway de l'Allemagne!'[12] This produced a most satisfactory response: a friendly welcome into the world of scientific networking to the aspirant from the acknowledged master. Banks expressed the hope that Humboldt should come and visit him again, and asked him for a small favour: to find someone 'to do my little commissions with punctuality & discretion.' In return, he promised, 'Should you have any commands here, I shall have great pleasure in obeying them.'[13] The connection must have been particularly pleasing to Humboldt: he had enjoyed his time in England so much that he had even entertained the thought of moving there. 'Should all my wishes come true, then I'll return to England in a year and a half. It would be a very congenial place to live,' he had written to Wegener just before Banks's reply arrived, in a letter enclosed with Wegener's own personal copy of the *Mineralogical Observations*.[14]

Humboldt left Hamburg without much heartache at the end of April 1791. As he had correctly observed when he arrived, the academy was on a downward trajectory, and, not long after his departure, suffered a further decline in its fortunes: there had been two fatalities among its students—not likely, as Humboldt observed, to enhance its reputation. 'Pepin and Metzer [. . .] will have hardly done the academy a favour with their deaths,' Humboldt commented; 'this sort of thing really tends to put parents off, and the whole Institute [. . .] now seems likely to fold.'[15]

In May 1791, Humboldt was back at Tegel. He can't have been surprised to find that being at home was not restorative: within days, he was ill with a high fever, and, as he wrote to his Hamburg friend Wilhelm Wattenbach, a swollen cheek.[16] As soon as he was better, he went out to resume the botanising and mineralising forays with Karl Willdenow. But Willdenow may have been less able to devote time to his student than he had been previously, for he had, according to Humboldt, acquired a 'dear simple wife.'[17] In general, Berlin seemed diminished and wanting. When he sent a present of a small piece of amber to the scientist Johann Reimarus, whom he had befriended in Hamburg, he accompanied it with the remark that it was 'the only mineral our Berlin deserts are able to provide.'[18]

He had reached a turning point: he reckoned that he was now, at twenty-one, 'of an age where I ought to decide on my field of activity.'[19] If he was to be a civil servant, it might as well be on his own terms. So he picked up his pen again and wrote to Baron Heinitz, asking him for a job in the mining department—if at all possible deferred for six months, to allow him to go to Freiberg to study with Werner. Heinitz was probably the one person who would not have thought such a request brazen—he himself had been involved in founding the academy some twenty-five years earlier, with a view to reforming the administration of mining through an injection of sound training and research. Heinitz replied post-haste, in a way that could not have been more accommodating or generous. He commended Humboldt on his desire to further his knowledge in the service of the mining department, and concluded with an order for Humboldt to present himself on his return from Freiberg, whereupon there would indeed be a post for him as an assistant inspector of mines.[20]

With his departure now imminent, time with Wilhelm became precious, and the brothers spent a busy and intense few days together at Tegel. They were both on the brink of major life changes.

Wilhelm had left Göttingen the year before without finishing his degree, but had been offered employment in the justice ministry in Berlin, which was very much the outcome his mother had hoped for. However, after not much more than a year at the ministry, he made quite a radical decision: in spite of excellent career prospects, he was going to take an indefinite period of leave. In fact, he wrote to the king, Friedrich Wilhelm II, to ask for his official discharge. His plan was to marry Caroline at the earliest opportunity and to buy a small estate away from the bustle of Berlin, where he would devote him-self to private study and generally live an 'independent, quiet, self-determined life.'[21] So while Alexander was packing his bags for Freiberg, Wilhelm was planning for married life. He reported on progress to Caroline, who was waiting at home in Erfurt:

> I have ordered a dozen wickerwork chairs, very pretty, and a sofa made from pear tree wood. The sofa will be upholstered with steel springs, and as it will make an attractive piece of furniture, it wouldn't have been nice to use the green canvas. Instead, I'll get some smooth, pale blue fabric [. . .]. I've asked Karl to buy a Wedgwood tea pot in Leipzig [. . .] of the type that is fashionable now.[22]

On the morning of June 3, 1791, a carriage took Alexander south towards Saxony. Later that day, Wilhelm, sitting at his desk at Tegel, wrote to Caroline, trying to put into words how his brother had struck him, now that he had seen him after what had amounted to a break of almost a year.[23] Alexander, he wrote, had 'turned out very well, though rather different from the way I expected.' Something seemed to be amiss. Was it the lack of a guiding principle or great purpose in Alexander that perturbed Wilhelm, or simply the void where a prospective wife ought to be? It wasn't that he found his brother cold; on the contrary, he thought him capable of affection and loyalty 'way beyond the ordinary.' But, as he imparted to the woman with whom he planned to share his own future, he wasn't confident that Alexander would find the same sort of happiness: 'I don't believe that anyone will capture his heart—while at the same time he would be cut out for such a way of life—and it's one of which he thinks so highly.' Worse, 'he'll never be content on his own, because he senses that he won't find fulfilment by himself. Every so often he's even made remarks to me in this vein, though mostly our innermost feelings were concealed as if by a veil, which we both saw, but neither dared lift.'[24]

Wilhelm and Caroline were to be married within weeks. His younger brother, Wilhelm could see clearly, was unlikely to follow a similar path. Was the explanation a straightforward one, that Alexander preferred the company of men? It seems unlikely that Wilhelm would have been too embarrassed to ask. The brothers communicated freely enough; Wilhelm even felt obliged, when sending one of Alexander's letters on to Caroline, to cut out some lines which he felt inappropriate for his bride's eyes: 'you know that what is thought delicate or indelicate is so different between our and your gender. Otherwise I wouldn't have been able to show you the letter.'[25]

Comparing his situation to that of his brother, Wilhelm must have felt that the difference between them amounted to more than simply sexual orientation. While he himself was in the process of arranging his life down to the colour of his sofa and the style of his teapot, Alexander seemed to recoil instinctively against everything conventional and regimented. It was a theme that was emerging with ever more clarity: the familiar tended to bore him, whereas the unknown attracted him strongly. Anticipating his stay in Freiberg, Alexander had written, with hardly concealed excitement: 'Again, I am going to a place where I do not know a soul.'[26]

7

The Compensations of Mining

'I am taking the liberty, my dear friend, of sending you my small paper on basalt, which was published (full of misprints!) while I was travelling in England.'[1]

Humboldt continued to use the *Mineralogical Observations* as a means of introducing himself. This time the target was a young man called Carl Freiesleben. Freiberg had a small student population—Humboldt enrolled as the 357th student since the academy's inception in 1765—and it was part of the programme to integrate the students closely into the community of miners and teachers. Accordingly, Humboldt was allocated rooms in the house of a high-ranking mining official, Carl Friedrich Freiesleben—the younger Carl's uncle. In fact, Freiesleben senior held a position of such distinction as to render it entirely untranslatable—at least to Humboldt, who wrote to his friend Archibald Maclean, in English, 'I am sure that you don't know what a creature is a *Obereinfahrer?*'[2] Carl junior, who had been born and raised in Freiberg, was steeped in mining, and Humboldt found him gentle and intelligent. And so, even though he was almost five years younger than Humboldt, the two fell into an easy friendship, one that was instantly cordial and affectionate: 'it will break my heart to leave this place,' Humboldt predicted.[3]

It was not the first time Humboldt had been inside a mine, of course—Carl von La Roche, for example, had taken him on a tour of his mining district near Magdeburg—but being part of the day-to-day business of a working mine was something quite new to him. It meant entering an environment that was utterly, and alarmingly, unlike life above ground: otherworldly and oppressive, men had no natural place here, and it was decidedly unsafe.

In *The Journey to the Harz* (*Die Harzreise*), the Romantic poet Heinrich Heine gave a vivid account of what it felt like to descend into a mine:

A miner, having lit his mine-light, conducts the visitor towards a dark opening much like that of a chimney, climbs down it until he's in up to his chest, explains about holding on to the ladders, and asks him to follow, and not to worry. [. . .] And now all of a sudden one is supposed to climb on all fours, the dark hole is very dark indeed, and God knows how long that ladder may be. It soon becomes clear that it's not just a single ladder, leading down into some black nothingness, but many, of about fifteen to twenty rungs, each perched on a small shelf on which a man can stand, and from which a new hole leads further down, to a new ladder. [. . .] The rungs are slithery with mud. And so it goes on down from one ladder to the next, while the guide, ahead, all the while assures you that it's not at all dangerous, as long as you hold on tight to the rungs, don't look down at your feet, don't become faint, and on absolutely no account step onto the plank where the barrel-rope hurtles up and where, a fortnight ago, a careless person had plunged down and, regrettably, broken his neck. I didn't descend to the deepest depth [. . .] but, between ourselves, it seemed deep enough to me—there was a continual roaring and rushing, an uncanny moving of machinery, a trickling of subterranean springs, water dripping everywhere and vapours rising like fog, while the mining lamp flickered ever more weakly into the lonely night. I felt numb, my breath was heavy, and I held on to the slippery ladder rungs with difficulty.[4]

Humboldt had arrived on June 14, 1791, and the following day he found himself down his first mine, named the Elector (after the local Saxon sovereign). Even though Freiesleben was by his side most of the time, helping and advising him, the pace was hectic, and it soon became obvious that the time-frame Humboldt had set for his studies wasn't realistic. Especially when, after only ten days in Freiberg, he announced that he was about to take off again, to 'embark on my little tour to Erfurt. I'll be back in eight days.'[5]

The reason, of course, was that Wilhelm and Caroline were getting married, in her father's house in Erfurt, on June 29. After the secret engagement in December 1789, in which Alexander had served as the witness, there had been a bit of cloak and dagger about the run-up to the wedding. Both of the couple's remaining parents—Frau von Humboldt, and Caroline's father, Karl Friedrich von Dacheröden—thought that their child might have made a better match elsewhere. And both would have preferred to see Wilhelm more firmly established in his career before the marriage, reacting with consternation when they heard that Wilhelm had left the civil service altogether. It had been left to Alexander's diplomatic skills to bring about a softening on both sides, even though Caroline had been reluctant to acknowledge his role:

> If he likes the idea that Mama's [Frau von Humboldt's] consent will be hard to obtain, and enjoys leading the negotiations, then let's not spoil it for him; and perhaps he's not so wrong after all. Mama may indeed have different plans for you, and schemes for a marriage more advantageous for your advancement.[6]

The wedding was small, attended by close family as well as the recently married Friedrich Schiller, whose wife, Charlotte, née von Lengefeld, was a childhood friend of Caroline.

Alexander was back in Freiberg within the week. He decided to extend his stay until February 1792. But still, the programme was very full: 'Every day, I get up at five in the morning, and, as it takes half an hour to forty-five minutes to get to the mines, I head out straight away. I am busy below ground for five hours, [. . .] and only this morning have been engaged with drilling and blasting.'[7] The work was physically hard and it was easy to get injured—a wound to his hand, from a drilling accident, incapacitated him for several days.

But he adjusted quickly, and, three weeks in, he was able to report that 'at least, I don't bleed any more.'[8]

The afternoons were set aside for lectures. Werner's academic career had reached the point where his celebrity had begun to out-pace his scientific competence, and Humboldt, who had courted him so assiduously in the past, was now alive to every weakness. Werner wasn't rigorous, he told Maclean; he was the type of person 'who calls nothing by its proper name.'[9] Lectures were repeatedly cancelled, as Werner was caught up in fussing over an elaborate dedication to the elector of Saxony in his new book.[10] When Humboldt discovered a new species of lichen underground, Werner decided that the plant should be sent to the elector as a present— though what he would have done with it was not at all clear. Humboldt also had no compunction in blaming Werner if, for example, he found himself short of mineral samples for acquain-tances. He wrote to the mineralogist Dietrich Karsten: 'In spite of all pleading and urging I have not been able to extract a single, not even the tiniest, inorganic particle from Werner.'[11] Humboldt found another teacher, Johann von Charpentier, 'a complicated character,' more interesting than Werner. With a cosmopolitan outlook and a wide network of friends, Charpentier was one of Goethe's advisers on the mine at Ilmenau, which formed part of Goethe's responsibil-ities as privy councillor in Saxe-Weimar-Eisenach. In Freiberg, Charpentier took Humboldt under his wing and invited him to spend evenings with him and his family.

Werner had the misfortune of having associated himself with not one but two theories that were both superseded in his own lifetime. Humboldt was already sensing that casting his lot with Werner over the question of the neptunic versus volcanic origin of rocks might have been a mistake. For the moment, however, he was still open to reviewing evidence that suggested that basalt, at least, might be of neptunic origin. In the controversy, basalt was establishing itself as the last stronghold of the Neptunists, as its provenance could still plausibly be explained in accordance with their theory.

In August 1791, Humboldt—accompanied by Freiesleben ('the only person I have any dealings with here!')—set out on a field trip to the mountains southeast of Freiberg.[12] They travelled on foot. Behind them walked a miner pushing a wheelbarrow, who transported their laundry, as well as any mineral samples the two picked up. The main haul yielded by the excursion was a large clump of marl. This had been found embedded in some basalt rock, and bore the imprint of what looked like a plant. Though this wasn't conclusive proof in either direction—the fossil was in the marl, not the basalt itself—Humboldt chose to see it as a point for the Neptunists. Still, he was careful to formulate it as a question rather than a statement when writing to Maclean: 'Could there be a plainer clue as to the watery origin of basalt?'[13]

The other theory Werner endorsed, that of so-called phlogiston, had been rendered obsolete by Antoine Lavoisier's discovery, in the 1770s, of oxygen's role in combustion. The phlogiston theory nevertheless managed to cling on for a while longer, particularly in Germany, where there was reluctance to accept a French theory in place of the German one. The latter, invented by Johann Becher in the 1660s and further developed by Georg Ernst Stahl in the early 1700s, postulated that phlogiston is a substance—contained in every flammable material—that is released in the process of combustion, leaving 'de-phlogisticated' matter, such as ashes, behind. The corrosion of metals was also understood as a form of burning, in which phlogiston escaped and rust, like a metallic ash, was left behind. Animals and plants had their own way of taking part in the process, when, during respiration, they removed the phlogiston part of the air they breathed.

Humboldt had encountered the first cracks in the edifice of the phlogiston theory in London. Henry Cavendish, a frequent guest at Banks's house, had, with his discovery that water was composed of two separate elements, hydrogen and oxygen, prepared the way for Lavoisier's theory of chemical elements. Now, in Freiberg, Humboldt met the Spanish-Mexican scholar Andrés Manuel Del Río, who referred Humboldt to Lavoisier's lately published *Elementary Treatise on Chemistry* (1789).[14] It contained a record of all the substances—many of them newly discovered—that, Lavoisier believed, could not be further broken down. Among these elements, as he called them, was oxygen, which immediately presented itself as a much more plausible candidate than phlogiston to help explain combustion. The *Elementary Treatise* made a deep impression on Humboldt—he read it three times in quick succession, and then declared that it had caused a 'total revolution' in his thinking: 'I am convinced that Lavoisier's discoveries about carbon and carbonised gas are going to lead to great things.'[15]

While out botanising, newly alert to the importance of oxygen, Humboldt began to look at his surroundings with fresh eyes. He had long wondered about the lichens growing in darkness inside the mines. Not all of them reacted to the lack of sunlight in the same way. Most of them were a ghostly, almost white, version of their counterparts above ground. However, there were exceptions: some of these underground plants were distinctly green, their colouring exactly matching that of the same species above ground. One of these exceptions was the oversized, clearly thriving lichen that Humboldt had found growing at the entrance to one of the mines—the prospective present for the elector. Another one, according to Humboldt, was 'very elegant, and, as I believe, as yet undescribed,' sporting shoots that were 'grassy green.' '[A]nd yet,' he noted, 'neither has ever seen a ray of the sun.'[16] Intrigued, Humboldt established a small vegetable patch inside one of the mines, arriving eventually at the conclusion that it was not the exposure to light, but instead the presence of oxygen, that was responsible for the green colour in plants. He recorded his observations, which were later published as a small volume entitled *Florae Fribergensis* (1793).[17]

It was not just Humboldt, or Heinrich Heine, who thought that his experience underground was worth writing about. The associations between writers in the Romantic period and mining ran deep. A tragedy that occurred in 1677 at the mines of Falun, in Sweden, seems to have proved almost impossible not to write about. It concerned a young man called Mathias Israelsson, who was killed in a mining accident just days before his wedding, and whose body could not be recovered. Forty-two years later, by chance, the body came to light, but nobody knew who he was. It was left to his fiancée, now an old woman, to identify Israelsson—he had been preserved in vitriol in the bloom of his youth. Gotthilf Heinrich Schubert, Humboldt's fellow student at Freiberg, wrote about the incident, and it was then seized upon by one Romantic writer after another. Johann Peter Hebel and E. T. A. Hoffmann each wrote a short story about it. Of the scores of poems it inspired, the best known are by Friedrich Rückert and Achim von Arnim.[18]

The interest in Falun was only the most prominent example of the Romantic preoccupation with mining. The poet Ludwig Tieck, who had travelled with his friend and collaborator Wilhelm Heinrich Wackenroder on foot through the Fichtel mountains in 1793, wrote a fairy tale called 'Rune Mountain,' in which the protagonist leaves his wife and children in favour of a woman who originates from within a mountain, and is made of stone. Wackenroder, like other German Romantics, went on to die young, at twenty-four years of age. Novalis, who only lived until the age of twenty-eight, introduced the motif of the Blue Flower, the most potent emblem of German Romanticism, in his novel fragment *Heinrich von Ofterdingen*. Here, the Blue Flower is reached by way of an underground passage through a mountain cave. The protagonist, Heinrich, is advised to become a miner if he wants to discover nature's deepest secrets. The centrality of the mining motif to German Romanticism seems intuitive. To gain true knowledge what is needed is a turn to the inside, to subjective experience.

There is, of course, a much more straightforward way of looking at the link between writers at the time and the practice of mining: a number of the writers of the Romantic period were employed in the mining administration. Clemens Brentano studied mining at Bonn, and Joseph von Eichendorff, whose uncle owned a coal mine in

Silesia, attended mining lectures at the University of Halle. Some writers had passed through Werner's mining academy at Freiberg. Theodor Körner and Novalis enrolled after Humboldt had left, while Gotthilf Schubert was a friend, as was the Romantic philosopher Franz von Baader.[19]

In the late eighteenth century, mining in Germany experienced a renaissance. This was mainly the result of increasing industrialisation, and the need for a steady supply of iron for construction work and machinery. Since coal had replaced wood in the smelting of iron, a demand for coal had arisen, too. Steam engines, which underwent rapid improvement during the 1790s, accelerated the process. In a relatively short space of time, the mining industry had made great strides in efficiency. The Freiberg academy, the first of its kind, further consolidated Germany's commitment to this newly flourishing industry.

Novalis's real name was Friedrich von Hardenberg (he was a distant relative of Karl August von Hardenberg, the Prussian minister and reformer). The author of *Hymns to the Night* (*Hymnen an die Nacht*), his prevailing image is that of a wraithlike young man, physically frail with long hair; but in fact he spent the majority of his time engaged in the practical concerns of an inspector of mines. Novalis arrived in Freiberg a few years after Humboldt, in 1797, the same year in which his child-fiancée, the fifteen-year-old Sophie von Kühn, died. In Freiberg, he met Julie, Charpentier's daughter, to whom he got engaged in 1798, in spite of his own grave doubts: 'In all truth, I'd rather be dead.'[20]

The miners in Novalis's *Heinrich von Ofterdingen* are pulled in two directions. On the one hand, a desire for a more profound knowledge draws them deeper and deeper inside the earth. At the same time, they are peripatetic, never staying at any mine for long, seemingly compelled to seek out new and unfamiliar ground. Elsewhere, Novalis had expressed his own desire for places apparently defined only by being unimaginably distant: 'Come, friends, let us flee / The shackles Europe builds, / And go to unspoilt Tahiti.'[21]

Humboldt seems to have been subject to these contrary forces, too. But while he protested to Wegener that the pursuit of science would keep him from human ties, he actually formed attachments easily. On leaving the Freiberg academy at the end of February 1792, he found, much to his surprise, that he had been popular. On his last evening, he was presented with a poem signed by fourteen of his Freiberg friends. Overwhelmed by this affection, he couldn't bear to say goodbye to Freiesleben: he tried to avoid everybody by hiding out in Franz von Baader's rooms, and eventually slipped away in secret. While his attachment to Freiesleben wasn't as intense as his relationship with Wegener had been, it seems to have occupied similar emotional terrain. In a letter, he assured Freiesleben that 'never have I loved a human being as closely and so much from my heart, as you,' and he even resorted to one of his favourite themes, a vague dream of living together: 'the thought of living with you in the future [. . .] cheered me up.'[22]

8

The Life of the Civil Servant

❧

On the morning of July 29, 1793, during a routine inspection of the so-called Loyal Friendship mine in Kaulsdorf, the young chief inspector of mines for the Prussian province of Ansbach and Bayreuth (near Nuremberg) met with an unwelcome sight. The pit props—the many bits of wood that were needed to support the seams—weren't where they should be. In fact, they weren't there at all. Investigation soon revealed that they had been stolen: the night before, twelve miners from the rival mining town of Saalfeld had made a foray into the mine and abducted most of the mining furniture. All of the pit wood and some of the winches were gone.

The Loyal Friendship was located half-way between Kaulsdorf and Saalfeld, but clearly within the town boundaries of the former. Thanks to Prussia's acquisition of the duchies of Ansbach and of Bayreuth in 1791, Kaulsdorf now fell under the jurisdiction of Prussia's local mining inspector, Alexander von Humboldt. Saalfeld, on the other hand, only a couple of miles to the west, was part of the duchy of Saxe-Gotha. The Loyal Friendship was a particularly promising cobalt mine, and Theodor Sommer, Saalfeld's mining administrator, clearly thought that the process of territorial reorganisation (with a young, inexperienced mining official in charge on the Prussian side) presented an excellent opportunity for appropriating it. So, less than a year and a half after leaving full-time education, Humboldt found himself in the midst of a quite unacademic dispute, which involved remonstrating with Sommer, making representations to his own provincial Prussian mining department in Bayreuth, and appealing for help to the local Prussian minister, Karl August von Hardenberg. Two days after the initial discovery, Humboldt was back at the mine, tearing out the Saalfelders' new boundary post with his own hands, and demanding the return of the pit wood in the name of the king of Prussia.[1]

Since his departure from Freiberg in February 1792, Humboldt's career had proceeded in an exemplary fashion—indeed, one could have mistaken it for the career of somebody who really meant to scale the highest peaks in the Prussian state administration.

At university, Humboldt had acquired a thorough knowledge of mining, but no formal qualification—in fact, he never sat an examination of any sort in his entire life.[2] Even so, he found himself eminently employable. Baron Heinitz had immediately made good on his promise and made Humboldt assistant inspector in Prussia's mining department. For one who entered public administration with so much reluctance, Humboldt's pleasure at this was remarkably genuine: he admitted that he was 'quite embarrassed to feel so elated at such a trifle.' For form's sake, he had voiced qualms about being promoted over the heads of the 'bevy of ancient students, cadets etc,' who had been biding their time in the queue—although he was told that, for his exact position, he hadn't been preferred to anyone.[3] This was, strictly speaking, true. Heinitz, as chief of mining in Prussia, didn't just want a position filled. He was aiming for a complete overhaul of the Prussian mining administration, which had been pervaded by nepotism and bureaucracy, hoping instead to put it on a proper scientific footing. This was to be achieved in part by the strategic deployment of a cohort of highly trained new recruits, handpicked by him. Humboldt, keen and with the relevant experience, was an obvious candidate. But, as Heinitz must have been well aware, promoting a godson of King Friedrich Wilhelm II would not upset the old order either. On his appointment, Humboldt specially requested that he be deployed outside the capital: after all, he pointed out, Berlin was about as suitable a place to be for a mining engineer 'as it would be for the location of a naval college.'[4]

His first encounters with the higher echelons of the mining administration, of which he was now a part, had not gone well. In April 1792, just two months after leaving the mining academy, he had returned to Freiberg, this time in an official capacity. In the past, he had made his own way on horseback, but this time he travelled by coach, wedged in between his superiors, Baron von Stein and Count Reden. Both men were part of the progressive new wave of civil servants employed by Heinitz, though nepotism wasn't going to be wholly eradicated: Reden, a prickly and combative character, was Heinitz's nephew. Humboldt had encountered him before, and found him less than impressive: he had a 'feeble body,' he remarked, before concluding that 'much about his character needs to be judged in the light of this.'[5] In the coach, he insisted on discussing mining techniques with Humboldt, advancing entirely untenable opinions and thereby betraying the blatant incompetence that existed at the highest levels of the mining administration. 'He asserted terrible things,' Humboldt wrote; for example, he claimed that 'a supporting structure was always wholly unnecessary' inside a mine.[6]

Stein, if anything, was the worse of the two. When Humboldt had met him several years earlier at the court in Brunswick, on his way to Göttingen, he had thought him slightly ridiculous. Now Stein was his superior, and he had to listen to him spouting appalling opinions concerning 'the harshness that is needed in order to drive people.' Both Stein and Reden had a tendency towards 'rash decisions about matters which, to me, seemed highly doubtful.'[7] As the light faded outside the carriage windows, so too did Humboldt's morale: 'my future hovered about me like the falling night.'[8] The contrast with his time in Freiberg and with Freiesleben,[9] to whom he had so recently said goodbye, was too great, and he found himself embarrassed when he could not hold back tears: 'much as I tried to hide it, Reden still enquired about my red eyes.'[10]

The trip did, however, helpfully establish Humboldt's convictions about the sorts of job he did *not* want: it was now clear to him that he did not want to be in an office, removed from practical mining, and that he did not want to work for Stein. Back in Berlin, he returned to live with his mother at Tegel, and waited to be assigned a task. His thoughts returned to Freiberg, and he employed himself by looking over Freiesleben's manuscript about minerals in Saxony, to help prepare it for publication. Plans formed in his mind that were of grand design but seemed to him easy to execute: he would find Freiesleben a publisher, he wrote in a letter to him, and would contribute a preface—'with the reputation that I have managed to conjure within the literary world, that should have some effect.' He went on to fondly sketch out the imagined title page, which would display both their names, Freiesleben's as author and Humboldt's as editor. The plan never came to anything.[11]

In the meantime, Stein had applied for Humboldt to join his office. Heinitz, however, probably aware of Humboldt's reluctance, decided to spare his new, young assistant inspector from involvement in Stein's large-scale survey of salt mines. Instead, he assigned him to Karl August von Hardenberg. The latter's career had been dogged by personal challenges. His first marriage had come to an end a few years previously, in 1788, after his wife, Juliane von Reventlow, had had a highly public affair with George Augustus Frederick, the prince of Wales and future King George IV. Gossip had hardly been given time to die down when Hardenberg, almost immediately after his divorce from Juliane, married again; his new bride, Sophie von Lenthe, had herself been obliged to obtain a divorce to be able to marry Hardenberg. A minister to the last margrave of Ansbach-Bayreuth, Hardenberg transferred to the service of Friedrich Wilhelm II of Prussia, and gladly accepted his mission of taking charge of Prussia's new province of Ansbach and Bayreuth.

In the space of a single year, the margrave, Karl Alexander, had (being heavily in debt) sold both his duchies to Prussia, buried his wife, married his English mistress (the author Elizabeth Craven), and departed for Britain, where he was to spend the rest of his life, dividing his time between London and Craven's estate in Berkshire.[12] The sale resulted in a strange geographical arrangement: two small specks on the map, near Nuremberg, were now part of Prussia, even though they were separated from the rest of Prussia by a large corridor. This isolated Prussian province became Hardenberg's personal fiefdom, and he made it the testing ground for the administrative reforms he was later to implement as Prussian chancellor.

So it was that, at the end of June 1792, the call Humboldt had been waiting for finally arrived. He was to report on the state of mining in Ansbach and Bayreuth.[13] He travelled by coach and, after a journey that lasted a day and a night, arrived at Erfurt. There he had time to meet Wilhelm and Caroline and their first child, also named Caroline, who had been born just six weeks earlier.[14] From there, Wilhelm and Alexander travelled to Jena together, staying for a few days with Wilhelm's new friend, Friedrich Schiller, and his wife, Charlotte.[15]

The assignment in Ansbach-Bayreuth proved to Alexander that he had been right about wanting an active post: he thrived, his health improved, and, in a letter to Freiesleben, he reported that he was having 'more fun than I can say.'[16] His days were hectic, and he found himself rushing from one mine to another, sometimes as many as six in one day: 'you'd better ask where I have *not* been [. . .] just think: in one day I walked to Saalfeld and back, and inspected the [mines called] Pelican, the New-Fortune, the Unexpected Joy, the Iron John, the Dinkler, as well as a bit of tunnel.' He walked until his feet were blistered.[17] His busy schedule never let up much, and in due course he was allocated two additional horses on account of his extensive travelling.[18]

With no friends or confidants close by, Humboldt seemed to talk himself into a steadily growing affection for the amiable and absent Freiesleben: 'I am full of longing for you, and every stone reminds me of you.'[19] As early as the end of August 1792, he was able to write to him that he had been promoted to inspector of mines, with personal responsibility for three local mining authorities.[20] The advancement was a direct result of the first reports he had submitted. He told his friend: 'I have completely covered myself in glory and have now been given the sole charge of all practical mining matters in the three departments of Naila, Wunsiedel, and Goldkronach. All my wishes, dear Freiesleben, have come true. I will devote my life wholly to the practice of mining and to mineralogy. [. . .] I'm reeling with happiness.'[21] He would have to spend periods of time in Bayreuth, the seat of the provincial mining administration, but chose for his headquarters the idyllic Bad Steben (a small village in the Fichtel mountains), where he moved into the former Margrave Karl Alexander's old hunting lodge.

In the autumn, before Humboldt could get properly settled, Heinitz sent him on a fact-finding mission to the salt mines of Bavaria, Austria, and Poland. On the way to Vienna, via the famous mines of Reichenhall and Traunstein, Humboldt found the Alps grander and more imposing than anything he had previously experienced: 'you think you've never seen mountains before once you've set eyes on those.'[22] They would lend themselves beautifully, he thought, to exploration with Freiesleben, who was now studying law in Leipzig and, surely, could come and collect him from Bad Steben—'it's perfectly feasible to manage it from Leipzig in the holidays. We'll hardly need six weeks to get there and back.'[23] A city at the forefront of science, Vienna too was exciting: 'The new chemistry is quite at home here. Everyone is busy oxygenising, the young Jacquin [Joseph Franz Freiherr von Jacquin] teaches it publicly, and the phlogiston [theory] has altogether disappeared.'[24]

That winter, 1792/93, he was back in Berlin, writing up his reports, working on his *Florae Fribergensis*, on the subterranean plants encountered in the Freiberg mines, and attending mining conferences with Heinitz. But he longed to be gone: 'I'm staying here, without any break, until April. You know what my domestic situation is like. It's all rather bleak, and so I'm always glad when I'm leaving my paternal home behind me. Solitude is preferable to living with people if one doesn't harmonise with them.'[25]

Wilhelm had also arrived in Berlin, and Alexander found that marriage had changed him. Caroline, possibly influenced by her childhood tutor, Zacharias Becker, had become drawn to German nationalism, and this attraction seems to have become more pronounced over time.[26] After her introduction to Wilhelm through Henriette Herz's Tugendbund, she had been steadily seeking to extricate herself from its influence, and it was noticeable that disparaging remarks she made towards its members were mostly directed against those who were Jewish, such as Dorothea Schlegel and Henriette herself. Wilhelm, too, was now showing signs of cooling towards his Jewish friends. He congratulated his friend Karl Gustav Brinkmann on an openly antisemitic poem he had written, and sarcastically proposed that they should go and read it out in the Herzes' salon.

When Humboldt submitted his official, comprehensive report on the state of mining in Ansbach and Bayreuth to Heinitz,[27] he discovered once again that he appeared unable to put a foot wrong: 'King Friedrich Wilhelm II,' the ministry in Berlin informed Humboldt, 'expresses his satisfaction with the report and with Humboldt's activities, and requests that he carry on with his good work.'[28]

In May 1793, Humboldt was back in the hunting lodge in Bad Steben: 'This Steben you won't be able to find on any map, [. . .] it is located in a wonderfully romantic area.'[29] He developed a real affection for the place, and wrote much later that Bad Steben was associated with the happiest memories of his youth.[30] But he was also aware that the area for which he was responsible presented challenges, and closer inspection revealed the true extent of the effort required to meet them: 'Everywhere here you are confronted with the monuments to glories past.'[31] A great many of the mines had been abandoned, some since the fifteenth century. The rest had been rendered unprofitable by outdated methods and bad practices, such as shoddy timbering, all of which was compounded by mismanagement and neglect at all levels.

Humboldt threw himself energetically into the rehabilitation of Ansbach-Bayreuth as a mining region. He unearthed files that had been festering in the nearby castle Plassenburg, and ordered that they be brought over to him—three crates full that hadn't been looked at for centuries. His decision to go straight to the source was rewarded with the discovery of a new gold seam: 'I've already been lucky enough to track down a side tunnel, entirely unsuspected, thanks to an old, unread mining report from 1544.'[32] He re-opened a previously abandoned mine, and superimposed the old reports on the up-to-date maps in order to discover new galleries: 'Never,' he wrote, 'did I feel a wish as vividly as I now feel the desire for ore.'[33]

A whole other domain that needed addressing was the poor training of the local miners, whose ignorance of even the most fundamental ideas and practices Humboldt found to be 'without limit.'[34] Often they were unable to distinguish between common ores; there was also a lack of basic safety procedures; and superstition reigned about natural phenomena, from the location of ore deposits to the weather. The problem, Humboldt saw, was simply a lack of education. To remedy this, he made a bold decision: he was going to open a mining school. While he knew that ultimately he could rely on Hardenberg, and even Heinitz, for funding, he initially put up the money himself, not wishing to expose himself to reproof in case it should all go wrong. But, like almost everything else in his mining career, it succeeded. The Free Royal Mining School, at Bad Steben, which, from September 1793, opened its doors every Wednesday and Saturday afternoon (so as not to interfere with the village school), was a runaway success, proving wrong all the sceptics who had advised against it.[35] 'It's incredibly hard work,' Humboldt wrote, 'but the enthusiasm of both the old and the young miners keeps propelling me on.'[36]

Humboldt trained one of his foremen, a young man named Georg Spörl, as a teacher, and involved him in the planning of lessons. Their content was carefully calculated to strike a balance between practical and local knowledge on the one hand, and a general, more ambitious education on the other. The curriculum included mathematics as it pertained to mining; how to determine the strike and dip of a rock face (the orientation of a rock layer towards a horizontal plane) without using an instrument; as well as handwriting, geology, mining law, and local mining history. Humboldt even wrote a textbook: 'some of it worked quite well, some rather less.'[37]

At the same time, appalled at the miners' poor living and working conditions, and particularly the catastrophic consequences of mining accidents for their families, he looked at improving their equipment. He devised a safety lamp that had a flame burning inside a protective glass cylinder, isolated from the potentially dangerous mine gases that might extinguish it or, worse, cause an explosion. Humboldt's lamp was widely adopted, and remained in use until it was eventually superseded by Humphry Davy's version some twenty years later. Humboldt also invented a respiration apparatus: through the application of a filter, it enabled miners who were surprised by poisonous gases to breathe for longer, and stand a better chance of being rescued.

The Saalfeld affair, in the meantime, refused to die down. Theodor Sommer, the administrator of the Saxe-Gotha region, had, when sufficiently pressed, apologised for the disruptive attack on the Loyal Friendship mine and promised to return the pit wood. However, he demanded that in return the Loyal Friendship would remain unworked until an official settlement had been reached. Wary of making concessions that might create a legal precedent, Humboldt declined.[38] Shortly afterwards, the Saalfeld miners made another sortie and had to be warded off by farmers from Kaulsdorf, whom Humboldt had placed as guards at the mine entrance. Two days later, he had to report that 'Saalfeld miners, thirty-eight of them and led by administrator Sommer,' had overpowered his fourteen Kaulsdorf farmers and made away with the pit wood for a second time. It was not until January 1794 that the episode was eventually brought to a close, and Humboldt was able to write that 'my Saalfeld quarrel has been decided most happily, and victoriously.

[. . .] I've occupied the pit with nine men and have already produced a respectable amount of cobalt and *fahlerz* [a grey crystalline copper-containing mineral]. But, dear God, how the mine has been fouled up!'[39]

Humboldt also reported impressively increased yields at his other mines: 'In the past eight years, an expenditure of 14,000 guilders produced barely 3,000 hundredweight of gold ore, whereas this year, with only 9 men, I mined 2,500 hundredweight, at a cost of less than 700 guilders.'[40]

Humboldt had been told to expect a promotion. But in a letter to Freiesleben, the tone struck is not quite that of a young official whose career is opening up before him. 'I'll be quite candid with you, my dear Carl,' he wrote to Freiesleben, 'I'll turn it all down. [. . .] My old plans remain unchanged; I'll take my leave in two years' time and go to Russia (Siberia), or some other place entirely.'[41]

9

Chemical Attractions

❧

'How I wish that one day I could hear Humboldt talk,' Ottilie, the sensitive young heroine of Goethe's novel *The Elective Affinities* (*Die Wahlverwandschaften*), confides to her journal, looking for guidance in difficult emotional straits. Goethe himself had indeed met Humboldt in March 1794.

That March, Goethe was emerging from a difficult year. A collection of his works to date had sold poorly, and he was having trouble finding anyone who would stage his plays *Iphigenia in Tauris* (*Iphigenie auf Tauris*) and *Torquato Tasso*. The political situation was not edifying either. The previous summer, Goethe had returned to Weimar from watching the siege of Mainz. As mentioned earlier, when the French conquered Mainz in October 1792 and established a republic based on the ideals of liberty and equality, they met with some enthusiastic local support—in the vanguard of which was Georg Forster. But the democratic experiment that became known as the Mainz Republic was short-lived and succumbed, after less than a year, to the siege and shelling by the combined Prussian and Austrian forces. Goethe had found himself an unlikely participant: his patron, Duke Karl August, was a general in the Prussian army, and Goethe had been called to come along as part of his entourage, with a vaguely defined role as a chronicler of events.

The personal connection with Forster was particularly poignant for Goethe. Not only had he greatly admired the account Forster had written of his and Humboldt's journey in 1790 to England, titled *Views of the Lower Rhine*, [. . .] *England and France*, he had also liked the man when he had made his acquaintance not long ago, in 1792.[1] Then, he had spent a happy evening in Mainz with the Forsters and Caroline Böhmer.[2]

It was therefore a source of relief to Goethe that, by the time he was watching the siege, Forster was no longer inside Mainz but in Paris (regarding the absorption of the Mainz Republic into France). But even so, witnessing the bombardment and eventual burning of the city was quite enough for Goethe. For a man upset at the sight of an orchard laid waste for purposes of defence, watching the siege and its aftermath, which brought the death of people he knew, was an experience that would haunt him for a long time.

While camping in a field outside Mainz, he wrote to his friend, the philosopher Friedrich Jacobi, that he could not wait to get home and to 'gather around me a circle that will let in nothing but love and friendship, art and science.'[3] So, in March 1794—even though Humboldt had ridden to Jena from Bayreuth mainly to see his brother, sister-in-law, and young niece newly settled in Jena—his arrival, full of energy and enthusiasm, and armed with the latest scientific ideas and experimental apparatus, could hardly have found Goethe in a more receptive state of mind.[4]

Humboldt had by now developed an almost obsessive interest in the idea of animal electricity, generally referred to as 'galvanism.' A few years earlier, Luigi Galvani, an Italian biologist, had come across a curious phenomenon as he was dissecting a frog. The steel scalpel he was using had by chance come into contact with the brass clasp that held the frog leg in position. At that moment, Galvani observed that the leg started to twitch. After further experimentation, Galvani was able to show that frogs' muscles would contract if there was electricity, such as lightning, in the vicinity. The fascination was obvious: could the workings of the nervous system be explained by electricity?

The experiments were quick to capture the public imagination. Humboldt, who had first heard them discussed in the salons of

Vienna, was deeply interested. Here, it seemed, the view opened, unexpectedly and exhilaratingly, on one of the deepest mysteries of life: the question of what exactly it is that separates living from inanimate matter. Indeed, Humboldt speculated, it seemed possible to 'come close to revealing the chemical processes of life.'[5] He replicated the experiments and tried out many different variations (to the detriment of countless frogs), fine-tuning them until he was able to elicit a reaction when the muscle was touched with a metal, or exposed to a fluid. Sometimes, he observed, even a mere breath—through the moisture it contained—was enough to cause a reaction.[6]

To Goethe, of course, all this was of great and immediate interest. In *Faust*, on which he worked for much of his life, the protagonist is possessed with the idea of discovering the secret of life—the thing that 'holds the earth together in its innermost core'—so much so that he sells his soul to find out. If a touch or even a breath was enough to cause an inert muscle to contract—a seemingly lifeless frog leg to jump—might one not be close to putting a finger, or rather a piece of metal, on the elusive substance that contained the key to life? Could the essence of life be as tangible as that?

Humboldt had taken his experimental equipment with him to Jena. After all, he explained, it was easy enough to carry: 'a few metal sticks, tweezers, sheets of glass and scalpels can be conveniently kept about one's person, even when travelling on horseback.'[7] Humboldt demonstrated his experiments to Goethe, who was captivated: 'the presence of the younger Humboldt,' he wrote, 'stirs up a flurry of anything that might be of chemical, physical or physiological interest,' he wrote later.[8] This marked the start of a joint pursuit of anatomy. The ducal court, and therefore Goethe's main residence, was at Weimar, but Jena, a few miles to the east, was the seat of the duchy's university. During Humboldt's stay, Goethe (as he frequently did) was spending time at Jena, and so the two men would walk together to Jena's *Anatomieturm* (anatomy tower)—a round tower in the medieval city walls that now served as an anatomical theatre—to attend lectures and demonstrations by Jena's young professor of anatomy,

Justus Christian Loder. Wilhelm got involved too: unable to pass up the chance to join in with Goethe's latest enthusiasm, he rather overshot the target, going as far as buying his own cadaver.[9]

Goethe's interest in science was in fact of long standing, but it had not met with the acceptance that he had been hoping for: it had mostly been regarded as the eccentric enthusiasm of a great poet. But there was a truly innovative aspect to his thinking about science, and one that tends to be overlooked. Goethe's instinct had always been to question the practice of observing facts in isolation, believing instead that phenomena cannot be usefully studied outside the natural relationships in which they are embedded.

In the spring of 1791, looking through a prism in his home in Weimar, he thought he had discovered a flaw in Newton's theory of colour. Newton had refracted white light through a prism, thus demonstrating that it could be split up into its component colours. Goethe's epiphany, however, was based on a misunderstanding of Newton's original experiment. Instead of refracting light with the help of a prism, Goethe looked through the prism itself, at a freshly painted white wall—which, contrary to his expectation, still appeared white. Goethe thought that Newton's claim, about white light being composed of light of different colours, went against the evidence of his own senses. Encouraged by this, and by experiments of his own, conducted using a garden hose, he tried to find further flaws in Newton's theory on colour. He noted in particular that colour is not constant when seen in different lighting. Indeed, the 'white' that Newton created by blending colours turned out, as Newton himself had conceded, to be a greyish, off-white hue. It did, though, look fairly white under bright illumination.[10]

The perception of colour, for Goethe, could not be properly understood if one did not take into account the perspective of the observer. In fact, every phenomenon had to be considered in its context. Plants and animals, for example, had to be seen in the context of their development. It was this thought that led Goethe to propose the idea of an *Urpflanze*, an archetypal plant in relation to which all other plants could be understood. On his travels in Italy, he even attempted to hunt down a live specimen.

But it was Goethe's anatomical studies that actually produced proof that living forms are subject to development. The intermaxillary bone is a small component of the upper jaw, holding the incisors. It is present in most vertebrates and can be observed easily in monkeys. But most contemporary physicians, among them Johann Friedrich Blumenbach, Humboldt's professor at Göttingen, denied the possibility of its existence in humans—indeed, this absence seemed to illustrate the distinction between humans and animals. In 1784, however, Goethe showed that the intermaxillary bone, while undetectable in adults, can be faintly discerned in the human embryo. This confirmed his thought that all living forms are interconnected and in a constant process of development.

There was a Romantic element in Goethe's misgivings about scientific studies of phenomena in isolation. He expressed this most perceptively in *The Elective Affinities*, published in 1809, after Humboldt's return from the Americas, and after Goethe had absorbed parts of Humboldt's experience there. He used Ottilie to give voice to the deep alignment in their thinking, which had begun in the first year of their acquaintance in Jena: 'A naturalist only deserves respect if he can depict and present the most strange and most foreign things in their locality, with all their neighbouring circumstances, always in their own peculiar element.'[11]

Goethe conceived of nature as a living entity, 'never dead and dumb,' which could not satisfactorily be grasped by quantitative methods alone.[12] And while Humboldt was concerned with imposing the scientific tools of the Enlightenment on what he saw—probably as completely and rigorously as anybody might have wished—there was also a deeper motivation for him, natural to somebody whose mind had been schooled in German Romanticism: the hope of encountering a hidden, deeper truth. More than this, Humboldt desired reciprocity—for whatever it was that he found to effect a change in him, too.

If everything in nature was connected, then the relationship between phenomenon and observer would go both ways. Ottilie continues: 'But even he [the naturalist] becomes another person. No one can walk beneath palm trees with impunity, and ideas are sure to change in a land where elephants and tigers are at home.'[13]

After his first stay in March 1794, Humboldt returned to Jena towards the end of the same year. His two visits frame the beginnings of one of Germany's great intellectual friendships—that between Goethe and Schiller. The meeting of both poets in July—the 'happy occurrence,' as Goethe was later to refer to it[14]—transformed, to the surprise of both of them, a well-established mutual antipathy into a deep friendship, which would last until Schiller's death in 1805. Wilhelm von Humboldt, as a friend and admirer of both men, had been concerned about their resolute failure to come to any sort of rapprochement. Schiller had been finding it increasingly difficult to hide his resentment at being ignored by the elder poet, whom he admired so much. Goethe, for his part, could not bring himself to extend the hand of friendship to the young firebrand whose quick fame, achieved through his play *The Robbers* (*Die Räuber*, 1781), plainly irritated him, and who, with his recent move to Jena, now seemed to be physically encroaching on his territory.

Wilhelm and Caroline carefully engineered the course of events. In late July, Schiller made an appearance at a lecture at Jena's Natural History Society, which Goethe was also attending. He caught Goethe in the doorway, the two men could not avoid talking, and a polite conversation turned into a long one, with Goethe expounding his theory of the metamorphosis of plants. Wilhelm seized on the favourable moment, and invited both men for dinner two days later.[15]

The encounter was the culmination of a lot of preparation. In June, Schiller had tested the ground by inviting Goethe to write for his new magazine, *The Horae* (*Die Horen*). Alexander, too, was asked for a contribution. The letter he wrote to Schiller to thank him for the invitation throws further light on the overlap between his thinking and that of Goethe. There is, again, the idea of a hidden principle underlying nature's workings. This assumption leads to the expectation that harmonies and similarities exist between the most remote phenomena. The congruence extends to human beings, who are perceived as standing inside nature. And they do so not just as purely physical entities, but also with their cognitive and emotional faculties:

> For as long as natural history is practiced the way that it has been until now—by clinging to differences of form, studying the physiognomy of plants and animals, and by imagining that identification and classification constitute true scholarship—then sciences such as botany, for example, can hardly make a fit object of study for people with an inquiring mind.

Instead, Alexander laid out his own vision:

> The general harmony of form; the question whether there is an original plant shape that expresses itself in myriad gradations; the distribution of these forms across the Earth; the different moods, cheerful or melancholy, that the flora evokes in the receptive person; the contrast between the dead, motionless rock, even the inorganic-seeming tree trunks, and the animate plant cover which puts, as it were, gentle flesh on the skeleton [. . .]. I do see that in parts I have expressed myself clumsily but hope that all in all you get an idea of what I mean.[16]

Alexander von Humboldt's promised contribution, when it materialised later, was entitled 'The Life Force, or The Rhodian Genius' ('Die Lebenskraft oder der Rhodische Genius'). It is a slightly heavy-handed allegory set in classical antiquity—in Sicily under the tyrant Dionysus, which also provided the setting for Schiller's earlier ballad on tyranny and friendship, 'The Hostage' ('Die Bürgschaft,' 1789). Although 'The Life Force' is not successful as a literary essay, its blurring of the boundaries between chemical and human relationships was something entirely new—and it was a model that Goethe would adopt when he wrote *The Elective Affinities*.

'The Life Force' begins by describing a mysterious painting, retrieved from a shipwreck. Believed to be from the island of Rhodes, it shows 'youths and maidens,' not 'heavenly or godlike,' but unmistakably creatures of the earth. They are wearing mournful expressions and are crowded around a 'Genius' in their midst, their arms outstretched towards each other, but unable to reach. Its meaning only becomes clear when a second picture, soon seen to be a companion piece of the first, is washed ashore. The same figures are depicted, but this time the Genius's head is 'drooping, his torch extinguished and reversed. The group of youths and maidens thronged simultaneously around him in mutual embrace; their looks were no longer sad and submissive but announced a wild emancipation from restraint and the gratification of long-nourished passion.'[17]

A philosopher is called on to solve the riddle. The Genius of the picture, he explains, represents the 'vital force'—an energy that holds in check the elements of inorganic matter of which all living beings are composed, preventing them from arranging themselves according to their own laws and desires. Only when the vital force flags or is extinguished, as in the second picture, will the 'earthy' youths and maidens, who represent the mineral world, give themselves up to the attractions between them: 'released from all bonds they impetuously follow their sexual instincts, and the day of his [the Genius's] death is to them a day of nuptials.' While ostensibly setting out to illustrate the forces of attraction in chemistry, the sexual undercurrent rather distracts from the science lecture.

By way of explanation, Humboldt added: 'In lifeless inorganic matter absolute repose prevails as long as the bonds of affinity remain unsevered, and as long as no third substance intrudes to blend itself with the others.' What happens if such a third, or indeed a fourth, substance intrudes, is the very question that informs Goethe's *The Elective Affinities*. While 'The Life Force' portrays chemical elements in human form, *The Elective Affinities* uses the reverse technique: Goethe puts his characters in the positions taken up by chemical substances in the course of an experiment.[18] Treating people as though they were molecules—a bit of clay or oxygen, say—and determining, by way of experiment, how they will fare, is not a friendly way of using them: some elements will be displaced by others; some will end up destroyed altogether. Bettina von Arnim, otherwise an unconditional admirer of Goethe, felt this acutely, when she struggled to see why the same laws should apply to people as to chemicals: 'I don't understand it, this cruel riddle, I can't grasp why they all court calamity, why they all serve a spiteful demon with a thorny sceptre.'[19]

Like 'The Life Force,' Goethe's novel is strongly preoccupied with the idea of an equilibrium that needs to be maintained. It begins with two people, Charlotte and Eduard, married and happily settled in the countryside. They are joined by Eduard's friend, the Captain, who is at a loose end and in need of company. Soon Charlotte finds that the presence of their guest has unbalanced their relationship— the Captain takes up much of her husband's time and attention. But a corrective presents itself almost immediately: Ottilie, Charlotte's niece, is unhappy at her boarding school.

A chemistry lecture provides a metaphor that appears amusing as well as educational. Eduard explains:

> You are the A, Charlotte, and I am your B: for do I not depend on you and come after you as the B does [to] the A? The C is quite obviously the Captain, who for the time being has to some extent taken me away from you. Now it would be right and proper [. . .] to provide you with a D, and that, without question, must be the amiable young lady Ottilie.[20]

Surprisingly, the characters really do behave like molecules, pulled by chemical attractions that are stronger than they themselves are. Unsurprisingly, however, the results are less benign than Eduard had fondly envisaged. Chemistry, following its inevitable course, quickly grows beyond the experimental setting and draws the characters into a destructive maelstrom. While Eduard correctly identified the characters and the elements they represent, the direction of the forces of attraction was poorly judged. An irresistible attraction develops between Eduard and Ottilie, and in turn between Charlotte and the Captain. The latter two are able, just, to stay within the bounds prescribed by society. Ottilie and Eduard, however, the weaker 'elements,' cannot withstand the forces of attraction and end up destroyed, foundering on the moral impossibility of living out their overriding desires. Ottilie fades away and dies, and is soon followed by Eduard.

When Humboldt returned to Jena in December 1794, to stay for the week before Christmas, Goethe came over from Weimar especially to see him. Together, they plodded through the deep snow to the *Anatomieturm* to take up their studies with Loder again. Even more flatteringly, Goethe wanted to take Humboldt back to Weimar with him.

But Humboldt declined. He wrote to Reinhard von Haeften, a young officer stationed with the Grevenitz regiment in Bayreuth, that 'much as I like being with Göthe (he is my preferred company here), this might easily have taken up the festive period. I should have had to wait another 6 days before being able to see you, and nothing in the wide world would make up this loss to me.'[21]

Humboldt was on the way to placing himself in the unenviable position of being an intrusive third party. Haeften was subject to bonds and attractions of his own—in particular, he was involved with a woman, Christiane von Waldenfels. Then again, unlike Goethe's characters, Humboldt was not a helpless chemical element, but an active participant, and was in a position to have a fair idea of what he was letting himself in for.

10

Exposed Nerves

Humboldt must have met Reinhard von Haeften at the very end of 1793 or early the following year. In March 1794, Haeften came to stay in Bad Steben and, about a month later, Humboldt let slip, in a letter to Carl Freiesleben, that in Bayreuth 'everybody knows that I live under one roof with Lieutenant Haeften, who is always around.'[1]

In November, another letter reached Freiesleben. Might he like to accompany Humboldt on a journey to Switzerland? They would be joined by a third party:

> This person is a Herr von Haeften, Lieutenant with the local Grevenitz regiment [. . .]. This Reinhard von Haeften has for a year now been my only, and hourly company. I live together with him; he comes to visit me in the mountains [at Bad Steben]. I have, to enjoy him the better, completely broken away from all other society.

A geological trip on which, as Freiesleben must have concluded, Humboldt's attention would mostly be devoted to an unknown lieutenant, can't have been an entirely attractive proposition. What followed is unlikely to have allayed his apprehensions:

> He has—in spite of outward appearances, e.g. he speaks French and knows how to comport himself in any sort of company—enjoyed only an indifferent education. He is trying to make up for this shortcoming,

and I am convinced that in two years' time he will be very knowledge-able. [. . .] I am inferior to him by far. [. . .] He doesn't know much geognosy, but is keen to learn; he is curious about everything that interests us, because he has a sense of how to place things even when he doesn't know much about them. [. . .] He loves me boundlessly, and he will love you too—he is already taking an interest in you, as I talk of you so often.

All in all, Humboldt concluded, 'I mustn't entertain any doubt [. . .] that you will come on the Swiss journey.'[2]

For a man who seemed to find great slabs of time to visit Humboldt in Bad Steben, Haeften, four years Humboldt's junior, led a complicated private life. At the time he got to know Humboldt, he was already involved with Christiane von Waldenfels—the wife of a Prussian officer—and had made her pregnant. Humboldt allowed himself to be drawn into his friend's affairs with his usual reluctance to do things by halves, and without much thought either for possible damage to his reputation or, it seems, his own feelings. When Christiane gave birth to a boy, Humboldt was godfather, and he later tried to act as an intermediary when Karl von Waldenfels, the wronged husband, instigated divorce proceedings. Checking up on the progress of the case in Frankfurt am Main, and surprised by Waldenfels's unexpected appearance in the city, Humboldt and Haeften effected a slightly dramatic escape by boat down the Main and then the Rhine.[3] Through all of this, Humboldt's own feelings for Haeften remained strong: 'I know that I live with and through you, my dear, only R[einhard], and cannot be entirely happy except when I'm near you.'[4] He can't have been unaware that the fulfilment of his friend's happiness, towards which he was working, was hardly likely to align with his own.

At this time, Humboldt was still intensely absorbed in his experiments on nerves, muscle fibres, and electricity, and he aimed to write a comprehensive summary on all that was known about the nature of animal electricity.[5] By trying variations of Galvani's experiments he had discovered that the nervous impulse existed (to some extent at least) in various animal bodies. Humboldt tried putting together parts of different animals, to see whether the impulse could be made to jump the boundary from one animal body to another. He found that it could: 'You can combine nerves of three different kinds of animals, warm- and cold-blooded, frogs and mice, with some of the elements turned back to front—the experiment always works. [. . .] Even a long mouse tail served as a conductor, as long as the hair had been scraped off.'[6]

Humboldt's instinct led him to go beyond the role of the uninvolved observer, and to dispense with intermediaries. 'The experiments are, in part, on myself,' he reported. The motivation, clearly, was to gain a more direct, unadulterated insight. Besides the scientific motivation, however, the experiments also had a distinct air of self-flagellation about them:

> I raised two blisters on the deltoid muscles of my right and my left shoulder. A prepared frog rested on the left wound. The one on the right was covered with zinc. The frog jumped (in spite of being eight inches away from the metal) the moment it was linked to the zinc by means of some silver wire.[7]

It is hard not to be struck by Humboldt's apparent disregard for the pain engendered by his investigations. Perhaps pain was part of the point of what he was doing. It introduced a certain measure of objectivity: what was felt so strongly was definitely, undeniably there. Pain, where it reached the limit of what was bearable, also pointed to a clear border—one that Humboldt seemed to feel a need to keep within sight. Another experiment was abandoned only when a doctor intervened, warning him that it would be dangerous to take things further:

> Both blisters were cut open, and the secreted fluid was examined carefully. [. . .] I was able to dip my finger into the liquid and draw figures and names on my skin, which, even when washed off, showed up, red as blood, for several hours. [. . .] they gained in intensity and size (up to two square inches) as we watched, so that the doctor, and even I, grew alarmed.[8]

Humboldt's involvement with Haeften was, in a way, not entirely dissimilar: he must have known that he could not fail to get hurt. But here too, perhaps, pain served as a measure. If love caused pain, that at least proved that it really existed. And if the degree of pain was in proportion to the importance of the thing that caused it, then, maybe, trying to avoid it would be beside the point.

In February 1795, Count Reden was promoted to a desk job in Berlin. Consequently, one of the most prestigious and covetable positions in the Prussian mining administration—that of director of the Silesian mines—became vacant. Heinitz was quick to secure the post for his protégé Humboldt, and he offered it to the young man with the happy assurance that 'adequate remuneration will not constitute a problem.' However, to Heinitz's surprise and consternation, Humboldt turned it down. What was more, in his reply he told Heinitz that he was 'about to change my situation entirely,' and to 'lay down almost all public duties.'

Such a decision was difficult to explain, and Humboldt himself struggled to give a convincing account of his motives. What could outweigh such obvious advantages as establishing his career, boosting his (as he admitted) 'not very plentiful' income, and pleasing Heinitz? The explanation offered in his letter—'a journey [. . .] a not entirely unimportant cause'—was nebulous and unpersuasive. But he was serious about leaving: 'it would be dishonourable to accept a new position, only to give it up right away.'[9] A little later, in March, he wrote directly to King Friedrich Wilhelm II, and asked him to accept his resignation.

Heinitz handled the situation with great tact, and managed to hold on to Humboldt for the time being. As a result, Humboldt found himself promoted to director of the Silesian mines. Heinitz granted him permission to visit Italy and Switzerland, no doubt hoping that, having indulged his longing for a journey, Humboldt would return to the fold, refreshed and somewhat more settled.

So in July 1795, Humboldt set off from Bayreuth, accompanied by Haeften. The objective of the trip, Humboldt told Goethe, was 'to see the Alps of the Tyrol, Lombardy, and Switzerland.'[10] But another perspective can be gained from a letter to Freiesleben, where Humboldt explained that he had arranged the trip with Haeften 'more for his sake than for my own.'[11] Freiesleben seems to have taken the hint and had opted to forgo the leg of the journey involving Haeften. After a first loop through Italy by Humboldt and Haeften, they would all meet in Schaffhausen, in Switzerland, as Haeften's leave of absence drew to a close. Haeften would then rejoin his regiment, and Freiesleben would take his place. (Even though the two overlapped only briefly, Freiesleben's concerns seem to have been well founded—even months later, Humboldt was still making excuses for Haeften: 'you have to put much of the blame for his sullen manner on his situation at the time.'[12])

From Munich, Humboldt and Haeften travelled south and finally arrived, via Innsbruck, in Italy. They stayed in Venice for two weeks ('I am not so keen myself, but Haeften will like it'),[13] continuing via Verona and Genoa to Pavia, where they hoped to meet Alessandro Volta. Not finding him at home, they tracked him down at his country house near Lake Como—where many more frogs were being sacrificed to science. They were usually skinned and dipped into wine glasses filled with water, 'their torso in one, the thighs in the other glass,'[14] as Volta demonstrated the fact that water was an effective conductor for nerve stimuli. Humboldt had suspected as much, but Volta proved it. From there they passed through Milan before coming into Switzerland and crossing the St. Gotthard Pass. They visited Luzern, Interlaken, Grindelwald, and other Swiss attractions, and in late September arrived at the Golden Eagle inn at Schaffhausen, the agreed meeting point with Freiesleben. (They had had to make a detour via Constance, since, as Humboldt explained to Freiesleben, it was in Constance that Haeften had left his suitcase.[15])

With Haeften on his way back to his regiment, Humboldt and Freiesleben set off from Schaffhausen to see more of Switzerland. The journey now assumed a more scientific outlook, except for a short period when Karl von Hardenberg unexpectedly joined them and insisted on seeing Chamonix. In Geneva, Humboldt and Freiesleben met the foremost authorities on Alpine research, the meteorologist Horace-Bénédict de Saussure and the physicist Marc-Auguste Pictet.[16] They specialised in the study of a relatively small area of the Swiss Alps, but had been able to achieve more exact elevation measurements than anyone before them.

Humboldt built on those measurements, and used them to present a wide sweep of the alpine landscape in the form of a relief. He then added its vegetation as a further dimension. Plants were represented according to the height at which they grew. This was a new way of looking at nature, but to Humboldt, with his professional background, it must have seemed obvious: 'I conceived of the idea to present whole countries in the manner of a mine.'[17]

On their way back to Schaffhausen, towards the end of October, they travelled through some of the places Humboldt had visited with Haeften only a few weeks before. Humboldt asked Freiesleben to walk ahead for a bit, while he pondered his recent experiences. He related them to Christiane (who had confirmed, in her letter to him, the safe arrival of 'our Reinhard' back in Bayreuth):

> Do tell Reinhard that I liked the lakes of Lucerne and Sarn just as much as I did when I saw them for the first time. It remains the loveliest area of Switzerland, and if we don't all go to America together, then this is the place for us to lead a quiet, happy life, far away from the so-called intellectuals.

He knew it did not sound like an obvious plan, but he meant it: 'The place, the plot for the house, it's all chosen. By all means smile at the idea,' he went on, 'but my castles in the air won't always remain there.'[18] Soon after that letter was written, he was back home in Bad Steben.

On October 29, Reinhard and Christiane married. Humboldt wrote to Freiesleben that the wedding celebration had been 'less dull than most weddings.'[19] By mid-December, he was ready to elaborate a little further. 'It was a sober day for me,' he wrote. 'Two days later, there was a hunt, it was all quite tiresome, and I fled.'[20] He organised a ball in honour of the couple, at the old castle in Bayreuth, which was attended by more than 130 people, before effecting a further escape—this time, to inflict various metals on exposed nerves in the privacy of his own rooms. He related that

> it caused a lot of pain, but worked out beautifully. The serum started out white and benign. After the wound had been stimulated for five to six seconds, an instant change took place, [. . .] the serum turned a deep red, and was so corrosive that it inflamed everywhere it flowed in red welts. By wiping it about it was possible to cause big, red-blue blotches that remained inflamed for several hours.[21]

But still Humboldt persisted with the notion that one day he and Haeften would live together. Early in January 1796, he spent several nights composing a letter to his friend, in which he recorded his feelings about their relationship, sketching out a hopeful plan for their future existence together.

Humboldt's subordination of himself does not always make comfortable reading, especially as it clearly wasn't even particularly welcome: 'Every day this love and affection increases, the expression of which is so often irritating to you.' Nonetheless, he suggested that Haeften retire from his regiment in the next few months, and that 'all of us (including my brother) move to Italy for a few years. [. . .] We'd fit perfectly into one carriage, and my brother with wife and child would fill the other.' Naturally, all would be subject to Haeften's whim and pleasure:

> [W]here and how you want to travel, how soon you'd like to leave Italy—I shall vouch for it with my character, as well as with the record of our relations thus far, that you can command over me as over your child, and will encounter obedience without so much as a grumble.

After their return from Italy, they would all settle down together —'it doesn't matter where, best in a place where nature is friendly and where old ties won't embarrass us. There's a lot to be said for Cleves [Haeften's home town, near the Dutch border].'[22]

Humboldt must have known that these proposals were unworkable. Even the present situation—a continuing intimacy with Haeften that involved treating his friend's marriage as little more than a minor distraction—was clearly unsustainable. In a world dominated by traditional patterns of living, there seemed to be no obvious place for him. But at no point it seems to have occurred to him to question his feelings, and the wisdom of letting himself be guided by them. And when, at the beginning of April 1796, he had a dream animated by the feeling that his path was full of mysteries, but that he was being led along it towards a greater revelation, he wrote it down carefully and related it to his old friend Henriette Herz.

In his dream, a venerable old man led Humboldt through a crowded city, 'to show him people,' he said. But everybody they saw was heavily veiled, making it impossible for them to tell men and women apart. Three of these figures caught his attention, evoking an inexplicable feeling of desire in him. Their talk, he thought, exhibited 'manly beauty,' so he believed himself to be listening to three young noblemen. However, he had been mistaken: 'I realised that I was in the company of women, and the three sagacious ladies now became ten times more interesting to me than the three sagacious youths had been before.' When the tallest of the ladies took off her disguise, an 'invisible power' prevented Humboldt from looking at her. He found himself back at the side of his ancient guide, who explained that, in the case of this lady, 'nature had set out to create a man, but got the register wrong and made a woman instead.'

'Anybody who doesn't think, feel, and speak with us, will have trouble interpreting this mysterious dream. But then it wasn't written for him!' It was an 'unripe fruit,' Humboldt told Henriette Herz, and as such contained some bitterness—but the choice of words implied his confidence that it would eventually come to ripen.[23]

II

The Loosening of Ties

✎

'In May I intend to go to Italy, whether my mother is alive or dead,'[1] Humboldt announced to Freiesleben in September 1796.

The state of his mother's health was indeed very grave. She had been suffering from breast cancer for about five years, and, in recent months, her condition had taken a turn for the worse. Early in the year, Alexander, Wilhelm, and Caroline had converged on Tegel to spend time with her. The sight of her suffering was upsetting to them all. 'My mother's fate is terrible,' Alexander wrote. 'It isn't only that there is no remedy, but there isn't even any kind of relief. I think that she will die in the autumn.'[2] In spite of this, there was little sense that his mother's last illness might engender a new closeness between them. Alexander's tone was pragmatic rather than despairing. In December 1795, just before things had become acute, he had written: 'My mother is very ill, but it's impossible to predict when she will die. So I fear that I won't be able to leave Germany.'[3]

In February, he dutifully arrived when summoned, but left the sick-bed for frequent excursions—most of them to the Spandauer Straße, to discuss his private life with Henriette Herz and his experiments on nerves and muscles with her husband, Markus. He also determined to use this involuntary sabbatical as an opportunity to complete his book on stimulated muscle and nerve fibres. But his mother didn't die during the visit. And when, after five weeks, she even showed some signs of rallying, everybody returned home.

On Humboldt's return to Bayreuth, he was immediately swept up by events. He was summoned away in the middle of the night, on a diplomatic mission. He hardly had time to pack more than a few belongings—and certainly not to package up and send the prototype of his miner's safety lamp. Haeften, he promised Freiesleben, would send a detailed description.

The Battle of Valmy (September 1792) had marked a drastic change in the direction of the Revolutionary Wars. The French army under General Dumouriez gained a victory so decisive that Goethe famously told the Prussian soldiers—or at least he later claimed that he did—that 'from this place, and from this day forth begins a new era in the history of the world, and you can all say that you were there to witness it.'[4] France went on to consolidate its power, occupying German territories to the left of the Rhine, such as Mainz and the Palatinate. In 1794 Prussia decided to negotiate rather than fight on, and, in the treaty of Basel (April 1795), was guaranteed a zone of neutrality. This, however, applied to northern Germany only, and the southern German states, such as Bavaria, were left exposed. When, in 1796, the Rhine-Mosel division of the French army, led by General Jean Moreau, advanced towards Bavaria, Humboldt was assigned the task of negotiating with Moreau and helping to secure the neutrality of the Prussian province of Ansbach-Bayreuth, which was bordering Bavaria.

Chasing after the French army and acting as a diplomat was not really what he wanted to be doing—it went 'straight against my nature and thinking,' he protested.[5] The assignment was 'as difficult as it is honourable'—and quite impossible to get out of. He knew that a successful outcome would save large parts of the civilian population from the ravages of war. Still, he hoped that 'the dance would not go on for too long.' In the meantime, he wrote to Freiesleben, he would be on his 'way to the French headquarters, accompanied by hussars and trumpeters. A Chinese delegation couldn't cause more of a spectacle.'[6]

Being in a state of war had become the order of the day and, to Humboldt, had begun to feel almost normal. Together with the other residents of Bayreuth, he was getting accustomed to being 'surrounded by enemy armies as though in an occupied fortress, and hearing the sound of shooting at all hours.' His sympathies did not divide strictly along fighting lines. On the one hand, he admitted that he hated seeing 'the Germans crawl before the French in the very heart of the [German] Empire'; on the other, he found that he had great respect for the French—common soldier and officer alike. He reported talking to a French sentry, 'barely twenty years old and bristling with dirt,' who condemned the Austrian troops' practice of executing prisoners. 'No, *citoyen*, one cannot be a soldier without being a human being,' he told Humboldt, who approved of the sentiment—'isn't this straight out of a tragedy by Racine?'[7]

With the French officers, too, Humboldt felt among kindred spirits. General Louis Desaix, just a year older than him, and with 'a head like Cromwell, but with more bonhomie,' was surprisingly well informed about the recent developments in chemistry—for example, the ousting of the phlogiston theory by Lavoisier's discovery of the role of oxygen in combustion. He also took a lively interest in Humboldt's mining lamp, in which Humboldt took pride ('it *never* went out! Through all of my experiments'), and of which, astonishingly, Desaix had already heard. He had an attractive character, Humboldt thought—a curious mixture of the 'gentle and melancholy [. . .] with an outward fierceness.'[8] The easy friendship between them made Humboldt's task easier, as well as more pleasant. It also meant that he was treated with courtesy and even amiability inside the French camp.[9]

Another officer, General Jean Reynier, invited Humboldt along on an *exercice de l'Aérostat*—an ascent by hot air balloon to reconnoitre the terrain. But Humboldt had to decline, with the greatest regret, as he had run out of time and couldn't keep his hussars waiting: 'I shall mourn the loss of this opportunity for as long as I live.'[10]

In late August, Humboldt, returned from the assignment, took Reinhard and Christiane von Haeften for a little sightseeing, to the gardens at Sanspareil, not far from Bayreuth—a gothic extravaganza of moss-covered rocks and artificial ruins. But his involvement with

Haeften was not doing him any good, and he knew it. Haeften had followed Humboldt's advice and taken leave from the army—but he had not yet decided what he would do with himself. Moreover, his wife was pregnant with their second child.[11]

It was against this background that Freiesleben, open in character and immersed in the practical concerns of mining, suddenly appeared to Humboldt as the embodiment of a better, simpler, and nobler life, 'the high mark of moral purity which I shall never attain.' The Swiss journey came back to him, this time remembered with a shifted emphasis, as a time when friendship with Freiesleben elevated him to a higher moral plane; Haeften was mostly excised from the picture. He evoked 'the evening near Lausanne by Lake Geneva, opposite the rocks that pointed to the sky,' and recalled their times working side by side in mines with names such as 'God's Blessing' and 'Happiness Bestowed.'

Measured against his friend's existence, his own, Humboldt felt, compared unfavourably. But while he meant to address this situation, his personal purification would not take place below ground, through a return to active mining: 'I grew more corrupt every year, as my circumstances became further entangled. But I will simplify them—I shall return from the palm forests as the person that I feel I may yet become.'[12]

Palm forests being unattainable for the time being, he applied himself to perfecting his mining lamp, a project satisfying in its usefulness, as well as presenting an interesting technical challenge. A hollow wick was the first breakthrough. Such a wick would necessarily come into contact with a greater amount of air than a conventional one; that way, if conditions below ground were poor, it would make the best use of whatever oxygen was available. Humboldt sent some wick samples to Freiesleben and asked him to put them to the test in some of the mines that were known for their dangerous, oxygen-poor air. He reserved some of the most adverse conditions for himself, and, as a result, almost ended up a victim of his own experiments.

Relating the incident to Freiesleben, he explained that, even though his experiments had been satisfactory on the whole, there remained one tunnel where the air was especially foul, and which 'still put up resistance to my lamp.' Humboldt modified the apparatus slightly, allowing more air inside the cylinder that enclosed the flame, which, as a result, burned more steadily. He then approached the dangerous spot on his own, while his deputy, Eberhard Killinger, stayed behind. Humboldt was delighted to find that his adjustment seemed to be working: 'I arrived, put my lamp down, and took great pleasure in its light. I felt tired, and incredibly languid, and giddy; I dropped to my knees beside the lamp. I called Killinger, they told me later; I remember nothing of it.' Luckily, Killinger heard him, and succeeded in pulling him out by his legs. Humboldt soon regained consciousness: 'when I woke up, I could see the lamp still burning. That was worth fainting for.'[13]

He successfully petitioned for a pay rise for one of his employees, 'the little Gödeking.'[14] However, when he himself was offered more money, he felt that he must turn it down. It was not as though, in principle, he was averse to the idea that princes and rulers should 'also do something for people such as me'; but with the state coffers rather empty, accepting more money for himself would send altogether the wrong signals. 'The more one sits in judgement on others' actions, the more strictly one has to follow the laws of morality oneself. So the one achievement I'll leave behind me will be that, at least, I won't have abused the favour of a minister for my personal advancement.'[15] Humboldt was clearly preoccupied with the reputation he was going to leave behind in Ansbach-Bayreuth. He was also anxious not to enter into obligations, on either a practical or a moral level. A period of his life was drawing to a close, and he was preparing for the transition. His book was nearing completion too—'the nerves are almost finished,' he told Freiesleben.[16]

On November 25, he wrote to Freiesleben again, with new thoughts on how to further refine the miner's lamp, after the latest round of testing. He suggested that Freiesleben might have been over-generous with the oil, drowning the wick, and told him that he would supply some further improved wicks: 'they are knitted with four needles, like a sock—I can do it myself.' Freiesleben worried about an unintended effect of the improved lamp: it might contribute to the greater exploitation of miners, who could now be sent into yet more dangerous environments. Humboldt argued that every innovation was open to the possibility of abuse. But so far miners had had to 'toil in the dark, and it takes three quarters of a year to excavate the shaft'; the lamp would reduce this period of toil. It was the task not of science, but of reason, to decide how an innovation should be used.

There was a postscript to the letter:

The only thing I have to add is that yesterday news arrived of my mother's death. I've long been prepared for it. [. . .] You know that my heart could not sustain serious damage from these quarters. We've always been strangers to one another, but it would have been impossible not to be moved by her unbearable, endless suffering.[17]

Frau von Humboldt had died on November 19, 1796, and now Humboldt's situation was changed utterly.

12

Goethe's 'Caravan'

~⇜⋇⇝~

Meticulous in life, Frau von Humboldt had planned carefully for death. As early as 1791, when she first knew that she was ill, she had bought a manor house in Falkenberg, a village to the northeast of Berlin. She never lived there, but oversaw the renovations to the local church. These involved the demolition of the medieval wooden steeple and its replacement with a brick structure 'in the Egyptian style.'[1] Under this distinctive elongated pyramid, at the base of the steeple, she established the family vault, and had both her husbands' remains transferred there, as well as those of a daughter from her first marriage.

She had also left a well-ordered will, and appointed Kunth, her boys' former tutor and then her assistant, the executor. Relations between her and her younger sons may have been strained, but her will not only acknowledged the life choices of both brothers, but implicitly encouraged them. While Wilhelm, having left the civil service to devote himself to private study, inherited the family home at Tegel, Alexander received a legacy consisting mainly of money and easily liquidated bonds—as well as the Ringenwalde estate, a possession so remote and holding so little emotional value that Alexander would have no qualms about turning it into money.

At the age of twenty-seven, and for the first time in his life, Alexander von Humboldt found himself financially independent. He was freed, too, from having to live up to his mother's expectations—though after so many years of treading a fine line between her wishes and his own, he had become rather good at it. Alexander did not attend her funeral on December 3, 1796, and it was Heinrich von Holwede, his half-brother, who put the death notice in the *Berlinische Zeitung* on behalf of the family. Less than a month after news of the death reached him, Alexander's travel plans were sufficiently advanced for him to announce them to his friend Willdenow:

> My journey is unshakeably certain. [. . .] I'll stay in Italy for a year to eighteen months to familiarise myself with volcanoes; then it's onwards via Paris to England, where I could easily stay for another year (I won't rush, and would rather arrive well prepared); and then with an English ship to the West Indies.[2]

At the end of December 1796, Humboldt resigned from his position, this time for good, and would have set off right away had the political situation looked more auspicious. However, during his conquest of Italy, General Napoleon Bonaparte had captured Mantua and was now in the process of invading the Tyrol, which rendered the proposed stay in Italy a lot less feasible. But if the political situation was volatile, this meant, equally, that circumstances might soon improve. For the time being, it seemed practical to start preparations closer to home while keeping an eye on the changing political landscape.

From January to May 1797, Alexander visited Jena several times; in April he was accompanied by Reinhard von Haeften, his wife, Christiane, and their two children to see Wilhelm and his family. Caroline had given birth to the Humboldts' third child, Theodor, some three months earlier, and had been dogged by ill health ever since. (Their second child, named Wilhelm, was born in 1794; the boy died in 1803.) Wilhelm, due in Berlin to attend to inheritance matters with Kunth, had delayed his departure until Alexander's arrival, so that Caroline would not have to be by herself. Alexander's absorption into family life was so quick that at first he did not even have time to see Goethe, and had to turn down an invitation to visit the mine at Ilmenau: 'My sister-in-law has begun weaning today, and since her delicate condition means that this may affect her badly, I am reluctant to leave her on her own.'[3] Once Caroline felt stronger, new calls on Alexander's time immediately arose to take over from the old. The Haeftens' younger child was recovering from a smallpox vaccination, so Alexander moved in with them to lend an extra hand.

Perhaps it was all this domesticity that propelled him back towards the anatomy theatre, where he had spent so much time during his stay in 1794. 'As I am now making serious preparations for my West Indian journey, and intend to occupy myself there primarily with the organic forces, anatomy is now my main pursuit,'[4] he wrote: 'I spent—as long as the weather was relatively cool—five to six hours a day with the cadaver.' 'Brain-water,' he observed, was different in appearance from any other organic fluid—and, if left undisturbed, crystals shaped like pillars formed therein, 'even though the soul does not swim in it.'[5]

Goethe was pleased to have Alexander von Humboldt back in the vicinity. Knowing that he would himself be called away by his employer, Duke Karl August, towards the beginning of May, he was particularly keen to 'put the latter half of April to the best possible use.'[6] His work on natural history, he wrote, had, through Humboldt's arrival, been 'woken from hibernation,' and he started on plans to follow up his essay *Metamorphosis of Plants* (1790) with a work on the metamorphosis of insects.[7] If plants moved through a succession of distinct stages, then the development of insects from eggs, through larvae, then pupae, to adulthood, would be the logical next object of study. So Goethe and Humboldt dissected caterpillars and beetles, and continued the experiments on frogs. With the latter's account of his galvanic experiments about to be published, others had begun to be interested in his work and to try to replicate his results—among them two brothers from the Virgin Islands, the medical students Christian and Friedrich Keutsch.[8] Humboldt had hopes that his research might come to form the basis of something quite new in science.

Goethe wanted to hold on to Humboldt for as long as possible: 'There are many things that I would like to ask you, and I hope to enjoy your expertise and your company.'[9] Together, they explored the new instruments Humboldt had acquired in preparation for his planned journey, among them a theodolite, which measured horizontal or vertical angles; a sextant, for establishing the angle of a celestial body in relation to the horizon; and a barometer, for measuring atmospheric pressure (and, indirectly, altitude). None of them was straightforward to use. The sextant, in particular, requires a complex interaction of measurement and calculation as well as knowledge of the movement of the earth in relation to the stars. It is impossible to use one successfully without a great deal of practice, and Goethe enlisted the services of the technically experienced Lieutenant Johann Vent. With the barometer, the altitude of 'every molehill' was established; the new electrometer, excitingly, possessed telescopic legs, meaning it 'could all be carried in a bag.' 'I have,' Humboldt wrote, 'returned to a proper student's existence, for my sphere is narrow and wholly confined to myself.'[10]

In spite of the unpredictable political situation, Italy remained the intended destination. They would all go together: the Haeftens and Alexander, and Wilhelm and his family. Goethe was asked, too, and initially made positive noises. Everybody, it seemed, was going for a different reason. Alexander's aim was to look at Vesuvius, an active volcano that had the advantage of being within relatively easy reach. Goethe was attracted by the idea of recapturing the experience of his Italian journey in the 1780s, and with it, perhaps, some of its creative impulses. For Wilhelm, the desire for Italy was at one remove: it was more in the spirit of homage to Goethe and the experiences that had been the inspiration for some of Goethe's best poetry. Travelling at Goethe's side, of course, would be an almost inestimable privilege, but even just retracing his steps would be worth the journey. What exactly moved the Haeftens, nobody quite knew—but it seemed that Alexander was still holding on to the original plan of an educational journey for Reinhard. In any case, he had laid down his commission, and so was otherwise unoccupied.

The journey to Italy would start with a slightly unlikely swerve to the east, to Dresden. Alexander wanted to meet the astronomer Johann Gottfried Köhler, who was then the director of Dresden's Royal Cabinet of Mathematical and Physical Instruments, and who had offered to give Alexander further advice on how to handle a 14-inch sextant. From Dresden, Alexander would also be able to fit in a visit to Freiberg, some twenty miles to the southwest, to see Freiesleben, as well as to catch up with his old teacher Abraham Werner.

But things did not go smoothly. Caroline's health had still not completely recovered, and it was the end of May before they finally set off. Goethe, who witnessed the preparations, made his excuses: on balance, he would rather go to Italy on his own. Having seen the travellers off, he wrote a cheerful letter to Duke Karl August (Goethe got the exact number of travellers wrong, but the main import, his relief at not himself being part of that number, is conveyed clearly enough): 'Mining Councillor Humboldt has now left for Dresden, with a veritable caravan, consisting of two mothers, two men, five children, two maids, and a manservant.'[11]

Alexander, it was planned, would travel in a carriage with the Haeften family, and Caroline with her three children in another (Wilhelm was to go straight from Berlin to Dresden and meet them there). In the event, though, the Haeftens had taken an extravagant amount of luggage with them, so that, as Caroline later related to her husband, Alexander had to squeeze in with her: 'the Haeftens, even though they've got one child fewer, hardly any servants and three times as much space to arrange themselves comfortably and spaciously, have stuffed their carriage full with so much luggage that there just simply wasn't any room for Alexander.'[12]

In Freiberg, Freiesleben was not at home, and it was his mother who opened the door. The Haeftens had taken their older child along with them, Alexander's godson Fritz. Frau Freiesleben must have expressed her astonishment at how big the boy looked: the

Haeftens had been married for less than two years, and Fritz, after all, was now three and a half years old.[13] Alexander had no compunction in lying to his friend's mother, making up a convoluted story about a secret wedding: 'I told your mother that they had been married earlier [than the official wedding date], but that the royal permission had not come through [. . .] and that it was only at that date that the marriage was made public.'[14] Alexander then travelled on by himself for another twenty miles to find Freiesleben in Marienberg.

In Dresden, Caroline suffered a further relapse, so the group had to stay for longer than planned. Back in Jena, when friends were told of the travellers' progress, the general sentiment was a gleeful satisfaction at not being part of the trip. 'It's likely to prove an agreeable journey now that they've used up all their time before they've even set off!' Schiller crowed to Goethe.[15]

In July, Alexander von Humboldt decided that he could wait no longer, and travelled ahead to Vienna, via Prague. The group he left behind was, in any case, an unlikely constellation for a scientific expedition. But then again, he could think of few candidates who would make an ideal companion. An old friend from Freiberg, Leopold von Buch, had been in touch. 'He wrote to me that he "will go to Italy, to cast off his skin and drink ether" (in which case he may yet turn out handsome). At what time he is leaving, where I may find him—he doesn't tell me any of that.' But apart from his eccentric nature, Humboldt thought him 'an excellent, brilliant person, who notices much, and observes it well,' and the two arranged to meet up in Salzburg and to spend some time exploring the surrounding mountains together; each would then travel further south alone.[16]

In the meantime, different prospective companions, for different kinds of journeys, seemed to turn up wherever Humboldt looked. In Vienna, he ran into Nicolaus Böthlingk, with whom he had coincided at Büsch's academy in Hamburg, and who had later resurfaced in Jena. He had enthusiasm and solvency to recommend him: 'he is still firmly of a mind to go to the West Indies with me,' he wrote to

Freiesleben. 'We are thinking to start the journey via Spain and Tenerife. He has an income of 40,000 roubles.'[17] About two months later, another candidate emerged. 'I have (this is a secret) the hope, almost the assurance, of a superb travelling companion, the young [Joseph] van der Schot, a wonderful young man of great botanical knowledge, and a noble character.'[18] Head gardener at the botanical gardens at Vienna's Schönbrunn palace, van der Schot had been a botanist on Nicolas Baudin's expedition to Australia, India, and the East Coast of Africa, and had returned with a large number of specimens that now stocked the gardens at Schönbrunn.

By now, it was difficult to overlook the fact that Alexander's original journey was spectacularly ill fated. The rest of the company had arrived in Vienna, and proceeded to succumb to one illness after another. Wilhelm was in touch with Schiller:

> Just imagine that of the thirteen persons that make up my brother's and my circle, one after the other—all, except little Li [Caroline, the Humboldt's oldest daughter] and I—have been unwell, and that there have hardly been even three or four days in succession where not at least one of us has been too ill to leave the house.[19]

Three months went by in Vienna, and still the Italian situation did not show any sign of resolving itself: Napoleon had now occupied Venice and established a client state in Genoa, and hostilities were unlikely to end any time soon. Alexander was probably the one who minded least, not having to look after young, illness-prone children, and being able to spend most of his time among exotic plants in the gardens at Schönbrunn. But for Wilhelm, who wanted to visit France as well as Italy, the dithering in Vienna made little sense. He decided simply to reverse the order of the journey, and go to France first. The group broke up. 'The caravan has, one and all, given up the journey to Italy,' Goethe informed Schiller.[20] It was in September of 1797 that Wilhelm left for Paris with his family. Alexander and the Haeftens, meanwhile, decided to persevere with the Italian plans. But 'Italy is so tumultuous as well as entirely lacking in coach horses, that no one can go there.'[21] With the safety of their small children in mind, the Haeftens were in any case nervous about approaching Italy while the political situation was so unstable, so, for the moment, the reduced group decided to spend the winter in Salzburg, and to try to reach Italy via the Tyrol in the spring.

They arrived in Salzburg in October. Buch, 'still encased in his old skin,' and still with hopes for Italy, ether and all, joined them shortly afterwards. Unlike the presentable Haeftens, he was not a success in society, and consistently made a bad impression:

> His whole manner is as though he came from the moon. [. . .] I've taken him round on visits, but on the whole that hasn't gone well. He tends to put on his glasses straight after the introductions are made, and to examine, in some far-away corner, the cracks in the oven glazing, on which he is keen, or he creeps along the walls like a hedgehog to inspect the skirting boards.[22]

Buch and Humboldt made the best of the enforced waiting period, gaining practice and fluency in the use of their geological instruments and measuring practically everything that there was to measure: they determined Salzburg's latitudinal position, examined the atmospheric density at different altitudes, and used a barometer to fix the height of the mountains around them, such as the Gaisberg, which overlooks the city from the east. The Austrian mountains were to serve as the dry run for Italy, which, in turn, was to be a preparation for Alexander's real destination. The latter was, for the time being, still labelled somewhat imprecisely 'West India,' which meant, in the convention of the time, South America—but mostly seemed to denote, rather less precisely, 'as far away as possible.'

Then, in November, an offer reached Humboldt that was unexpected and unconventional, but altogether too intriguing to dismiss. Frederick Hervey, 4th earl of Bristol, 'half mad, half genius,' had heard of Humboldt's travel plans.[23] He was planning an expedition to Egypt, which so far lacked a scientist, so he invited Humboldt to join him. They would set out from Naples:

He wants to set sail in August, has his own ship, armed men, painters, sculptors etc., cook and cellar on board. He plans to go up to Syene [Aswan] in upper Egypt. The journey is to not cost me anything, and in the spring of [17]99 we'll be back, via Vienna and Constantinople. An offer such as this cannot be turned down.[24]

Here was another not-quite-ideal travelling companion. What Lord Bristol lacked in scientific grounding, he made up for in extravagance. Apart from the luxurious conditions in which he proposed to travel, he attracted scandal. As well as Humboldt and an archaeologist, Lord Bristol planned to take with him the Countess of Lichtenau, a former mistress of King Friedrich Wilhelm II. Humboldt was not altogether comfortable with providing the respectable veneer to a somewhat dubious enterprise. As a precaution, he stipulated that he would pay his own way, so as to maintain at least some degree of independence. In the circumstances, though, it seemed the most realistic plan: France had now instigated a sea war against the United States, in response to the latter's refusal to repay its debts to the new Revolutionary regime. 'The war at sea,' Alexander wrote, 'prevents me from embarking on my West Indian journey. So I will likely spend this winter in Egypt.'[25] He reasoned that Egypt would give him experience of tropical conditions, too, and, in any case, 'I am tired of the never-ending waiting. I am getting older all the time, and have to use the moment.'[26]

Of course, even with this plan, Humboldt would still have to negotiate Italy to make the rendezvous. What made this slightly more feasible was the fact that he was now by himself. Following 'a hideous period of indecision,' the Haeftens had finally given up on the idea of travel.[27] After the trouble and worry of taking two young children through Europe during the Napoleonic Wars, it was surely easier to appreciate the charms of a less adventurous life. And there was another thing: Christiane was expecting the couple's third child. The couple went to the Northern Rhineland to live quietly on Reinhard's ancestral estate near Cleves. 'So it is earlier than antici-

pated (you are aware of the entire situation) that I find myself unat-
tached,' Humboldt wrote to Freiesleben.[28]

Although he was now resolved to take part in Lord Bristol's expedition, he still had serious reservations. He asked his friend, the
Danish diplomat Christian Bernstorff, whether he would be able to
call on the Danish consul in Cairo if things went wrong. But, he
begged, 'you won't, please, give this Egyptian journey any publicity
whatsoever!'[29]

Towards the end of April 1798, Humboldt left Salzburg and set
off for Paris in order to update his collection of instruments so as to
be properly prepared for Egypt, and to say goodbye to his brother. It
was at this time that Napoleon left Italy and returned to Paris, from
there to direct his attention to Egypt. The timing was not, of course,
a coincidence. France's attempts to challenge England's dominance
in the Middle East had been closely watched by London. Lord
Bristol's journey to Egypt was probably a front for his activities as a
British spy.

This, at any rate, is what the French thought. Halfway to Paris, at
an inn in Strasbourg, Humboldt opened a newspaper to discover that
Lord Bristol had been arrested: 'I was about to buy a few more
instruments in Paris, when the French go and catch my mad Lord
near Bologna and lock him up in Milan, to make him (who has an
income of £60,000) pay a decent ransom.'[30] He travelled on to Paris
anyway.

Humboldt happened to arrive just in time for the ceremony—held
in Lieusaint, a little south of Paris—that concluded the plan, begun
in 1790, to establish the metre as the new basic unit of measurement.
The metre was defined as being one ten-millionth of the distance
between the North Pole and the equator. The calculation of this
quadrant rested on the exact measurement of the section of it that
ran from Dunkirk to Barcelona—and which also passed through
Paris. Humboldt witnessed the completion of the last measurement—that of the stretch between the towns of Melun and
Lieusaint—and was made welcome by the leader of the project,

Jean Baptiste Delambre. Also present in Lieusaint was Louis-Antoine de Bougainville, the explorer who had circumnavigated the earth between 1766 and 1769. The book he had written about the journey, *A Voyage Around the World* (not to be mistaken with Georg Forster's similarly titled book), had become hugely popular, and had influenced the public perception of native societies as well as the thinking of Rousseau with its depiction of the South Seas as a world unspoilt by Western civilisation. Now nearly seventy years old, Bougainville had been put in charge of another expedition, again a voyage around the world, this time with a particular focus on the South Pole. Humboldt's reputation as a scientist was established enough for Bougainville to offer him a place on his expedition almost immediately—in fact, as Humboldt later put it in a letter to his friend Willdenow, he 'persuaded me to follow him.'

This invitation represented an almost incredible turn of fortune for Humboldt, who had so far seen all his plans thwarted. And even though the South Pole had never been part of any plan, it immediately appeared to him as a perfectly logical place to go: 'since I had an interest in investigating magnetics at that time, a journey to the South Pole made a great deal more sense to me than one to Egypt.'[31]

But circumstances changed yet again. The French government decided to widen the scope of the expedition. It was now proposed that it should last five years and, before the attempt on the South Pole, should take in South America, Mexico, and California. After the South Pole, it would go on to Madagascar and conclude on the coast of West Africa. Bougainville was considered too old for a journey of that length and was replaced by Nicolas Baudin. Bougainville, who had planned to take his fifteen-year-old son with him, instead now entrusted him to Humboldt's care.

Baudin was a rather less heroic figure than Bougainville, and indeed was touched by scandal. Courtesy of his friend Joseph van der Schot in Vienna, Humboldt was better informed than Baudin could know. He was aware, for example, that on a previous expedition commissioned by Austria, Baudin had opportunistically given most of the samples he had collected to France instead. He had also used the journey to traffic slaves, for his own profit. All in all,

> the character of Captain Baudin was not apt to fill me with confidence. [. . .] But as I would not have been able, out of my own means, to undertake such a long journey and see such a beautiful part of the world, I decided to join the expedition and take my chances.[32]

Again, Humboldt found that his renown as a scientist smoothed his path wherever he went: 'all the national collections were opened for me, so that I could pick whichever instruments I wanted. As to the choice of the scientists, of everything that concerned the equipment, I was asked for my opinion.'[33] The three ships that formed the expedition had been designated, farewells had been said, and the members of the party had been introduced to each other: 'how keenly each looked at the other when he saw him for the first time! Strangers at first, but soon, for so many years, we were to be bound together so closely!'[34]

In Paris, where the expedition had been the talk of the town, most people believed that it had already sailed—when it was abruptly called off. Now that war with Italy seemed likely to flare up again, funding a scientific expedition was suddenly less of a priority. 'Having had all my hopes cruelly snatched away, with a single day seeing off the plan that I had been nurturing for several years, I decided to leave Europe as soon as possible, and whatever the circumstances.'[35]

One evening, arriving back at his hotel in the rue Colombier, Humboldt fell into conversation with a young man who was also staying there; it may have been the stranger's botanising equipment that first caught Humboldt's attention. Aimé Bonpland, four years younger than Humboldt, was originally from La Rochelle on the Atlantic coast, from a family of apothecaries. He had come to Paris to train at medical school (one of his teachers there, Jean-Nicolas Corvisart, would eventually become Napoleon's private physician). When Bonpland's education got interrupted through the French

Revolutionary Wars, he spent his military service as a ship's surgeon. However, it was collecting and studying plants that held his chief interest, so on his return to Paris, he supplemented his medical studies with botany, at the Jardin des Plantes. Bonpland, it turned out, had also wanted to join the Bougainville–Baudin expedition: 'He has served in the navy, is very solid, good-natured and has a flair for comparative anatomy.'[36] A few months later, Humboldt described him to Freiesleben as 'a good man [. . .] who however leaves me rather cold—that is, my relationship with him is purely scientific.'[37]

13

Departures

The prospect of being part of a grand voyage of exploration, with the full backing of the French government, and in the congenial company of other scientists, had been an exciting one, and its loss a severe blow.

Help came unexpectedly in the person of Mathias Archimboldus Skjöldebrand, the Swedish consul, who arrived in Paris in October 1798. He had strong links with North Africa: besides having excellent contacts at the court in Tripoli, he was at that moment on his way to deliver gifts from the Swedish government to Algeria's dey, Baba Hassan. Moreover, he had a small stake in the business aspect of the Hajj: each year, he sent a ship to pick up pilgrims at Tunis and convey them to Mecca. Without great difficulty, Humboldt secured for himself a place on Skjöldebrand's ship, to take him as far as Egypt.[1]

For several years now, Humboldt had been ricocheting between borders that always closed just in front of him. Napoleon's campaigns, it seemed, might have been launched with the express purpose of frustrating him. By now, his longing for escape had become so strong that he seized on Skjöldebrand's offer, even though it severely reduced his options—it was yet another compromise. Bonpland, also at a loose end, was easily persuaded to throw in his lot with Humboldt.

The new plan took shape almost instantly. Humboldt and Bonpland were to travel on board the ship taking Skjöldebrand to

North Africa. The winter of 1798/99 would be spent in the High Atlas mountains in Morocco, an area worthy of exploration in itself: 'so far, no mineralogist has studied this high mountain range.'[2] Skjöldebrand's connections would secure them a permit that allowed them to travel freely there. In spring, they would embark at Tunis to join the pilgrims on the ship bound for Mecca, but get off at Egypt. With the French already established at Cairo, Humboldt hoped to find the same friendly reception that he had experienced in Paris. From there, he and Bonpland would travel up the Nile.

Once the decision was made, events moved rapidly. They had learned only on October 12 that Baudin's expedition was cancelled. The Swedish frigate, the *Jaramas*, was expected in Marseilles before the end of the month. Skjöldebrand would be able to hold it for them for a few days if necessary, but not beyond that. Humboldt and Bonpland had to be quick, so they left Paris in haste on October 20. Wilhelm and his family had kept Alexander company until then, and, even though the leave-taking had been anticipated for a long time, when it happened it felt abrupt and awkward. Both brothers tried to keep any anxiety to themselves; Wilhelm and Caroline were determinedly cheerful. This helped: 'Strength from others is uplifting.'[3] The baby nearly did it for him, though: 'When Li [Caroline] lifted the little one [Theodor] up to me, I almost lost my composure. But it was only for a moment. We all behaved as one ought to in such situations.'[4] He gazed reflectively at Bonpland, 'with whom I was to undertake such a long journey.' As the coach moved off, he turned and sought out Wilhelm, looking steadily at him until he passed out of sight. He reassured himself: 'a secret voice told me that we should see each other again.'[5] In that, at least, he was right—though almost everything else he had imagined about his journey would turn out differently. As he wryly noted when the journey was over, 'I left Paris intending to embark for Algiers and Egypt; but, as chance rules over the lives of all men, I saw my brother again after returning from Peru and the Amazon, without ever even having set foot on the African continent.'[6]

They arrived in Marseilles on the evening of October 27 and rushed straight down to the port in the hope that the ship was still there. All was well: the *Jaramas* had not yet even docked. A few days later, there was still no sign of her. They busied themselves checking their instruments: 'a terrible sight, the theodolite in pieces, as was the *éboulloir* [an instrument to determine altitude], and almost all the thermometers. I spent several hours unpacking broken instruments. Bonpland was even more distraught than I was.'[7] They climbed, once a day, up the hill of Notre-Dame de la Garde, Marseilles's highest point, to scan the sea for a sign of the *Jaramas*: 'we got excited at every sail that appeared on the horizon.'[8]

To break up the waiting time, Humboldt and Bonpland travelled further along the coast to see the towns of Toulon and Hyères. Skjöldebrand promised to send a messenger straight after them should the *Jaramas* appear. Walking by the harbour at Toulon, they spotted a frigate whose name they recognised: it was the *Boudeuse*, Bougainville's ship, being readied to sail to Corsica. This was the ship that had carried Bougainville around the world thirty years earlier. The crew was already on deck, the sails were being hoisted, and Humboldt and Bonpland were acutely conscious that they were still waiting for a ship to take them on what was, by comparison with the round-the-world voyage, an extremely short journey: 'It is hard to describe my feelings when I saw the ship that had carried [Philibert] Commerson [or 'Commerçon,' the botanist on Bougainville's journey] to the South Sea Islands. There are certain moods in which everything is shot through with a sensation of pain.'[9] Humboldt staged an emotional little moment for himself. He climbed down into the cabin and spent ten minutes sitting by the window, looking out onto the sea, until the others noticed his absence and called for him. 'I could have cried, as I was so vividly reminded of our lost hopes.'[10]

After two more months of waiting in Marseilles, their fears were confirmed. The *Jaramas* wasn't coming. She had been damaged in a storm off Portugal, was currently in Cádiz awaiting repairs, and was not now expected in the French port before the spring. The thought of staying on in Marseilles for such a long time, waiting for a ship that might or might not materialise, was, they felt, more than they could bear. In addition, Tunis had in the meantime become a far less attractive prospect: there were reports of a plague, which was spreading from Oran, in Algeria, towards Tunisia.

They had clearly exhausted all the possibilities Marseilles had to offer. Where might they go, now that they were here? Corsica and Sardinia would be of considerable botanical interest, but were 'too small, too isolated, too immediately leading back to France.' Turning towards Spain was the other obvious option. How about spending the spring there, 'in Valencia or Cádiz, and from there or from Lisbon find an opportunity to get to Tenerife, to the Cape of Good Hope, to Brazil?'[11]

In spite of the obvious appeal of these options, Humboldt couldn't quite let go of North Africa, now that they had got so close. 'I did appreciate that it wasn't the wisest thing to do, but Tunis was where I wanted to go, and that was that.'[12] Bonpland, on the other hand, thought that the idea had run its course, and that it was time to abandon it. But Humboldt dragged him down to the port anyway, and indeed turned up a ship headed for Tunis: the *Speranza*, which sailed under the flag of the Republic of Ragusa.[13] Invigorated by the prospect of departure at last, Humboldt could find no fault with the ship: 'As usual, I thought that everything was wonderful.' Bonpland was less enthusiastic, and found the ship 'generally quite pig-like— and indeed we found a black sow lodged in the cabin that was to be allocated to us.'[14] They negotiated their fare and were a day from sailing when news reached them that the atmosphere in Tunisia had turned. Once again, the cause was Napoleon. His invasion of Egypt had put France on a war footing with the Ottoman Empire, and the bey, an Ottoman vassal, had to fall in line. Everybody who arrived from a French port was liable to be arrested and imprisoned. 'I had everything to fear for Mr. Bonpland—and for myself, too, as the collecting of plants, when the Mamelukes and French were at war, might be thought a French undertaking.'[15] In any event, the decision was taken out of their hands: the port authorities would not allow the ship to depart. Still, Humboldt could scarcely bring himself to accept the realities of the situation, and to give up on his plan for good:

> The decision may have been wise and prudent, but no less mortifying for that. Had I been alone, had Bonpland shown enthusiasm rather than reluctance, then I should have carried out my plan. It was reckless, certainly, but will anything ever get done if one isn't prepared to take a risk?[16]

To compound Humboldt's frustration, the *Speranza* now stayed in port for another six days. 'Whenever I went up to the observatory I couldn't prevent myself from looking at her,' he complained. 'In fact, all ready for departure, she had positioned herself in the middle of the harbour. I would much rather she had been concealed behind other vessels.'[17]

So Spain it was. As they left Marseilles, the weather turned. A tempest erupted, raging for more than a week, and, making their way west along the coast, they kept seeing debris of ships that had come to grief—a sight that helped alleviate the intensity of Humboldt's disappointment about the *Speranza*. They reached Barcelona in January 1799. The jagged, finger-like rocks of the Montserrat mountains in Catalonia were too enticing to pass without at least a cursory exploration: 'The Montserrat itself consists from foot to peak of a conglomerate, mostly gritty; [. . .] as the sandstone is very susceptible to weathering, cones have formed, of which there are always five to six bunched together in the strangest formations.'[18]

The African coast seemed to have brought them a lot of trouble for no return, and, with the political situation still uncertain, another idea occurred to Humboldt. He remembered the Keutsch brothers, the medical students he had met in Jena in 1797, and who were now back at their home in the Virgin Islands. Perhaps now was the time to make use of the connection. The Spanish territories in the West Indies were inaccessible: nobody who was not Spanish received permission to go there. The Keutsch brothers, on the other hand, were perfectly located on the island of St. Thomas (a Danish colony at the time), and would be sure to make them welcome. In any case, there was little point spending the winter isolated in some Spanish port. Much better to await spring in Madrid, trying to establish connections and making further preparations. Furthermore, Humboldt was in need of money, which, if it were to be sent from Berlin, would have to go to a reliable bank in the Spanish capital. Even so, there were difficulties: Kunth was unable to persuade a bank in Berlin to send Humboldt's money to Madrid. But old friends from Henriette Herz's circle stepped in: Joseph Mendelssohn (Moses Mendelssohn's oldest son), who had by now established his own very successful banking firm, together with David Friedländer, was ready to transfer, 'without bail or bond, any amount for Humboldt to the Madrid banker d'Iranda.'[19]

In Madrid, letters were waiting for him from Reinhard and Christiane von Haeften. Their third child had been born. Humboldt was relieved that everything had gone well.[20] The affection in his reply comes over as strong, though it is clear that it also benefits from the effects of distance. The relationship was safely back in the realm of the ideal, where Haeften's marriage and steadily expanding family only added to the love everybody—including Humboldt—felt for each other: 'If only I could embrace those children for a moment, and you, Reinhard of my heart.'[21]

Humboldt and Bonpland had no good reason to believe that being based in Madrid would speed up the arrangements for their journey to St. Thomas. But things were looking auspicious—much more so than they could have hoped at this stage. Almost straight away, Humboldt ran into somebody he knew of: Baron Philipp Forell, whose brother he had met in Dresden. Forell was Saxony's envoy at the Spanish court. Working on a book on the geology of Spain, he was delighted to meet Humboldt and happy to take him and Bonpland under his wing. He steered them in the direction of Mariano Luis d'Urquijo, King Carlos IV's newly appointed secretary of state, who had taken up his post just days before Humboldt and Bonpland's arrival in Madrid. Should things with Urquijo go well, Forell hinted, there might be an undreamed-of possibility opening up: the chance to visit the Spanish overseas possessions after all, as a private person, and on the condition that Humboldt carry the cost of the expedition himself.

Urquijo, it turned out, was somebody else with whom Humboldt could claim a modest degree of acquaintance: the Spaniard had lived in London at the time Humboldt had been there with Forster, and their paths had crossed, albeit fleetingly. Urquijo also had a nephew, Don Raphael d'Urquijo. The latter was about to be appointed secretary of the Spanish legation in Berlin. He had not yet arrived in Berlin, but his uncle probably knew of the plans for him and was keen to smooth his passage. (In 1802, Don Raphael and Rahel Levin would enter into a short-lived engagement.[22])

Whether because of these connections or because Humboldt—being personable and aristocratic—was not difficult to promote, Urquijo 'removed all obstacles.' Since Humboldt was not attached to a research programme of any rival nation, such as France, there was no reason to keep him away from the Spanish colonies. Humboldt stressed that Urquijo's support had been purely the result of a 'love for the sciences.'[23] Certainly Urquijo was a reformer, opposed to both the Inquisition and to slavery, so perhaps Humboldt's generous assessment wasn't so wide of the mark.

An audience with the king was arranged. Humboldt, as instructed by Urquijo, presented a document that laid out his reasons for wanting to travel to the 'new continent.' There was, of course, his 'burning wish' to see South America. But the petitioner also confidently sketched his programme. Instead of merely studying 'different species and their characteristics—a subject that is still being pursued far too exclusively,' he had a more ambitious agenda: to discover the underlying forces that governed those phenomena. This reached beyond cataloguing and counting: it was something much closer to Goethe's desire to find the forces underlying everything. Seeking 'his Catholic Majesty's protection,' Humboldt talked about 'the influence of atmosphere and its chemical composition on living things, the fabric of the Earth, the correlation between the strata in countries at the furthest remove from each other—ultimately, the great harmonies in nature.'[24]

His success was greater than he could possibly have imagined; when seen against the setbacks of the past year, it was spectacular. Within days, Humboldt found himself issued with a passport. In his own account of his South American journey, *Personal Narrative of a Journey to the Equinoctial Regions of the New Continent* (which was part of Humboldt's 34-volume *Voyage aux régions équinoxiales du nouveau continent*, which he published between around 1807 and 1850), he gives a precise summary of the document—so extraordinary was the extent of what, at a stroke, he now found himself expressly permitted to do:

> I was authorised to make use of my physical and geodesic instruments with complete liberty; I was allowed to take astronomic measurements in all Spanish possessions, as well as survey the altitudes of mountains, collect the products of the soil, and do whatever I thought would serve the furthering of science.

In short, 'never had a traveller received a more comprehensive permit, never did the Spanish government show greater trust to a stranger.'[25]

In mid-May 1799, Humboldt and Bonpland were on their way to La Coruña, a port in northwest Spain, hoping to embark for Cuba. They could profitably have stayed on in Madrid for a while longer, especially as they had been granted access to several excellent collections of Latin American minerals and natural products. But dried plant specimens, even 'the greatest collection of herbs ever assembled in Europe,' had lost a lot of their attraction now that they had a new, still quite miraculous-seeming permit burning in their pocket: 'For a year now I had met so many obstacles that I could hardly believe that my most fervent dream should become reality.'[26]

On June 3, with the breeze blowing calmly but steadily from the west, and in surprisingly rough seas, they were on board the *Pizarro*. There they waited for two days until the wind turned. There was nobody in Europe who had an exclusive claim on Humboldt, and whom he could not have left behind with a fairly easy heart. Even so, by his own account, he was deeply affected by his departure. Perhaps it served as a reminder, as much as anything, of the lack of such binding ties: 'Separated from those we love, about to step into a new life, we instinctively retreat into ourselves, and are overwhelmed by a feeling of loneliness such as we have never felt before.'[27]

Just after two o'clock on June 5, a cannon shot sounded, and they were off. Once again, Humboldt fixed his eyes on what he was leaving behind. This time it was the forbidding fortress of San Antón, a prison which held, as he knew, the Italian explorer Alessandro Malaspina (who had served in the Spanish navy). 'As I left Europe, I would have rather seen something better, something more apt to instil a good opinion of humanity.'[28] At nine o'clock in the evening, they saw a last light on the mainland, coming from a fishing hut somewhere near Sisarga. As it got darker, the wind increased, and they were on their way.

14

Across the Atlantic

✦

The *Pizarro* was bound for Cuba, via a brief stopover in Tenerife. As she left the harbour of La Coruña, most of the crew scanned the horizon for any sign of an English ship. This anxiety was prompted by Spain's recent switch of allegiance. Originally part of the First Coalition against Revolutionary France, Spain suffered a heavy defeat at the hands of the French in the War of the Pyrenees, a powerful sign that it might be wiser to enter into an alliance with France instead. This put Spain in direct opposition to the other European powers, foremost among them Great Britain, which had retaliated by imposing a naval blockade preventing trade between Spain and her American colonies.

For the first three days, all was quiet, and the crew were relaxed. Humboldt noted in his diary that Bonpland was 'completely seasick,' whereas he himself 'didn't suffer from the sea, even though it was very rough.'[1] In the evenings, porpoises appeared and swam alongside. Humboldt and Bonpland observed the phosphorescence of the sea, particularly visible on the foam-tipped crests of the waves: 'it looks like fire sparked from steel.'[2]

It wasn't until sunset on June 8, as they were having dinner, that a cry went up from the lookout on the mast: sails had been spotted. It might be a frigate, possibly English; and it seemed to be coming towards them. The drill was to immediately extinguish all lights on board while the crew tacked. 'This precaution,' wrote Humboldt, 'which is observed on board of all merchant vessels [. . .] was to cause us deadly boredom on many of the sea crossings we had to undertake within those five years.'[3]

During the night, the other vessel having been shaken off, the *Pizarro* returned to her course, and on the following day, a Sunday, mass was celebrated on deck: 'Next to the priest stood some chicken baskets, as well as a dead ram. All except the helmsman were on their knees, and, as the ship was rocking quite a bit, the novices were thrown sideways.'[4] Two days later, on the 11th, a shoal of luminescent jellyfish floated by. Bonpland dunked a basket into the sea and caught a few. Humboldt spent the rest of the evening subjecting them to galvanic experiments:

> The jellyfish themselves don't glow, except when you poke, shake or rub them. [. . .] Having rubbed a board with a jellyfish, it will stop glowing after a while, but can be made to glow again, though less brightly, when the same bit is rubbed with a dry hand. The third time, there is no more glowing, even though the spot is still very moist and sticky.[5]

They were carried along the African coast by the Gulf Stream, and Humboldt and Bonpland admired the clear night sky: 'The double stars Mizar and Alcor were clearly visible to the naked eye. And the light simply poured out from the almost perfect sphere of the moon! [. . .] Countless shooting stars fell out of a cloudless sky, seemingly at a lesser height than at home.'[6] Forty miles east of Madeira, a 'luckless swallow, endlessly exhausted' sat down on their topmast, too weary even to try and evade capture.[7]

As they approached the Canaries, Humboldt 'galvanised' a mysterious leathery organism. It had been dredged up in the as yet uncharted sound between the two small islands of Alegranza and Montaña Clara, north of Lanzarote, which they had explored using a plumb line. Both he and Bonpland were unsure whether it was animal or vegetable. However, when exposed to galvanic treatment, it failed to show a reaction. So they gave it a name, *Fucus vitifolius*, and grouped it, provisionally, with the algae. It had grown at a depth of 192 feet, and yet it was green—just like the lichen that had grown underground at Freiberg, which had so intrigued Humboldt eight years earlier.

Even with entities as remote as this, Humboldt made comparisons almost compulsively—there were few things he encountered that did not remind him of something else. Connections seemed to be everywhere, some only dimly perceived, others taking shape as he studied and pondered them. For example, the small islands north of Lanzarote somehow managed to put Humboldt in mind both of the landscape of Venetia, as well as the shore of the river Rhine, near Bonn. Local customs had the same effect on him. Lanzarote's native population, he was told, had a long tradition of polyandry: 'A husband was recognised as such only for one orbit of the moon, then another would take over the office straight away, with the first getting absorbed back into the household staff.' Such a practice, Humboldt thought, was found only here and in Tibet.[8]

The Gulf Stream, of course, was itself a hidden connection made manifest. It provided ample evidence that the furthest reaches of the Earth stood in some communication with each other. In the fifteenth century, two dead bodies had arrived on the Azores, 'belonging, to judge by their physical attributes, to an unknown tribe of humanity.'[9] Fruit of the Antilles often appeared on the shores of two of the westernmost Canary Islands, Gomera and El Hierro; and, just before Humboldt's own arrival on Tenerife, a tree trunk, with lichen still attached, had been washed up on the beach there—a *Cedrela odorata*, which only grew in the tropics. On the coast of Scotland, charred parts of the wreck of the *Tilbury*, a ship that had gone up in flames near Jamaica, had been found. Barrels of French wine, from ships wrecked in the Antilles, appeared on the coast of the Outer Hebrides—and even tortoises were not unknown there.[10]

On June 16, land was finally sighted—looking, at first, 'like a small cloud on the horizon.' By five o'clock, with the sun already low, Lanzarote lay before them, stippled with tones of gold and ochre. From the ship, the island was visible in such detail that Humboldt was able to measure the height of 'a cone-shaped mountain, majestically surpassing the other summits, and which we held to be the great volcano that had caused such destruction on the night of September 1, 1730.'[11]

Instead of heading straight for Tenerife, the *Pizarro* was to land first at Lanzarote, so that the crew could establish whether there were English ships lying in wait at Santa Cruz, Tenerife's port. Humboldt and Bonpland were too excited to sleep, and spent most of the night on deck: 'the moon shone on Lanzarote's volcanic peaks, whose ash-covered slopes gleamed like silver.'[12] After midnight, heavy clouds moved in, obscuring the moon, and, in the darkness, they could see lit torches being carried along the shore. These probably indicated fishermen preparing to sail, but the scene put Humboldt in mind of a more exalted adventure: 'these moving lights reminded us of those that Pedro Gutiérrez, a page boy of Queen Isabella's, saw on the island of Guanahani on that memorable night that the New World was discovered.'[13] The notion may have been far-fetched, but it was not without its own hidden connection: it was from the port of San Sebastian on Gomera in the Canaries that Christopher Columbus had departed on his epoch-making voyage in 1492.

By the reckoning of the *Pizarro*'s captain, they were approaching Lanzarote's main port of Teguise. They hoisted the Spanish flag and fired a shot to salute the small fort overlooking the bay in front of them. Their salute was not returned, so they set out by cutter, hoping that, with the fort so close, they would find someone who could tell them whether English ships lay ready. Humboldt and Bonpland, excited to 'step on African soil, [. . .] possibly to encounter strange animals and plants,' joined the party on the cutter, and, with 'eight seamen and the fat Catalonian canvas merchant rowing incredibly fast,' they approached the shore.[14] As they drew nearer, it became clear that what they had saluted was not a fort at all, but a large basalt rock. The rock was not even on Lanzarote itself, but on the little island of Graciosa, just off Lanzarote's northern tip. However, they did make out a fisherman—who, terrified at their approach, threw away his fishing rod and tried to run off. Only when they had assured him that they were harmless did he confirm that no English ship had been seen on the open sea for weeks. Back on board the *Pizarro*, Humboldt was hoping to examine the beautiful blood-red fish he had bought off their informant, but the ship's cook had already de-scaled them, and, what was more, 'they turned out to be entirely unpalatable.'[15] They made for Tenerife without further ado.

As they approached Santa Cruz, the light haze that they had noticed ahead thickened into a heavy fog. They inched their way forward, using the plumb line, and were about to give a salute when the clouds above them tore apart, revealing a beautiful blue sky, 'and in the midst of the blue, as though it didn't belong to this earth and the view opened into a different world, there appeared the Pico del Teide in all its majesty'[16]—some 3,700 metres high. The peak of the Teide seemed to be covered with snow—a common misapprehension that Humboldt himself laboured under at first. In fact, the upper slopes were under a layer of pumice, dazzlingly white in the sun-shine. As they hurried to the foredeck to enjoy the spectacular sight, four English ships became visible, steering into the murk: under cover of the fog, the *Pizarro* had unwittingly sailed past them unob-served. It was sheer luck that had saved them from being sent back to mainland Europe: 'indeed it would have been bitter for a natural-ist to have seen the coast of Tenerife from afar without being allowed to set foot on its volcanic soil.'[17]

After this close call, the *Pizarro* made for the protection of the harbour of Santa Cruz. 'A vast caravanserai en route to America and the Indies,'[18] it was also the place where, as Humboldt noted, just two years earlier Horatio Nelson had lost his right arm in his failed attempt to seize Tenerife's main port. On stepping ashore, the crew immediately found themselves the object of the attentions of 'La Capitana,' the chief of a band of local women, who offered to come aboard to help 'counter the disorder that might be caused by drunken sailors'—a request which they politely declined.[19] But even licen-tiousness, Humboldt observed, assumed some form of order here:

La Capitana had an excellent reputation for making sure that sailors turned up on board orderly and on time when their ship was about to sail, and was often the first person a captain would consult if any of his crew had defected.

Thanks to their Spanish passport, Humboldt and Bonpland were made welcome by the local dignitaries. Colonel José de Armiaga, commander of an infantry regiment, invited them to stay with him. In his garden they were thrilled to see plants thriving that previously they had encountered only in greenhouses. Tenerife, on the edge of the tropics, not only offered an enticing glimpse of what was to come but also had a beauty all of its own: 'no place in the world seems more apt to cure melancholia.'[20]

The captain of the *Pizarro* had agreed to remain at Tenerife long enough for them to climb the Pico del Teide. However, the English blockade meant that they could not stay safely for longer than four or five days. So, on June 20, Humboldt and Bonpland hurried across the island to the town of Orotava. This was the traditional starting point of any ascent, and they had been told that they would find guides there.

Santa Cruz had been uncomfortably hot. Now, as they moved west across the island, the valley of Orotava opened up before them, cool and verdant. Vines covered the slopes of the hills, the coast was lined with palm trees and, higher up, bananas grew, as well as the famous dragon trees, 'the trunk of which is often compared, rightly, to the body of a snake.'[21] (In Orotava, they would visit the town's famous dragon tree. They were impressed by the girth of its trunk, which in the fifteenth century, they were told, had already been more or less as they saw it now. Given its extremely slow rate of growth, Humboldt reckoned that it must be one of the oldest life forms on the planet.) Orange trees, covered in blossom, were dotted around the landscape, as well as myrtles and cypresses, and farmers bordered their plots of land with agaves, serving as fences. 'The whole coastline is cultivated in the manner of a garden.'[22] Over all this presided the peak of the Teide. Even after Humboldt's return from South America, where, he conceded, he had seen grander spectacles of nature, still, he had 'never looked at a tableau that was so varied, so attractive, and so harmonious.'[23] Even this paradise was not untainted, though:

> It is sad to relate, however, that the prosperity of the inhabitants doesn't correspond to their efforts, nor to nature's bounty. Those who farm the land are mostly not those who own it: the fruit of their labours belongs to the nobility, and the way of life that has made Europe unhappy for so long now still keeps the people of the Canaries from prospering.[24]

In Orotava's botanical garden, they ran into another European near-acquaintance: the French vice-consul Le Gros, who had been with Baudin on his expedition to the Antilles. When Baudin had been forced to dock at Tenerife during a storm, Le Gros had gone ashore, and never returned. Now happily settled in Orotava, he retained an interest in science. He had written an account of a volcanic eruption—that of the Chahorra on the western flank of the Teide—which had taken place just a year earlier, on June 8, 1798. Humboldt was able to engage Le Gros as a guide, together with an English gardener, also a resident, who had been a student of William Aiton, director of Kew Gardens near London.

On the morning of June 21, Humboldt and Bonpland began their ascent, along with Le Gros; his secretary, Lalande; the English gardener; and local guides. The weather was not auspicious, and the peak was shrouded in heavy cloud. There was only one road up the mountain, so, as Humboldt noted with mild frustration, they followed it just like everybody who had gone before them. 'Climbing the Pic[o] is just like visiting the Chamonix valley or Etna: you have to follow your guides and only get to see what other travellers have seen and described already.'[25]

During the climb Humboldt carefully noted the changing vegetation. First they passed through a chestnut grove, and then a stretch covered with heather as high as small trees. Ascending further, they entered a region of ferns. The roots of the humble *Pteridium aquilina* (common fern, or bracken) were edible. Dried, ground into powder and roasted, they formed a substance called *gofio*, 'a foodstuff so primitive as to give a good picture of the miserable state in which the common people of the Canaries live.'[26]

Beyond the ferns was a grove of junipers and firs. This was the place where the English traveller John Edens, who had climbed Teide in 1715, had reported (in his account to the Royal Society) seeing flames or, indeed, 'fire running downwards in a Stream.'[27] There were no flames in 1799. Humboldt did not dismiss Edens's observations out of hand, but did suggest that his notion that they were caused by the sulphurous atmosphere must have been the result of 'the physical ideas of his time.'[28]

Further up, a 'great plain of gorse' opened before them. So far, the slopes of the Teide had been verdant and welcoming, with nothing to indicate the presence of a volcano beneath their feet. The plain they entered now was littered with pumice stones and small sharp blocks of obsidian. As they walked, their steps raised clouds of dust, which soon covered their hands and faces. It was all quite desolate: 'The barren area of the Pic[o] measures about ten square miles, and as the lower regions, seen from afar, appear foreshortened, the whole island presents itself as an enormous heap of burnt rock, surrounded by no more than a narrow belt of vegetation.'[29] They struggled for more than two hours across the gorse-and-pumice plain before they reached, a little higher up, the place where they were to spend the night.

The Estancia des Ingleses was so named because Edens and his companions had camped there some eighty years earlier. The Estancia was not much more than a cave formed by two overhanging rocks, offering very minimal shelter—something that became painfully clear when the temperature dropped to 5°C (41°F) that night. The guides lit a fire with some bits of gorse, but the wind drove the smoke straight back into the faces of those huddled inside the cave. A protective screen, fashioned from cloths and blankets, was positioned too close to the fire, and by the time they noticed that it was burning, it couldn't be saved.

They rose at three o'clock in the morning and, by the dim light of pinewood torches, set off on the final part of the ascent. After two hours' hard climbing they reached the Alta Vista. This was a small plateau used by the *neveros* (ice sellers) as a base from which to climb into the ice cave—a huge cavern filled with ice and compacted snow. As the sun rose, they could see above them the *malpaís*, a steep and desolate landscape denuded of topsoil and strewn with volcanic rock. The climb was arduous, and the rock, with its razor-sharp edges, hurt their hands and sometimes gave way beneath their feet.

In addition, their relationship with the local guides was becoming increasingly strained. Only the day before, the guides had tried to dissuade Humboldt and his companions from climbing beyond the Estancia des Ingleses. Aggrieved that their advice had been ignored, they now made a point of sitting down every ten minutes to rest. Perhaps explaining why they were reluctant to continue the ascent, it now emerged that none of them had ever climbed all the way to the summit. Relations were hardly sweetened by the travellers' habit of picking up mineral samples as they went—which the guides were expected to carry. Humboldt made the painful observation that, time and again, their samples of volcanic obsidian and pumice were thrown away down the side of the mountain whenever the guides thought that nobody was looking.

After a gruelling three hours, they arrived at la Rambleta, a small plateau, from which rises the Pitón de Azúcar, the Teide's sugarloaf summit. It was here that they observed small gaps in the rocks—locally known as *les narices del pico* (the nostrils of the peak)—out of which curled hot vapours. The party examined these emissions and found them to consist of pure, odourless water, with a temperature of 43.2°C (109.76°F).

Now the steepest part of the ascent—the Pitón—was before them. The slope was so rugged that climbing it would have been impossible had it not been for an old lava run that emanated from the crater itself, and which now formed a solid wall that led through the layers of ash and rubble. Its crags were so heavily weathered that what they tried to hold onto often broke off, and it took them half an hour to climb a distance of less than 200 metres.[30]

At eight o'clock in the morning, exhausted, numb and cold, they finally reached the peak. The wind from the west was blowing so hard that it was a struggle to stay upright. The centre of the crater was still obscured from view: the lava had formed a crest around it, 'like a small cylinder on top of a truncated cone.'[31] After a while, a narrow gap towards the eastern side of the crest was discovered—created, Humboldt thought, by an ancient lava flow—and the group climbed through it to reach the bottom of the crater.

No direct heat could be felt, except over the steaming crevices inside the crater. There they also recorded hearing a curious humming sound. When a thermometer was placed inside, it rose to 68°C (154.4°F), or even 75°C (167°F): 'it undoubtedly registered an even higher temperature, but we were only able to look at the instrument once we had taken it out again, so as to avoid getting our hands burnt.'[32]

There was no sign of recent eruptions: none of the small cones of slag and ash above narrow vents that are often observed on volcanoes between eruptions were present. Only centuries of weather appeared to have left their mark: lava walls had crumbled, leaving large slabs of rock scattered over the surface. All recent activity, therefore, must have been at the side openings—such as the 1798 eruption of the Chahorra described by Le Gros.

However, Humboldt sought something else from the experience of being at the summit, something that went beyond measuring the phenomena he encountered. Like many young people of his generation, Humboldt had read Jean-Jacques Rousseau's novel *Julie, or the New Heloise* (*Julie ou la Nouvelle Héloïse*).[33] His mind had been schooled by this key text of early Romanticism, and so he would have had certain expectations of being on a mountain summit. A place as exalted as this surely would have the power to lift the mind to higher, sublime contemplations. Teide, however, failed to conform to Romantic expectations: while it provided 'ample opportunity for interesting observations,' Humboldt wrote, 'it isn't in itself an impressive sight.'[34]

Before making their descent, they looked down at the island below. They were at an altitude three times higher than the clouds, so the whole of the horizon was visible, uninterrupted even by the highest of the mountains on the surrounding islands. Humboldt quickly calculated that if the crater were to spew fire, 'the Pic of Tenerife would serve as a beacon to sailors for a distance of more than 260 miles.'[35] The port of Orotava was intermittently visible through the shifting clouds, as were the barren slopes of the Pico and the cheerful-looking settlements by the coast; in between, the different temperature zones were discernible thanks to their changing vegetation.

The coastal area seemed unnaturally close, so that even the rigging of the ships in the harbour could be clearly seen. Here, again, Humboldt's thinking was perhaps coloured by his reading of *Julie*. When Saint-Preux, the male hero, climbs to the top of a mountain in the Swiss Alps, having been sent away by Julie, he observes the same phenomenon. The consistency of the air is different, 'pure and subtle.' This affects how things appear: it makes 'colors more vivid, outlines sharper, brings all lines of sight closer; distances appear shorter than on the plain, where the density of the air covers the earth as with a veil.'[36]

From the Teide, Humboldt described what he saw in strikingly similar terms. The fact that everything seemed close together—'the villages, the vineyards and gardens by the coast'—had much to do with 'the transparency of the air,' he thought. The houses, the ships, the plants in the plain, seemed to 'glow in the most vivid colours.' He made the comparison with the Swiss mountains himself, but thought the effect even greater in the subtropical and tropical zones: 'given an equal distance, the reflection of a lake, or a broad river, will glitter less when seen from the ridge of the high alps in Switzerland, compared to from the top of the cordilleras in Peru or Mexico.' It was columns of dry air, rising over Africa and blown west by the wind, that gave such an extraordinary transparency to the air of the Canaries: 'it heightens the brilliance of the plants' colours and increases the magical effect of their harmonies and contrasts.'[37]

They lingered for a while, hoping to be able to see the whole archipelago, but the cloud cover over Lanzarote got thicker. It was, in any case, hard not to feel chastened by the inhospitable nature of the place. There was no sign of life at the top of the volcano—no insect, moss, or even lichen; all they encountered were dead bees, stuck to tiny crevices in the rock through which were emitted sulphuric gases. Humboldt guessed that the bees were carried up the mountain by the wind, and 'end up roasted when they, incautiously, come too close to the fissures they approach for warmth.'[38] The explorers themselves did not feel a great deal more comfortable: the biting wind had not let up, and while their hands and faces were rigid with cold, the soles of their shoes were blistering on the hot rocks. The descent down the sugarloaf summit was rapid, 'involuntarily, in part, as we often slid on the ashes.'[39] The *malpáis*, with its loose lava rubble, did not provide much relief. Nor did the next stretch, through short grass so slippery that they had to lean backwards to keep their balance. The temperature, measured as 22.5°C (72.5°F), seemed stiflingly hot after the exposed conditions at the top. They were out of drink, too: their guides had decided to lighten their load by drinking the wine they had taken, and by breaking the water bottles. 'Fortunately,' Humboldt wrote, 'the bottle containing the sample of air from the crater had remained intact.'[40]

15

Decisions and Typhoid Fever

꒰ ꒱

Humboldt left the Canaries not without regret:

It is almost with tears in my eyes that I depart; I'd like to settle here—
even though I have hardly left Europe behind me. If you could see these
fields, these thousand-year-old laurel groves, these vineyards, these roses!
The pigs are fattened on apricots, and camels roam the streets.[1]

From the way Humboldt wrote to his brother, Tenerife had joined
the list of idealised places that he seemed to keep in his head. As
with the imagined house by a Swiss lake where he had proposed to
settle with the Haeftens, it was as though he was trying to prove that
there were places that might allow him to live in closer harmony with
his own nature than those places that he had left behind. In any case,
Humboldt was sorry to be moving on. He might come back one day
though, he thought, perhaps on the return journey. As it happened,
he never did.

On June 25, they were back on the *Pizarro*, bound for Cuba. After
a couple of days they crossed the Tropic of Cancer, and soon after,
Humboldt noticed for the first time that his shadow on the ship's
deck fell to the south. It was during the nights, while watching the
stars, that he was most alive to the feeling of passing from his familiar world into another:

It is a strange, quite novel feeling, to see, on approaching the equator, and especially when passing from one hemisphere to the other, how the stars, familiar from earliest youth, sink ever deeper and eventually disappear. Nothing puts the traveller so vividly in mind of the immense distance from home as the sight of a new sky.[2]

A few nights later, on July 4, the skies were clear enough for them to see the Southern Cross constellation, very much tilted and only intermittently visible through the clouds. It was an important moment for Humboldt—and, as he freely admitted, for emotional rather than scientific reasons. He had longed to see the Southern Cross for many years, a craving conditioned mostly by his reading. When the time came, he recalled the fateful moment in *Paul and Virginia* (*Paul et Virginie*), the Romantic novel by Jacques-Henri Bernardin de Saint-Pierre, at which 'Paul and Virginia speak to one another for the last time by the source of the palm-tree-river [on Mauritius], and where, at the sight of the Southern Cross, the old man admonishes them that the time to part is at hand.'[3]

Over the next few days, Humboldt made notes on almost everything he encountered. All natural phenomena were potentially significant; fragments of information were to be collected in the expectation that they would, in time, fit with some new data, whether contributed by himself or others, and point to underlying, invisible laws. When there was a heavy hailstorm, for example, he thought it might be 'a very important fact, that it hailed during the night. Hasselquist on his voyage to Egypt also observed the phenomenon of hail in the night-time.'[4]

He applied himself to measuring longitude and latitude. And he was struck by the colour of the sky one moonlit night: it was of 'a blue the purity of which is never seen in the North. I took an air sample.'[5] One morning, a shoal of flying fish appeared. These were followed by a flock of tropical birds; the latter proceeded to eat most of the former. Humboldt and Bonpland struggled to obtain a flying fish for themselves, having struck the same problem they had had with the red fish off the coast of Lanzarote: fish 'regularly evades study, as it tends to get eaten almost as quickly as it is caught.'[6] Eventually they secured a young specimen, cut it open and were able to examine its air bladder—'more than half the volume of its entire body.'[7] Unfortunately, the strong movement of the ship prevented them from analysing the air therein. And, once more, they had the company of a swallow: it caught up with the *Pizarro* and travelled for two days with them, mostly resting on the sails, before flying off.

They skirted the African coast, following the traditional route established by Columbus. Having passed the Cape Verde Islands, they struck west to cross the Atlantic. From there, the passage was easy. Once they were in the path of the trade winds, the ship was practically carried across the ocean: 'the sailors hardly need touch the sails.'[8] It was as easy to navigate as steering a ship down a river. In fact, the passage was known among sailors as 'El Golfo de las Damas'—the idea being that it was so easy to navigate that even a woman might manage it.

Humboldt's calculations concerning the *Pizarro*'s position differed from those of the sailors by as much as one degree longitude. On July 12, he was confident enough to predict that they were about to see land—though, given the considerable discrepancies between the French, Spanish, and English maps, it was hard to be sure where exactly they were on the South American coast. The sailors smiled at his predictions of land immediately ahead and asserted that they were another two or three days from landfall. 'It was therefore to my great satisfaction,' Humboldt wrote, 'when I heard, on the 13th, at six o'clock in the morning, that a very steep shore had appeared before the masts, though shrouded in mist and hard to make out.'[9] It was the island of Tobago, off the coast of modern-day Venezuela (which in Humboldt's day formed part of the Spanish viceroyalty [colonial province] of New Granada).

Since they had entered the tropics, the temperature on board had risen steadily: Humboldt had measured 36°C (96.8°F) on the steerage deck, where a lot of the passengers and crew were quartered. They were only about a day or two from Tobago when typhoid broke out on board. Humboldt and Bonpland were taken aback at how poorly prepared the ship was for such an eventuality. Even when more passengers fell ill, no one took any of the obvious measures, such as fumigating the ship: 'I talked about spraying with vinegar, or installing an air pipe near the main mast. The captain found these ideas very amusing, and nothing happened.'[10] There was no Peruvian bark on board—the bark of the cinchona tree, containing a raw form of quinine, which was mainly used against malaria, but had general fever-reducing properties—and Humboldt and Bonpland themselves had been too preoccupied with their instruments to think of bringing any. In any event, it had not occurred to them that a Spanish vessel sailing to the Americas would not be equipped with it.

One of the sailors was so ill that his death was thought to be imminent. The 'fat surgeon, who sat about all day with his hands folded over his stomach,' restricted himself to blood-letting, thus exacerbating his patient's weakness, while the captain dealt with the problem by declaring that, in his twenty-five years' experience, people didn't get ill on courier vessels.[11] Humboldt thought that the captain's and the surgeon's actions amounted to 'the most criminal negligence'—especially when it became clear that the correct administration of the last rites constituted a far greater concern. Sleeping quarters were so cramped that the sailor, lying in his hammock awaiting death, was wedged with his face about five centimetres below the planks of the deck above him. As it wasn't feasible to perform the last rites properly in such a confined space, a pallet was made up for the man by the deck hatch to facilitate the 'clerical spectacle.' Uniforms were donned, lights were lit, and a procession accompanied the stricken sailor outside for the solemn ceremony. 'He was asked a hundred and one things, which he was supposed to believe in, and which we answered in his stead.' The ceremony, Humboldt believed, saved the sailor's life:

He breathed cooler, purer air. He got better day by day, and I was touched when, on the morning of the 13th, pale-faced and with a long beard, he peered out on deck wanting to see the island of Tobago—and, he said, to give thanks to God that he was allowed to set eyes on dry land again, and such a green and beautiful one at that.[12]

A nineteen-year-old Spanish passenger was less lucky. He 'had an open, happy, and gracious aspect. He was also said to be well educated.'[13] Everything seemed to conspire to make his case as tragic as possible: he was the only son of a poor widow and had been extremely reluctant to leave his native Asturias. His mother, however, had selflessly entreated her son to seek a better life and join an uncle who had emigrated to Cuba, where he had done well. The young man's illness progressed rapidly: he fell into a frenzy, then lost consciousness, and died a mere three days after exhibiting the first symptoms.

It was the only fatality, but it was enough to change the atmosphere on the *Pizarro*: 'there was not a person on board who wasn't affected by the fate of the young man, whom we had seen vigorous and well just a few days ago.'[14] In the evening, Humboldt stood on deck, looking at the land that they were approaching:

[O]ur eyes were resting on a rocky, wild shore, illuminated by the occasional ray of moonlight that fell through the clouds. There was no sound but the monotonous cry of some large seabirds, as if searching for land. A deep calm reigned in this forlorn place; but the calm in nature contrasted starkly with the painful feelings that moved within us.[15]

The death knell slowly tolled, the body of the young man was laid out on deck overnight, and, at first light, with a sandbag tied to the feet, it slipped down a plank into the sea.

Afterwards, there seemed little desire among the passengers to stay on board the contaminated vessel for longer than was absolutely necessary. During the night of July 14/15, Humboldt and Bonpland made their decision: they would leave the ship at the next port, Cumaná (in Venezuela), and stay there for a few weeks—'it would have pained us to land in Cumaná or La Guaira [another major port, near Caracas] without setting foot in the interior of a land that has been so little visited by naturalists.'[16] Then they would travel on to Havana. Once again, one of their most momentous decisions had been made as a consequence of chance: 'instead of a few weeks we stayed for a whole year in Tierra Firme; without the epidemic on board the *Pizarro*, we would never have reached the Orinoco, the Casiquiare, and the very border of the Portuguese possessions at the Rio Negro.'[17]

Having rounded the North Point of Tobago, the *Pizarro* headed further west, towards the island of Margarita. There was an almost perfect reprise of the incident at Lanzarote (when a large basalt rock had been mistaken for a fort), when the sailors declared that the landmass ahead of them was undoubtedly Margarita. Humboldt noted in his diary:

> We looked in vain for houses. There was nothing but high cacti and some fishing boats, which promptly fled when we fired a cannon in order to ask for help. Soundings were taken and the seabed was detected in 3 brazas [5 metres]. Consternation all around. The ship was brought to anchor, a boat was to be sent out. Arguments.[18]

The impasse was resolved when a further cannon shot flushed out two pirogues manned by native Indians. They had broken cover when it had become clear to them that the *Pizarro*, by virtue of its incompetence, could not possibly be an English warship. The sailors had mistaken the small island of Coche for Margarita, and had therefore manoeuvred themselves into the wrong channel: the shallow, difficult-to-navigate sound south of Coche. '[A]s ever,' Humboldt observed, 'ignorance rendered us original.'[19]

The Indians were happy to trade some of their supplies—fresh coconuts, calabashes, and some fish, 'the colour of which we could not admire enough. What treasure, to us, did the barges of the poor Indians contain!'[20] The skipper of one of the pirogues offered to come on board and pilot them into Cumaná. Humboldt discovered that the man, Carlos del Pino, spoke Spanish, and the two men sat on deck talking late into the night.

This set the tone for Humboldt's relationship with the indigenous people he encountered: he met them as equals, the difference in their lives a source of fascination to him, rather than a means of classifying them by European standards.

Asked about the fauna and flora of his native land, del Pino delighted his new acquaintance by confirming that it boasted 'two very different species of crocodiles, as well as boas, electric eels, and several types of tiger'[21] (Humboldt means to refer to jaguars when he uses the word 'tiger').

As day broke on July 16, 1799, a verdant coast was spread out before them. On their approach, Cumaná's fortress, San Antonio, was coming into view, gleaming white among the palm trees. The whole scene was framed by mountains rising out of the morning mist: 'At nine o'clock in the morning,' Humboldt recorded, 'forty-one days after our departure from La Coruña, we cast anchor in the port of Cumaná.'[22]

16

A New World

Whenever he thought of Spanish America, Humboldt said later, it was the image of Cumaná and its surroundings that appeared before his inner cye:[1]

> How colourful the birds are, the fishes, even the crabs (sky blue and yellow)! We've been running about like mad things, and in the first three days couldn't identify anything at all—we're forever throwing away one thing so as to be able to pick up another. Bonpland assures me that he will lose his mind if the wonders aren't going to cease soon. [. . .] I can feel it, I shall be very happy here.[2]

The onward journey to Cuba would take between eight and ten days, and there seemed to be no particular urgency to get there right away. In any case, as Humboldt explained in a letter to his brother, the climate in Cuba would be at its hottest from now until October, so it made more sense to stay around Cumaná for a while. Indeed, his plans seemed to adjust, and expand, as his pen moved across the paper: only a few paragraphs later, he wrote, 'I don't know yet how long I'll stay here; three months, I think, here and in Caracas; but perhaps much longer.' And in any case: 'it's important to take in what is close at hand.'[3]

Humboldt and Bonpland had managed to engage Carlos del Pino as a guide. A native of the Cumaná region, he belonged to the Guayqueríes tribe—a name that, according to Humboldt, was acquired as the result of a misunderstanding. Apparently, Columbus's men had met some local people who, at that moment, were harpooning fish with a sharpened stick tied to a string. Asked the name of their tribe, they mistook the question and gave the name of their harpoon: 'Guaike, Guaike,' signifying 'pointed stick.'

Del Pino now guided them from the place where they had anchored, by the mouth of the Río Manzanares, to Cumaná itself. The walk was about a mile across a barren plain, and it was very hot—Humboldt stuck his thermometer into the white sand and measured 37.7°C (99.86°F). It was truly a new world:

> The feathered palm fronds stood out against a blue sky, untouched by the merest haze. The sun rose quickly to its zenith. A dazzling light permeated the air and rested on the whitish hills, scattered with cylindrical cacti; and the sea was deeply calm, its shores alive with pelicans, herons, and flamingos. The radiant daylight, the colourful plants, the shape of the flora, the gay plumage of the birds—all announced the magnificent character of nature in the tropics.[4]

The first part of the town they passed through was the Indian quarter, where del Pino took the opportunity to show them his house and garden—though the latter looked, to Humboldt, 'more like a copse than land that has undergone cultivation.'[5] The neighbourhood had a well-ordered, friendly aspect: the streets were 'straight and studded with small, new houses.' The pleasant appearance was built on calamity, however: this part of town had only recently been reconstructed after a catastrophic earthquake in December 1797. Once they left the Indian quarter, signs of destruction were still apparent everywhere, with 'new buildings rising out of the rubble of the old.'[6]

In the centre of town they were introduced to Don Vicente Emparán, the provincial governor. They presented their passport and, once again, it worked like a charm: Emparán seemed delighted with Humboldt and Bonpland's intention of spending time in the region. But more than that, Don Vicente was actively interested in the scientific purpose of their journey: did they not think, he inquired, that in the tropics the air contained less nitrogen than in Spain? That iron oxidised more quickly and that this was due to the greater moisture content of the air? At that moment, Humboldt wrote, nothing could have sounded lovelier to their ears than 'the words nitrogen, ferric oxide, hygrometer'—nor could they have hoped to find such an enthusiastic welcome.[7] And indeed, as Humboldt reported later, 'the public signs of respect that he showed us during our long stay in his region did play a great part in the gracious reception that we encountered everywhere in South America.'[8]

They rented a house; they unpacked their instruments— astonishingly, undamaged. The area around Cumaná was a naturalist's dream. Thick hedges of prickly pear cacti formed impenetrable screens, called *tunales*, which 'did not just detain the natives, who are naked above the belt, but is feared by those who are fully clothed, too.'[9] The *tunales* were also breeding grounds for rattlesnakes, and were thus used, Humboldt noted, for defensive purposes, just as crocodiles were encouraged to live in moats.

Earthquakes, with reminders of their impact all around Humboldt, became a natural focus of interest for him. Although they were not confined to South America—even in Europe, the catastrophic earthquake of 1755 in Lisbon was still a vivid memory—their occurrence here was so frequent that Humboldt regarded them as one of the New World's particular contributions to the understanding of nature's deeper workings:

> Each part of the globe furnishes science with its own special subject, and if we cannot hope to divine the causes of a natural phenomenon, then we must at least try to discover its laws and, through the comparison of a great array of facts, to distinguish common, repeating patterns from that which is variable and random.[10]

The task of comparison, however, wasn't as straightforward as might have been hoped: as a result of infestation by white ants and termites, Cumaná's archives did not go back beyond 150 years. Since then, the most devastating—and, Humboldt noted, the scientifically most interesting—earthquake had been that of October 21, 1766, which was still commemorated with an annual church service and procession. Humboldt tried to establish its defining characteristics and context as well as he could. There had been a long drought preceding it. The quake itself had intermittently lasted for fourteen months, so that Cumaná's inhabitants had spent much of that time living on the streets, 'and began rebuilding their houses only when the quakes had let up enough to occur on a monthly basis.'[11]

During that earthquake, and also the one that followed it, in 1794, the earth had moved with a wave-like, horizontal motion. The great earthquake of 1797 was different—this time, there was a vertical thrust from below. This quake was preceded by a roaring sound; having studied the reports of witnesses, Humboldt compared it to an explosion deep inside a mine. It could be heard the loudest in the southern part of the city, on the hill on which the San Francisco monastery was situated—and this was also where, only about half an hour before the eruption, people had noticed a strong smell of sulphur.

True precursors of a quake were not always easy to disentangle from popular superstition. Humboldt was told that those earthquakes that caused the most devastation announced themselves by very faint vibrations of the ground. There was also said to be a rushing, buzzing sound in the air, and animals, such as dogs, goats, and pigs, would behave strangely. Pigs were thought to be particularly sensitive, displaying restlessness, or even screaming, at an approaching earthquake. However dubious the scientific justification for these claims, Humboldt didn't think it impossible that animals, being closer to the ground than human beings, might be better able to hear underground noise, or be affected by leaking gases. In any case, he thought it worth noting that 'it is very rare that a false alarm is raised by somebody who is native to the area.'[12]

Such beliefs and observations were valuable to Humboldt above all as clues to a larger, more global system of interconnecting forces.

Understandably, many people thought that the area most strongly affected by an earthquake must be its centre of origin. In Cumaná, for example, it was believed that the monastery on the hill must have been built on top of great reserves of sulphur and other combustible materials. But Humboldt was able to see beyond local conditions. He recognised that the great speed at which the vibrations of the tremors travelled in all directions, even across the sea, made it likely that the centre of an earthquake lay at a considerable distance from the earth's surface.[13]

Not only were individual earthquakes connected to each other but they were also, he suspected, linked to the activity of volcanoes. All these phenomena, then, must be regarded as the outward expression of unseen forces. At the time that the great earthquake of February 1797 in Ecuador was devastating Riobamba, Quito and the surrounding areas, Humboldt noted, 1,500 miles away 'the inhabitants of the eastern Antilles were startled by tremors of the earth that lasted for eight months.' Indeed, the tremors only stopped when the volcano on Guadeloupe erupted in September. That eruption, in turn, was followed by a persistent underground roar, which lasted until the December earthquake that destroyed Cumaná. The Riobamba quake also seemed to be directly linked to the activity of another volcano, Galeras, near the town of Pasto in southern Colombia. For several months, a thick black pillar of smoke had risen from it, 'which disappeared in the same hour that, sixty miles further south, the cities of Riobamba, Hambato, and Tacunga were destroyed by an enormous strike.'[14]

While they collected plants, examined rocks, and gathered information about earthquakes, Humboldt and Bonpland acquired a modest degree of celebrity. Towards the end of July, Humboldt started a series of astronomical measurements. Ever since he had realised, on board the *Pizarro*, how little the existing maps corresponded to his own measurements, he had had a suspicion that Cumaná's position—in fact that of the entire coast—had been drawn too far to the south. This, he thought, must have been a consequence of the strong northward currents near Trinidad, which distorted the sailors' readings of their instruments. Indeed, he was able to confirm that Cumaná's true position differed by half a degree in latitude from the map based on the measurements of Thomas Jefferys, published a mere five years earlier.[15] The two exotic men standing on the terrace of their house with various instruments set up around them were natural objects of curiosity:

> We were constantly prevented from working by visitors, and if we didn't want to give offence to people who were so delighted to view lunar spots through the Dollond [the telescope developed some decades earlier by the English optician John Dollond], to see two gases consume each other in a eudiometrical tube, or watch a frog move as a result of galvanic stimulation—we were forced to answer their often irrational questions and to repeat the same experiments for hours.[16]

In time, they found themselves easily absorbed into the social life of the town, which itself mixed the strange and the familiar in a way that must have been attractive to Humboldt. Most evenings, the two explorers joined a 'circle of very respectable people' enjoying a bath in the Manzanares River. By the light of the moon, chairs were placed into the gently flowing waters, where both men and women, 'lightly dressed, much as in some North European spa towns,' sat for a few hours, all the while chatting about the weather, untroubled by the small crocodiles, known as *bavas*.[17] Only the occasional dolphin would cause a mild disturbance, when it spouted water at the bathers through its blowhole.

There was also dancing: Humboldt wrote home to Haeften that he and Bonpland were invited to balls almost daily. The fashion was to blend formal Spanish dances with African-influenced rhythms. Humboldt even thought that he recognised a version of a dance he knew, the *Menuet à la Reine*, the local variation of which was known as the 'Minuet Congo.' It was just as well that he had practised it with Henriette Herz in Berlin.

Humboldt and Bonpland's house, 'so advantageously situated for observing the sky and meteorological events,'[18] also afforded another view, towards the town square, where the sale of enslaved Africans took place—not often, but with enough frequency for Humboldt and Bonpland to witness several sales. Those individuals being sold were young: fifteen to twenty years of age, Humboldt guessed. He clearly found it painful to watch this 'degrading custom,' and described how buyers would appraise the health of their prospective purchases 'as if at a horse market,' yanking open their mouths to assess the state of their teeth. A guest in the country, he was not in a position to interfere, and noted, with some resignation, that 'we counted ourselves lucky that at least we were in a place and among a people where such a spectacle occurs quite rarely, and the number of slaves is generally negligible.'[19]

After a month in Cumaná, Humboldt and Bonpland felt that it was time to venture further afield. The Araya peninsula, which reaches like an arm across the Gulf of Cariaco north of Cumaná, was the site of a famous salt mine that Humboldt wanted to see. Every Sunday night, a ferry carried the workers from Cumaná over to Araya, in time to begin work early on Monday. So on August 19, Humboldt and Bonpland joined the ferry for its night crossing. Jaguar furs had been spread out on deck for the night—but still the two men were so cold that they could not sleep. Humboldt checked his thermometer and was surprised to find that it registered 21.8°C (71.24°F). They had spent less than two months in the tropics, but already their perception of what was normal had been radically recalibrated.

The extensive salt flats of the Araya peninsula had been exploited by the Spanish early in the sixteenth century, and by the Dutch in the seventeenth. Now, more than a century later, the mine was reduced to a small-time concern—primarily, Humboldt observed, as a result of less than impressive management: 'The saline inspector spends his life in his hammock, from where he issues orders to the workers, and takes receipt of his provisions, which are brought to him via a *lancha del rey* (royal barque) from Cumaná each week.'[20]

The people on the Araya coast were keen to show off their foremost attraction to the visitors: the *piedra de los ojos* (stone of the eyes). The thing was believed to be half stone, half animal:

> It is found in the sand, where it doesn't move; if you pick one up, however, and place it on an even surface, a pewter or Faience plate, say, it will move if it comes into contact with lemon juice. If you put it in somebody's eye, the ostensible animal will perform a full turn and drive out any object that may have got into the eye [. . .]. They offered to put some sand into our eyes, so that we could satisfy ourselves of the efficacy of the thing.[21]

They declined.

The 'stones,' Humboldt and Bonpland saw quite clearly, once they put them under the microscope, were very small conch shells. But, they found, 'these explanations were not at all what the inhabitants of Araya wanted to hear. Nature seems the grander the more mysterious it is, and popular science rejects anything that is simple.'[22]

17

'The American Alps'

The New World elicited two distinct types of response from
Humboldt. What he encountered would often strike him as
uncannily similar to what he knew from Europe: the Río Manzanares,
for example, was 'very like the river Saale near Jena.'[1] Conversely, and
often at the same time, he found it utterly different, possessed of a
quality that made it fundamentally unlike all that he was familiar
with. Europe was his point of reference, but he was also seeking
something beyond it, something that transcended the confines of
what he knew—and it was the tension between these two positions
that seemed particularly to hold his attention.

At five o'clock in the morning on September 4, 1799, Humboldt
and Bonpland set off to explore the interior of the country. Before
moving further south, into the Orinoco Basin, they would travel
across a triangular slice of the country, mostly via the mission stations established by the Catholic order of the Capuchins. There was
the prospect of a fabled cave of night birds, probably new to science,
as well as the chance of encountering indigenous tribes that hadn't
been described before. The paths, they had been told, would be difficult, and they would be able to take only the barest necessities. So
they travelled with a painfully reduced load of scientific instruments:
a sextant; an inclination instrument,[2] as well as one for determining
declination (the difference between geographic, or true, north and
magnetic north); a thermometer; and a hygrometer (to measure

humidity);[3] as well as quantities of paper for storing and drying plant specimens. Finally, they also carried a barometer, which, being the most sensitive of the instruments, was given into the special charge of a porter employed exclusively for that purpose, who walked alongside the mule that carried it. '[T]hese were the instruments to which we generally confined ourselves on our smaller expeditions.'[4]

On crossing the mountain range that separated the coast around Cumaná from the interior, the changing rock formations put Humboldt in mind of Switzerland and the Tyrol. Indeed, he declared, they were 'in the American Alps'![5] On the summit of its highest peak, they turned to look back. They could see all the way to the coast and beyond, where the Araya peninsula lay in the distance. Among the almost vertical rocks the estuary had dug itself a path like a twisted riverbed. The view that was spread out before Humboldt's eyes was entirely new to him, of course, and yet, it seemed effortlessly to find a place in the network of meaning he was at home in: 'This strange sight is reminiscent of the fantastical landscape that Leonardo da Vinci used as the background of his famous portrait of La Gioconda [Mona Lisa].'[6]

They descended into a densely wooded region, and, as they walked on beneath a green canopy, everything seemed magnified—bigger, louder, and more vivid than in Europe. Not only was this new continent vast, but it had also been filled with a generous hand: 'everything is of gigantic size, mountains, rivers, and masses of vegetation. [. . .] It is as though the ground is so overloaded with plants that there isn't enough space for them all to grow.'[7] Vines climbed up into the treetops, which were more than 100 feet high and so thick they often completely blotted out the sky. The roaring of the streams rushing down from the mountains was overlaid with the screeching of parrots. Bonpland fretted that their stocks of paper wouldn't be able to cope with all the riches they encountered; his worry was so urgent that, Humboldt wrote, 'it almost spoiled my enjoyment.'[8] A messenger was sent back to Cumaná for an extra 800 sheets.

Their first stop was the mission station at San Fernando. The people of the Chaima tribe who lived there had been settled into huts, tidy and uniform, and arranged along a narrow grid of streets. It may have seemed an unlikely place to call to mind Gnadau (near Magdeburg), the settlement of the Herrnhut community he had visited as a student, and yet this is exactly what it did to Humboldt: 'the serious, taciturn character of the inhabitants, the exceptional cleanliness in their dwellings, all that is reminiscent of the towns of the Moravian brethren.' The missionary, when they met him, was a cheerful and corpulent Spanish Capuchin, who, Humboldt judged, treated his wards with gentleness and forbearance. However, he was unable to discern the purpose of Humboldt's and Bonpland's journey—'it seemed altogether reckless to him and, at the least, quite pointless.'[9] The focus of his attention was almost exclusively directed towards a cow. He kept trying to make Humboldt and Bonpland inspect the animal, and held forth about good beef being the most exquisite pleasure life had to offer. The next morning, they had to witness the gruesome spectacle of the cow's slaughter: she was brought down with a cut through the knuckles before having her throat slit.

The next village, Arenas, had somehow managed to mislay its mission station—but had retained its church, complete with murals depicting armadillos, caimans, and jaguars.[10] A local, Francisco Lozano, had achieved modest fame for having supposedly reared his son on his own breast milk. Lozano was not at home when Humboldt and Bonpland called, but they met people who knew him and were able to corroborate the story.[11] Would it prove, as it had been contended by some Europeans, that the indigenous Americans were somehow less manly?[12] Humboldt gave a robust defence: 'I can affirm that such a case does not occur more frequently on the [new] continent than the [old].' The phenomenon, he stated, had also been observed in Russian peasants, 'and the Russians have never been thought of as weakly or effete.'[13] And in any case, Lozano wasn't even a Chaima, but, from what Humboldt understood, was mostly of European descent.

The principal mission station in this region was Caripe. The monastery was built straight onto a steep rock wall, surrounded by wooded mountains, and the whole area was picturesque, 'indeed romantic.' It reminded him 'vividly of the valleys in the county of Derbyshire, as well as of the cavernous mountains near Muggendorf in Franconia.' In fact, it was just like Muggendorf, except not quite: in place of the German beeches and maples, here reigned the 'grander shapes' of tall *ceibas* and palm trees.[14]

In spite of his reservations about the missionaries' influence, Humboldt found that it was difficult to say anything bad about the Caripe mission, or in fact about most of the Capuchin missions they encountered. The monks welcomed them and permitted them to store their instruments in the cloister. The fact that Humboldt hailed from the obviously Protestant Prussia, about which he had been mildly anxious, failed to raise an eyebrow. And while there was a certain amount of coercion—the Indians were obliged to work in the monastery garden most mornings—there was fairness, too: once the produce was sold, a good proportion of the profits was apparently shared.

Caripe's real attraction was its famous cave, filled with night birds, the *guácharos*. Humboldt was not expecting much. His career as a mining inspector had taught him that, on the whole, one cave was much like another. Moreover, having seen the majestic caves at Ojców in Poland, and Castleton in Derbyshire, he thought that, as far as caves were concerned, nothing could astonish him.[15] But of course they would have a look at the cave at Caripe, not least because 'the moment the traveller alights at Cumaná, he is told ad nauseam about the eye stone at Araya, the child-nursing peasant at Arenas, and the Cave of the *Guácharo*, which is said to be several miles long.'[16] There was even some minor historical significance, Humboldt learned: the Capuchin monks had, on their first arrival, been so afraid that they might be attacked by local tribes that they had spent their first forty days hiding in the cave, before working up the courage to approach the locals. Their first encounter with them seemed to have passed without incident. The 'cave, from which a river takes its source, and in which thousands of night birds live, whose fat is used for cooking in the mission stations,'[17] was undeniably a place of wonder and mystical significance.

It was about two hours from the monastery, with the last part of the way particularly hard to negotiate. The narrow path followed the river that emerged from the cave. Often, their animals had to wade upstream through the riverbed, or mount the steep, slippery banks. Four hundred feet from the cave, the entrance was still not visible, and they came on it unawares. The sight opening before them was 'grand even for eyes familiar with the picturesque scenery of the Alps.'[18]

A cave might always be just a cave, but, again, the pull between the similar and the different held Humboldt in thrall. Trying to put his finger on what accounted for the difference this time, he identified the tropical vegetation as the main factor: 'inorganic nature indeed is the same in all climate zones, but the way in which it contrasts with animated nature, when the two abut each other, is as different and manifold as there are regions under the sun.'[19] The effect was not just a difference in appearance: it changed the atmosphere and the emotional impact of a landscape. The tropical vegetation lent the cave entrance a majestic aspect, something that was utterly lacking in the 'caves of the north, shaded as they are by oaks and gloomy larches.'[20] The gaping blackness of the entrance was surrounded by pothos plants and orchids; out of the forest canopy hung suspended the huge orange flowers of Angel's Trumpets; and red-and-yellow Heliconias crowded into the cave as far in as there was light. Here, too, it is Humboldt's frame of reference that catches the eye: he gives the height of the cave as 'lower in height by about a fifth than the colonnade of the Louvre.'[21] With post-Revolutionary Paris an important scientific hub, the proportions of the Louvre were not at all an unreasonable point of comparison. But, at the same time, he was tying his new experiences into a net of meaning that went beyond purely scientific discovery.

The entrance to the cave, garlanded with flowers and verdure, led to a stark underworld. Near the entrance, some plants were still holding on—pale and ghost-like on tall stalks, reminding him of the etiolated plants from his Freiberg days.[22] Almost at the same time as the daylight vanished, the cries of the birds became audible, getting louder as they went deeper into the cave: 'even somebody who has seen many thousands of crows roost in high fir trees, can hardly have a conception of the furious racket.'[23] Their name, *guácharos*, was onomatopoetic: it was an approximation of the hollow cries that reverberated off the walls of the cave. The effect, Humboldt thought, was uncanny.

The Chaima must have felt similarly: for them, Humboldt wrote, the cave was a very tangible sort of underworld, a local entrance to hell. The *guácharos* were regarded as birds of the netherworld—Humboldt called them 'Stygian birds,' in open analogy to the under-world of the ancient Greeks.[24] In the Chaima language, he noted, saying that somebody had 'gone to the *guácharos*' was a synonym for having died. Unsurprisingly, Humboldt and Bonpland found it hard to persuade their local Chaima guides to accompany them into the farther, darker reaches of the cave.

The 'fat harvest,' the local practice of oil extraction, took place once a year, on the feast day of St. John.[25] Young men from the Chaima tribe set out for the cave, where they climbed up to the nests of the *guácharos*, or simply brought them down with long sticks. The adult birds tried to defend their young, but most fell out and were immediately clubbed to death. In this way, Humboldt wrote, thou-sands of birds were killed each year. The chicks, fat and flightless, were processed in situ. Their abdomens were sliced open and their fat rendered over a fire to make an oil known as *manteca*. The annual harvest, Humboldt noted, came to 150 to 160 bottles. While he was careful not to pass judgement, he remarked that the yield bore no proportion to the carnage by which it was obtained. All in all, he thought that it was just as well that the further reaches of the cave remained untouched—otherwise, there would hardly be a breeding population left.[26]

The Chaima people did the slaughtering, but it was the 'fat-craving' monks who instigated the practice. Indeed, all the dishes in the mission station were cooked using *manteca*. The Chaima were obliged to provide a token amount of the oil for the church lamp, and the monks bought whatever they needed for their own consumption separately—with the prices fixed by the monks. This was clearly a murky business, and Humboldt was under no illusions about the nature of such transactions: 'it is well known,' he remarked, 'the manner in which monks "buy."'[27]

But they, too, did not leave without shedding some blood. Keen to get hold of some specimens, they fired their guns almost at random, aiming at the sound of screeching and flapping wings. Bonpland eventually managed to shoot two birds, which, disturbed and con-fused by the light of their torches, had fluttered after them. Their beaks featured a double 'tooth,' and they had no skin between their toes; they were sufficiently different from their nearest relatives, the *Caprimulgus*, Humboldt decided, to constitute a species of their own. He gave them the name *Steatornis caripensis* ('fat bird of Caripe').[28]

Since the reluctance of their guides made it impossible for them to advance any further into the cave, they turned back. On the whole, they were not sorry. Their eyes were hurting from the smoke of their torches, and the noise and dark had been oppressive: 'we were glad to be away from the hoarse screeching of the birds, and to have left a place behind us where darkness was entirely uncoupled from the soothing sensation of rest and quiet.'[29]

Back in the monastery, it was impossible not to entertain doubts about the effectiveness of the monks' mission. The Chaima didn't understand much Spanish, and the missionaries knew even less Chaima. Even the most basic concepts were prey to confusion. The Spanish for 'hell' is *infierno*, and for 'winter,' *invierno*. As winter for the Chaima was the wet season, the monks, Humboldt observed, had succeeded in teaching the Chaima to think of hell as a place where, mostly, it rains.[30]

On September 22, they left Caripe, to begin their path back up to the coast. It was time to be gone. The monks' manners and hospitability had been so delicate that Humboldt and Bonpland realised only very belatedly that they had been a strain on their hosts' resources. Wheat was an imported luxury—they eventually noticed, 'with a shudder,' that the monks had been denying themselves, and, on their last day, had gone without both bread and wine. 'They pleaded with us to stay on, but only quite feebly.'[31]

The journey back was laborious. They travelled north in the direction of the town of Cariaco, which was situated on the eastern shore of the inlet that had Cumaná on its western side. About half-way to Cariaco, the descent from the high plateau down into the valley near the village of Santa Cruz was so steep that the mules they were riding were forced to slide down the hillside on their hindquarters, 'any old way.'[32] This took seven hours. Down in the valley, they were back in the forest. It smelt of fog and wet weather, and, above them, they could see small low clouds, shred-like, clinging to the tops of the trees. They walked on in the half-light created by the canopy, the air thick with moisture, which, 'in spite of the heat, the air seemed unable to absorb.'[33]

A change in the weather announced itself with the sound of rolling thunder, joined by the mournful cries of the howler monkeys, the *araguatos*.[34] Humboldt liked this particular type of monkey; it looked a bit like a bear, he thought, and so he named it *Simia ursina*. Its blue-green face, however, was very human in aspect, and Humboldt risked a generalisation: the more closely monkeys resemble humans, the more mournful they tend to look.[35]

They arrived at Cariaco the next day, having passed a mountain whose peak reminded Humboldt of 'the needles and horns of the Swiss Alps.'[36] From there, they caught a pirogue to cross the Gulf of Cariaco and return to Cumaná. They spent the night on the little boat and slept badly, squeezed in amid a cargo of bananas, sugar cane, and coconuts. Their crates of instruments had been wedged in with difficulty. The next morning, on September 24, they were back at the mouth of the Río Manzanares; they were greeted by the bright skies of Cumaná and by vultures lazily roosting in the coconut trees, 'in rows, like chickens.'[37]

The stay in Cumaná during the autumn of 1799 was prolonged by unexpected financial troubles. Nobody, it turned out, was willing to pay out money against Humboldt's draft, made out for Havana. There were weeks of uncertainty that did not, he confessed, 'belong among the sweetest ones of my life.' He thought he would have to leave for Cuba, without having had a chance to see the Orinoco. 'My whole enterprise, my entire journey all of a sudden seemed very reckless and doubtful.'[38] Relief came when the governor, Don Vicente Emparán, privately lent him money to tide him over.

Then there was the incident with what Humboldt called the 'Zambo.' On the night of October 27, Humboldt and Bonpland were walking along Cumaná's waterfront. Hearing steps behind them, Humboldt turned and saw a man, 'the colour of the Zambos' (a person of mixed African and American-Indian heritage), wielding a club.[39] Humboldt jumped aside, with the result that Bonpland received the full force of the blow. The attacker, bending down over his felled victim, picked up Bonpland's hat and walked off with it. Bonpland had only been stunned by the blow—he was able to get up and join Humboldt in giving chase—but the sight of his travelling companion stretched out on the ground as if dead had shaken Humboldt.

The 'Zambo,' when he was eventually apprehended, told a good story. Or the sort of story that appealed to Humboldt's sensibility. Part of the crew of a privateer from Santo Domingo, he had been treated badly, fallen out with the captain, and been deliberately left behind when the ship sailed from Cumaná. Embittered with all things French, he had, on hearing Humboldt and Bonpland converse in that language, been 'unable to resist the urge to deal them a good blow.'[40] Since the course of justice was slow, and a defendant might have to wait seven or eight years until his case came to trial, Humboldt was, on the whole, glad when he heard that their attacker, only a few days after their eventual departure from Cumaná, had escaped from prison.

In spite of the incident, the next day found Humboldt out on the terrace at five o'clock in the morning, recording a total eclipse of the sun. There were conspicuous changes in the atmosphere, Humboldt noted—a reddish mist, followed by black cloud and thunder. Humboldt measured the electricity in the air, but found it no different to European thunderstorms. Later, two strong tremors shook the ground; Bonpland, who was leaning over a table examining their yield of plants, was almost thrown over; Humboldt, who often seemed to find himself in a more favourable position, felt it too, 'strongly, even though I was lying in a hammock.'[41]

18

Taking Rousseau to America

❦

By now, they had their next few months mapped out more clearly. They would wait out the rainy season in Caracas before heading south, crossing the great plains (the Llanos) to reach the Orinoco. They would travel up the Orinoco and search for the Casiquiare canal—the fabled waterway that was thought to link the great water-systems of the Orinoco and the Amazon—whose existence was to some extent still doubted in Europe. They would then return to Cumaná via the town of Angostura (today's Ciudad Bolívar), on the Orinoco.

As luck would have it, just before they left, they met a young missionary, a Franciscan named Juan Gonzales, who had only recently returned from the Orinoco. In the election of a new head of his original mission station, he had supported what turned out to be the wrong candidate, and, in the subsequent purge, had been sent to the least popular location: La Esmeralda, on the upper Orinoco, as remote as could be, and notoriously plagued with insects. He had repeatedly suffered from malaria, and so he was well placed to pass on his experience of living in a difficult climate.

Humboldt and Bonpland left Cumaná on the evening of November 18, 1799. The open-topped trading boat they were travelling on floated out to sea past the fortress of San Antonio—the first thing they'd seen when they had arrived in Cumaná four months earlier—and into the Gulf of Cariaco, on the way to Caracas.

Humboldt felt, he said, as though he had lived in Cumaná for many years. He had certainly grown fond of the place; Cumaná for him represented 'the first country that we had entered in that part of the world for which I had yearned from my earliest youth.'[1] And as if to prove that this longed-for land of his desires agreed with a deep, irrefutable part of his nature, he returned to what had become a personal article of faith for him: that he never got seasick: 'my travelling companions suffered badly; I however slept soundly, as I—by some rare good fortune—never get seasick.'[2]

On their approach to La Guaira, the port of Caracas, the coastal mountain chain was so steep that it seemed, Humboldt thought, 'as though the Pyrenees, or the Alps, were rising straight out of the water'; the pass that led through them resembled, Humboldt thought, the St. Gotthard pass in Switzerland.[3] One of the mountains that had been visible from the sea was the Silla. Shaped like a saddle (*silla* in Spanish), it was made up of two peaks of different heights. It was an obvious, tempting target—a good project to start the new century with. On January 1, 1800, Humboldt and Bonpland stationed themselves on a coffee plantation at the foot of the Silla. They planned to set off at five o'clock in the morning, but nevertheless hoped to observe the three eclipses of a satellite of Jupiter the night before. They stayed up late—and then missed them all, having got their calculations slightly wrong.

The ascent itself was a study in pain, endurance, and absurdity. Accompanied by guides and some curious citizens of Caracas—a group of eighteen in all—they left according to plan at five o'clock, and reached the lower of the two peaks within two hours. With the morning bright and pleasantly cool, their guides—none of whom had made the ascent before—confidently predicted that another six hours would see them to the top of the higher one. The second ascent proved much steeper, however—they had to tilt their bodies forward to make any progress at all. The dense grass had an odd, slippery quality. Several among their party fell behind. As Humboldt and Bonpland waited for them to catch up, they were dismayed to spot them in the distance, moving down instead of up. A young Capuchin monk, who had been conspicuous for his pronouncements on the physical superiority of Spaniards over Hispano-Americans, was the first to give up. Impeded by his long, heavy robes, he chose to follow the progress of the remaining party through a telescope, from the comfort of a nearby plantation. Unfortunately, however, Humboldt and Bonpland had put him in charge of organising the provisions, and so the climbing party ended up without food or water for more than ten hours. (In his account of the episode, Humboldt went to the trouble of sketching out the Capuchin's subsequent fate: only a few years after their encounter, he was murdered on the banks of the Apure River.[4]) Humboldt and Bonpland, for their part, returned after fifteen hours of almost continuous walking, the soles of their feet bloodied, but with a crowd ready and waiting to hear about their exploits. The Silla, they were able to confirm, was lower in height than the highest point of the Pyrenees—a scientific fact that did not find an appreciative audience.

About a month later, on February 7, they were ready to leave Caracas. In twelve years' time, the city as they had known it would no longer exist: the great earthquake of March 26, 1812, killed several thousand inhabitants. The catastrophe happened on Maundy Thursday, just before the procession was due to take place. The churches were full, and a great number of people died in the collapsing buildings.

Earthquakes captured the European imagination. While the novella 'The Earthquake in Chile' ('Das Erdbeben in Chili') by the German writer Heinrich von Kleist was almost certainly inspired by Kant's description of the Lisbon earthquake of 1755, Kleist chose to situate it in South America. (The novella was probably written in 1806, and published the following year.)

The successful uprising of enslaved Africans in the French colony of Saint-Domingue (Haiti) was also taken up by Kleist, in his novella 'The Betrothal in Santo Domingo' ('Die Verlobung in St. Domingo'). Published in 1811, it is set in 1800, at the same time that Humboldt had Saint-Domingue on his mind. Kleist, who felt the constraints of the Prussian way of life strongly, repeatedly looked towards the Americas. It is as though, for the European Romantic mind, South America provided an imaginary place where emotions were more striking and more vivid. Not only did nature seem magnified, in the way that had struck Humboldt when he first travelled through the forests of the new continent, but human fates did too.

Their first way station towards the Llanos, the great plains, was Lake Valencia, west of Caracas. This large lake was bordered by shrubs, the fruits of which released scores of tiny red hairs that floated above the lake in clouds and greatly curtailed the enjoyment of bathing in it. They were called *picapica* and were exactly that: on contact with human skin, they caused severe itching. They were popular, the explorers were to find out later, during Carnival, when it was considered amusing to carry bags of them around and blow them into the faces of passers-by.

Humboldt measured the water level in the lake and established that it had been falling: in recent years, three new islands had emerged. These islands were locally believed to be of miraculous origin. Humboldt assumed a less mysterious and less benevolent cause: that of human activity. The clearing of woodland and the cultivation of indigo had robbed the soil of its ability to retain water, and reduced the amount of water the lake received from its tributary rivers.

After he had taken note of all the local specifics and analysed the condition of the lake scientifically, he looked again and what he saw was—Lake Geneva. The two lakes were at a comparable height above sea level and had a similar shape (even though Lake Valencia was somewhat smaller than Lake Geneva). Lake Valencia's northern shore resembled the corresponding Swiss shore of Lake Geneva, being attractively cultivated and fertile. Its southern shore, by contrast, had a forbidding and desolate aspect—in this it was to Humboldt much like the mountainous French side of Lake Geneva. The rock faces of Lake Valencia reminded him of 'the ravishing descriptions, to which Lake Geneva and the cliffs of Meillerie have inspired a great writer.' The writer, of course, was Rousseau, and the cliffs were those below which one of the most famous scenes of *Julie, or the New Heloise* plays out: the boating trip in which Saint-Preux and Julie almost come to grief.[5]

At the same time, Humboldt had an acute sense of the limits of comparison. In each part of the world, he stressed, nature had its own, distinctive character, and the very thing that was singular about it eluded the power of comparison.[6] This distinctive, essential but elusive quality did not answer to the methods of science, but to something more immediate and fundamental: his own senses. 'What speaks to the soul, and evokes such deep and manifold sensations, is beyond our measurements, as well as what we can express in words.'[7] Humboldt was trying to put his finger on something that transcended the boundaries of what he knew, and perhaps also what could be known through scientific methods.

On March 9, they entered the Llanos, which separated the coastal area from the forests inland. It looked like a sea of grass, vast and unvaried; Humboldt found the impression oppressive, as though nature had been numbed and deadened.[8] During the rainy season, they were told, the area was lush and green; in early March, it wasn't. It looked like a desert: 'the grass crumbles to dust, the earth cracks open, and crocodiles and the big snakes lie buried in the dried-up mud.'[9] Under a baking sky, with the air tasting of dust and a horizon that seemed to be constantly receding as they moved towards it, their progress was slow and arduous. They tacked the leathery leaves of the *rhopala* tree to their heads for protection, which helped somewhat.

After five days, they reached the town of Calabozo, about half-way through the Llanos. Here, they were intrigued to hear about the presence of electric eels. Humboldt, with his interest in electricity, animal or otherwise, had been curious about these 'living electrical machines' ever since his arrival in the Americas.[10] He'd been promised specimens on many occasions, but this had never come to anything. The one fish he had obtained in Cumaná had been particularly disappointing. It had not been an eel at all, but a ray, which had swum about in a lively enough fashion, but emitted only the weakest electrical currents.

In Calabozo, not only were there real electric eels, but a new way of catching them had been pioneered, too. The new method was not efficient, and cruel. The idea was to let the fish discharge as much of their electric power as possible before you touched them. The locals drove wild horses from the Llanos into the muddy pool in which the eels were lurking. The panicking horses tried to flee, but were prevented by men screaming and waving sticks; the eels defended themselves by discharging their electricity while pressing themselves against the horses' bellies, thus stunning their vital organs. Within the first five minutes, two horses had drowned. Humboldt was convinced that, if this had continued, all the horses would have perished; he does not say whether he would have stepped in to prevent this happening. In the event, the electric power of the eels weakened markedly, and Humboldt got several specimens to experiment on.

The electric shocks Humboldt experienced from the weakened animals on his study bench seemed to him not unlike those those he had suffered in his experiments as a student, when he had administered electrical charges to muscles on his shoulders. But now the pain was fiercer, and was most definitely unsought: 'I don't recall ever having suffered, even from the discharge of a big Leyden jar, such a terrible shock as when I inadvertently placed both feet on a *gymnotus* that had just been pulled from the water.'[11] The experience left him feeling sick for the rest of the day, and he had vivid pain in his joints, particularly his knees.

Generally, the electric eels were not popular locally. Roads frequently had to be re-routed when they attacked—and on occasion killed—mules that forded a river. They weren't even good to eat: some of the flesh was tolerable, but most of their large bodies consisted of the electric organ, which was slimy and unpalatable.

On March 24, 1800, the explorers left Calabozo, and three days later arrived at San Fernando de Apure, located on the banks of the river Apure, a tributary of the Orinoco.

19

Very Far from Prussia

❧

San Fernando was the main mission station on the Apure. Located not too far from the Apure's junction with the Orinoco, it was a hub for trade along both rivers. Humboldt learned that San Fernando had been founded as recently as 1789—while Caracas, on the coast, dated from the sixteenth century. But here, less than 300 kilometres to the south as the crow flies, the monks had managed to gain a foothold only so recently. In fact, even this foothold was less impressive than official reports suggested: keen to show their successes overseas, both the church and the Spanish government had somewhat over-represented their presence along the Orinoco and nearby rivers. Humboldt and Bonpland passed villages that had never developed beyond the point of having their names printed in the maps that were published in Rome and Madrid.

They had entered an entirely new domain—a green and watery network of tributaries to the Orinoco. As they were measuring the width of the Apure on March 28 (they measured 206 *toises*, equalling 400 metres), they noticed clouds drawing up, which announced the first thunderstorm of the season. Humboldt proceeded to measure the electrical charge of the thunderstorm, holding an electrometer six feet above the ground for twenty minutes. The electrometer featured small balls (or 'globules') fashioned from lilac wood marrow and suspended by silken threads next to two metal plates.[1] As the thunder gathered strength around Humboldt ('I saw the lilac mark globules fly apart mostly just a few seconds before the flash of lightning'),[2] and the sky turned first indigo, then grey, he observed freshwater dolphins and crocodiles coming up to the surface of the water.

On March 30, they were in a small boat following the Apure down to the Orinoco. This first part of the river journey began in almost leisurely style: they had a steersman, as well as four people to row. On board, they fashioned a structure much like a small hut covered with palm leaves, spacious enough to accommodate a little table and chairs. Their provisions included generous quantities of bananas, manioc flour, and cocoa, as well as some live chickens. They anticipated being able to hunt—at least before it would become too humid for them to deploy their firearms. There were good game birds along the Apure, the *pauxi* and the *guacharaca*—the turkey and the pheasant of the country, according to Humboldt.[3] He was quietly thrilled with their new mode of travel, though for the moment he was content to watch and to record his impressions:

> The Indians (quite naked, with only pubic area and bottom artfully in a pouch) were cheerful in the way that boat people are. As there was a constant headwind, they rowed with colossal strength, all the while joshing and jesting prodigiously, ducking underneath the oars while slapping their bottoms.[4]

As they drifted along the river, small freshwater dolphins passed their boat in long rows, as did groups of birds sitting on pieces of driftwood, catching fish as they went along. The view to the shores was picturesque, 'like an English garden,' bordered by 'a hedge that was of an even height everywhere, as though it had been cut (though it's hard to conceive why that should be so).'[5] Openings had been broken into this hedge, and occasionally animals from the forest would emerge through them and, unperturbed by the boat gliding by, come down to the river to drink.

Humboldt's enjoyment of all this went beyond that of a naturalist. He had come very close to what he was looking for: a world nearly untouched by Western civilisation. Here was nature, direct and up close. More than that, it was beautiful. And it was as though it was presenting itself especially for his benefit: jaguars, tapirs, and peccaries, as well as herons and rheas, all 'promenaded' along the riverbank, taking their young to the water. 'It is like being in paradise,' averred the steersman. Humboldt was inclined to agree—though he was aware that, on closer inspection, matters were more complicated. For one thing, Humboldt noted, the steersman had been brought up by a clergyman. Further, a closer look at animal behaviour revealed that paradise relied on precise checks and balances: 'the creatures fear and avoid each other. The golden age is gone.'[6]

Among the less obvious denizens of paradise were the crocodiles, which were present in generous numbers. Every few minutes, the travellers now encountered groups of about five or six of them. When a few dead ones washed up on the shore, Humboldt examined them with Bonpland: they were definitely not caimans, but true crocodiles, with articulated feet, similar to the crocodiles on the Nile, even though this particular species had not been described before. He was fascinated to observe such strange animals up close: when they moved, one could hear a faint dry rustling, produced by the plates on their skin rubbing against each other; their locomotion was straight, like an arrow, from one point to another; but their turning circle was surprisingly narrow. In the water they were less nimble and could not turn fast. This became clear when the party's mastiff, Turco, jumped into the river to chase a capybara and put himself in the way of a crocodile. With much shouting, he was persuaded to swim towards the shore; the change of direction slowed down the crocodile, and Turco made a narrow escape.

The capybara, or *chiguire*, was the crocodiles' main prey. This large rodent, Humboldt noted, was 'about half-way between a pig, a bear, and a hare' (it was bristly like a pig, walked like a bear, and its face, with its cleft lip, was reminiscent of a hare's).[7] These 'unhappy animals,' Humboldt wrote, 'possess no means of defending themselves; while they do swim faster than they walk, in the water they are eaten by crocodiles, and on land by tigers [by which Humboldt meant jaguars].' When swimming, they lifted their heads, much like dogs. Running seemed an even less successful venture: 'as their hind parts are higher than the front, they move in a short gallop, but make so little progress that we were able to catch two'; and while running, they emitted a low sigh, as if they found it hard to breathe.[8] Goethe, and his idea of gradual development, was not far from Humboldt's mind: he found 'no tail as such but (very remarkable that, Göthe!), a rudimentary tail—if one bends back the bristles, there is a half-inch-long cone of wrinkled flesh, but quite hairless.'[9] Apart from being easy to catch, capybaras also had the advantage—from the missionaries' point of view—of being, arguably, aquatic animals, which made them suitable for consumption during Lent. (The church allowed eating fish and shellfish during this period of fasting.) Humboldt thought that the ham produced from this source had a 'very unpleasant, musky odour.'[10]

Late one day, they passed a small banana plantation and were invited by its owner to stay the night. Don Ignacio, who prided himself on some remote Spanish ancestry, kept telling Humboldt and Bonpland how lucky they were to have found him: they would be able to spend the night among people of suitable standing. Humboldt and Bonpland had brought a capybara along as an offering to their host; Don Ignacio would not tolerate what he called 'Indian game' in his house, however, and served them deer—*Cervus mexicanus*—instead. It was delicious, Humboldt had to admit. He was interested in his dinner's chemical properties, too: he thought 'the muscle fibre less charred, more oxygenated' than that of deer he had eaten in Europe. Throughout the evening, their host lectured them on the 'superiority' of *nosotros caballeros blancos* ('us white gentlemen'), boasting about his campaigns against the tribes of the Meta River, as well as his grand lineage and the refined manners of his wife and daughter, Doña Isabella and Doña Manuela. All of this must have grated on Humboldt, who in his diary contrasted his host's exalted boasts with the fact that the whole family was walking about 'naked-arsed.'[11] Perhaps Humboldt would have felt more generous towards this deluded small-time farmer had the rest of the evening gone better. In spite of Don Ignacio's eager hospitality, he had failed to erect even a simple roof of palm leaves. During the night, a sudden downpour soaked the party to the skin, and a desperate cry issued from Bonpland's hammock. Happily, it was not a jaguar, but Doña Isabella's cat, which had dropped out of the tree above and landed on him.

Further down the Apure, they stopped at a small mission station, grandly recorded in the mission records as 'the village Santa Bárbara de Arichuna,' but in reality consisting of, Humboldt reckoned, sixteen to eighteen tiny huts constructed flimsily out of palm fronds.[12] Humboldt paints a striking picture of their night there. 'Crocodiles were lying on the shore,' he writes: 'they had arranged themselves so that they could see the fire.'[13] He might be describing an evening in his drawing room, with his dog stretched out before the fireplace. As far from Prussia as he could possibly be, Humboldt presents himself as part of a picturesque, and curiously homely, tableau.

A few days later, he got as close to untamed nature as he could have hoped. This time, it was actual physical danger. The jaguar was lying under a *ceiba* tree, half-hidden by leaves. Humboldt might have walked straight into the animal had he not bent down to pick up small samples of glimmering mica schist and noticed fresh jaguar tracks. Raising his head, he found himself looking straight at the large cat—'never had a tiger appeared to me so enormous,' He made a swift retreat. Though shaken and slightly panicked—'there are instances in life where it's futile to call on reason for help'—he managed to recall the instructions he had been given by their guides.[14] He walked on slowly, avoiding moving his arms as far as possible, and describing a wide arc away from the jaguar. Resisting the temptation to look around to check whether he was being followed, he allowed himself to walk faster the further away he got. He arrived back at the camp, out of breath and flustered, to find the guides unimpressed by his adventures. They took their shotguns and walked for a bit in the direction of the *ceiba* tree, but when it was clear that the jaguar wasn't waiting for them there, gave up the effort.

April 4 was their last day on the Apure. The river had become steadily less welcoming. It was so silted up and shallow in places that they ran aground several times. The mosquitoes had become harder to ignore—here, at the mouth of the river, there was a particularly aggressive sort, called *zancudos*, which settled on the travellers' hands and faces. At night, they approached the hammocks from below, with their long proboscis easily penetrating even the thickest clothing. Worse, just as Humboldt and Bonpland were about to set up their hammocks, jaguars were spotted behind the trees nearby, so they spent the night on a small island close to where the Apure joined the Orinoco. But the next day 'we saw, with some emotion, for the first time what we had dreamed of for so long: the waters of the Orinoco.'[15]

A huge expanse of water was spread out before them, almost as far as the eye could see. All seemed quieter: 'it was in vain that we looked for water birds [. . .]. We hardly saw a crocodile.'[16] The Orinoco had a peculiar atmosphere all of its own, which was hard to describe. As Humboldt explained, 'an experienced sailor can guess by the shape of the waves, by the colour of the water, the appearance of the sky or the clouds, whether he is on the Atlantic, the Mediterranean or the tropical part of the Great Ocean.'[17]

Now their direction was upstream, towards the place where, Humboldt believed, the upper Orinoco would come very close to the Amazon—or rather one of its major tributaries, the Rio Negro. They were lucky: there was a strong wind from east-northeast, which propelled them against the current.

They hadn't gone more than a few miles when they encountered something that interested Humboldt deeply: the mysterious rock of Encaramada. On one of the large islands in the Orinoco stood a very tall, steep rock, painted with representations of animals and other hieroglyph-like signs. The paintings were so high up, however, that they seemed impossible to reach without scaffolding. When asked, the local people explained, as though this was an obvious matter, that this was a remnant of 'the time of the great waters,' when their ancestors had been able to circle the top of the rock in their canoes. For Humboldt, this was another instance of the tension between the familiar and the unknown—one that he now formulated in terms of the universal and the individual. In the same way that he noted the parallels between the underworld of the ancient Greeks and that of the Chaima people, now here was the myth of the flood transposed into a new setting. There was a general principle, one that united human culture and the natural world:

> Just as certain plant families hold on to the imprint of their particular type, in different climes and in the most disparate altitudes, in the same way do the cosmological myths of people everywhere have the same characteristics—a similarity that is astonishing. So many different languages, seemingly isolated from one another, pass on the same stories to us. In their basic ideas [. . .] the legends hardly differ from one another, but each people gives them a local tint.[18]

The fame of the Isla de la Tortuga, an island on the Orinoco a little further upstream, was of an altogether different nature—it was founded on the innumerable river turtles whose nesting ground it was. Humboldt and Bonpland happened to arrive just in time for the great annual turtle-egg harvest, at the beginning of April. Having travelled in a state of near-isolation after leaving San Fernando de Apure, they suddenly found themselves in the middle of a large encampment. The shores were populated by different tribes, resting and waiting. Interspersed were traders from the cities, most of them from Angostura, the great trading post much further down, towards the mouth of the Orinoco. The atmosphere was that of a great trading fair—or that is how it struck Humboldt: 'this part of the Orinoco is visited in much the same way that one attends the fairs at Frankfurt or Beaucaire [France].'[19]

There was another analogy: Humboldt was reminded of mining. By tapping a thin stick into the earth it was possible, through the sudden lack of resistance when it reached the layer of turtle eggs, to determine exactly how far that layer reached. Informed by investigations carried out in this way, the missionary in charge (*comisionado del Padre*) demarcated lots and allocated them to the tribes present. The whole thing was as well organised as any industrial process, but it was not an edifying scene. The eggs, dug up by hand, were boiled down in huge wooden vats to produce a clear odourless oil; in this pure state, this oil kept well and was widely used for cooking, much like the oil extracted from the *guácharos*, the oil birds. However, the purity of the oil was mostly a fiction: 'It is difficult to obtain pure turtle oil. In most cases, it has a putrid smell, the result of eggs that had been exposed to the sun for too long and in which young turtles had begun to form.' The oil they took with them for their own use was like this: 'it had fibrous dregs at the bottom, the sign of an impure turtle oil.'[20]

However, this rationalisation of the turtle-egg harvest did not represent a linear sort of progress, Humboldt felt impelled to note. Before the arrival of the missionaries, the traditional egg harvest by the tribes had by no means been perfect: the ground had been dug up any old way, huge numbers of eggs were broken, and more were harvested than could be transported, resulting in wastage: 'it was as though an iron mine had been exploited by inexpert hands.'[21] The Jesuits had introduced some measure of regulation: they had made sure that at least part of the island remained untouched, to allow the turtles to reproduce. Now, under the Franciscans, all was dug up carelessly again, but with frightening efficiency: 'it was thought to be noticeable that the yield became poorer year on year.'[22]

As they left the island, things went badly wrong: the steersman, taking the chance to display his skill to a larger-than-usual audience, attempted to push into the middle of the stream via an elegant manoeuvre that involved sailing close to the wind. This would have gone well had it not been for a sudden gust, which threw the small boat on its side. All was under water, with diaries, books, and plant specimens floating around them. Humboldt believed they might be about to die: 'My thoughts turned to Wilhelm, the Haeftens [. . .]. I felt moved more than frightened.'[23] Bonpland saved the day.

Calculating that the shore might be reached by swimming, he caught hold of Humboldt and reassured him that they would be safe: 'ne craignez pas mon ami, nous nous sauvons.' Humboldt later noted down Bonpland's exact words, but did not mention quite how pertinent they were: Humboldt had never learned to swim. Just in time, the rope holding the sail tore, the boat righted itself, and, by what seemed a miracle, nothing was lost—expect for one book, Johann Schreber's *Genera Plantarum.* The steersman, in answer to reproaches, voiced his confidence ('rather coolly,' Humboldt thought) that 'the white gentlemen won't lack for sun to dry their papers.'[24]

The stretch of the Orinoco they now entered—between two of its tributaries, the Arauca, which they had just passed, and the Atabapo, before them—had its own local name: the Baraguán. They entered it with the uncomfortable knowledge that, while they had several months of dangerous, often uncharted, waters before them, they had almost come to grief after a mere three days on the Orinoco. The Baraguán was full of life: myriad insects swarmed around them, and on the shores were geckos and iguanas, and a large amount of different types of birds. Yet, in the midday heat, when everything was swathed in a reddish haze, there was an eerie silence. Only when he stopped and listened very carefully did Humboldt become aware of a low, steady humming sound, as if every bit of matter in the forest around him were animated: 'all of nature is breathing, life pervades the dusty, cracked ground in a thousand forms, in the lap of the waters as well as in the air around us.'[25] The Baraguán, however, was also an area devoid of springs—something they noticed when the quality of their drinking water declined sharply. Drawn from the river, it had a strange, offputtingly sweet and altogether repugnant taste. 'It's the rind of the caimans,' one of their guides explained, referring to the leathery skin of dead caimans rotting in the river. 'The older the caiman, the more bitter the rind.'[26] It was the persistent musky smell that was the worst of it, Humboldt felt: 'If in this hot climate, and constantly plagued by thirst, one has to drink river water of 27 to 28 degrees [Celsius], one wishes, naturally, that such a warm water, tainted with sand, should at least be odourless.'[27]

On April 9, they anchored at Pararuma, another turtle-egg harvesting site. They found a conglomeration of local egg hunters, traders, and missionaries; many in this last group were suffering from malaria. The way they looked, Humboldt thought, didn't inspire confidence about the wholesomeness of the area for which he and Bonpland were heading. It was at this stage that their steersman, who had so recently almost drowned them, informed them that he would not go on beyond Pararuma; he was unfamiliar with the area beyond, he said, but perhaps he had simply had enough of this particular adventure. Astonishingly, the problem resolved itself almost immediately: one of the sick priests was Father Zea, who was in charge of the mission station near the great rapids further upriver. He was keen to return there, and even talked about accompanying them further, to the Rio Negro, as the climate there was supposed to be healthy: 'he spoke of those regions with the enthusiasm that, in the colonies, is afforded to everything that is far away.'[28]

Here, in Pararuma, looking at the gathering of tribes, Humboldt allowed himself to admit—with a frankness that contradicted his belief in cultural and ethnic equality—that some of the tribes on the Orinoco did not conform to his hopes and expectations of people untouched by Western civilisation. The people he met were not the 'noble savages' promised him by his reading at home. Bernardin de Saint-Pierre's *Paul and Virginia*, especially, makes the point that neither Paul nor Virginia are 'educated,' with all their knowledge deriving instead from their mothers and from living in the midst of nature. This, Bernardin de Saint-Pierre holds, is principally what accounts for their charm and uncorrupted simplicity. In Humboldt's view, not all of the people he encountered on the Orinoco were like that. In some cases, he felt, there was an uncomfortable mismatch between expectation and observation: 'One baulks at the idea that this state of societal infanthood [. . .] should represent the original form of our species! Human nature here does not confront us clad in gracious simplicity, as portrayed so strikingly in the literature of all languages.'[29]

Humboldt arrived at a conclusion that could be reconciled both with his scientific training, building on observable phenomena, and with his Romantic grounding and its search for direct, unmediated experience. The problem, he decided, arose when native people became estranged from their origins, mostly through the efforts of the missionaries. The thing to do was to seek out members of native tribes who had only recently been subjugated, and then establish contact without interference by third parties: 'there can be no doubt that direct contact with the natives must be more instructive and more reliable than when an interpreter is used.'[30] Together with Bonpland, Humboldt took the idea of direct contact further, right up to the demarcation line he liked to take things to: that of his own skin. Talking to some locals, and getting on to the subject of their facial paintings, the two of them asked to have some drawn on their own faces. It turned out, however, that these were harder to remove than they had at first assumed, and weeks later, when they arrived in the downriver town of Angostura, they did so with remnants of black colour across their faces.[31]

20

Across the Watershed

The group left Pararuma in considerably less comfort than they had been in when they arrived. They needed to change into a different boat, as light and as small as possible, so that it could be carried overland where necessary. Their new craft was a dugout canoe, or pirogue—a hollowed-out tree trunk, so only two people were able to sit next to each other. The pirogue was easily unbalanced—each time Humboldt or Bonpland wanted to get up from where they were sitting, they had to ask an oarsman to balance out the movement. Should they want to open any of their cases of luggage, the whole crew had to get off. To maximise the area on board, a lattice enclosure had been tacked on to the stern. Its leaf-covered roof was low, so Humboldt and Bonpland couldn't even sit up straight beneath it. 'One had to sit in a hunched-over position, or else stretch oneself out on the floor, but then it was impossible to see anything.'[1] When they were in the latter position, their legs stuck out, so when it rained, half of their bodies got soaked through: 'it is difficult to picture quite how wretched it is to travel on such a vehicle.'[2]

Their space was further constricted by their scientific apparatus: their sextant, compass, and meteorological instruments were all stowed under the lattice roof too, as was their luggage and bundles of dried plant samples. Undaunted, they weighed the craft down even further with the purchase of some animals: on board were two rock chickens and several cages with birds, some of which were fastened to the lattice enclosure, and others to the bow of the pirogue.

There was also a squirrel monkey, a 'titi of the Orinoco,' on board.[3] Whether it served any scientific purpose is unclear. Humboldt fondly described his features, noting how 'no other monkey's face resembles that of a child as the titi's does; it's the same expression of innocence, the same roguish smile, the same rapid transition from joy to sorrow. His big eyes fill with tears when something frightens him.'[4] Humboldt and Bonpland spent some time reading to the titi and showing him the plates in Georges Cuvier's *Elementary Survey of the Natural History of Animals*, with the ostensible notion of investigating his intelligence. Even though the illustrations were only black and white, 'the titi swiftly reached out his little hand, hoping to catch a grasshopper or a wasp, whenever we showed him the eleventh plate, which featured those insects.'[5]

This stretch of the Orinoco was heavily plagued by mosquitoes, and, for some temporary relief, Humboldt and Bonpland resorted to sticking their heads under a blanket for minutes at a time: 'on this part of the journey, Bonpland and I were not able to take in all the observations that our surroundings, no doubt rich in scientific treasure, offered up.'[6] The mosquito problem became worse as they travelled up the river—at certain points, they couldn't speak without ending up with a mouth full of insects. In fact, the mosquitoes made it difficult to think about much else. Humboldt distinguished different types. Apart from the common mosquitoes, there were *zancudos*, *jejen*, and *tempraneros*, all, it seemed, equally intent on stabbing through their clothes and crawling inside their mouths and noses. Of these, the *zancudos* possessed 'the longest feet,' as well as the most painful sting. The local people, meanwhile, were said to be able to tell the different types of mosquitoes apart 'by their song.' Mosquitoes were so much part of the fabric of life that they provided a subject for formal small talk: people would greet each other in the mornings by politely inquiring, 'How did you find the *zancudos* last night?' or 'How are things with the mosquitoes today?' Missionaries who fell into disfavour, as had happened to their acquaintance Juan Gonzales, were often sent to the outpost at La Esmeralda on the upper Orinoco, a procedure commonly known as 'being sentenced to the mosquitoes.'[7] And, clearly now devoting an obsessive amount of time to their tormentors, Humboldt dreamed up the idea of an 'insect clock': since different types of insects were active at different times of the day, he thought that he might be able to tell the time just by the degree and character of the pain they inflicted.

Above the great rapids of the Orinoco, the country was largely unexplored by Westerners. For them, it was a land of myths and fanciful beings: there were said to be people with only one eye in the middle of their foreheads, and others with mouths situated near their stomachs. It wasn't easy to argue against such beliefs, Humboldt found: whenever he attempted it, the clincher in every discussion was, 'the Padres have seen it—but it was far beyond the Great Cataracts.' This was, in its way, understandable, he thought, missionaries being by 'virtue of their profession not inclined to scepticism.'[8]

The 'Great Cataracts' (which include the rapids of Atures and, further up, of Maipures) were the result of the Orinoco breaking through a granite mountain range—the mountains of Parima. These rapids were an extraordinary sight: on all his further travels, Humboldt declared, nothing, not even the Andes, could dim for him the memory of what he felt when he saw the rapids at Atures for the first time. It looked as though the whole wide river was suspended above its bed.

The author of *Paul and Virginia* was still a guiding light: 'for moments at a time, I felt I had been transported into the hermitage of the old man, described by Bernardin de Saint-Pierre as one of the most beautiful parts of the island [of Mauritius].' For Humboldt, Bernardin de Saint-Pierre had achieved a degree of truth in his portrayal of Mauritius (where he had lived for some time) that would not have been accessible to the mere cataloguer of scientific facts: 'he was able to represent nature, not because he knew her as a scientist, but because he had a deep sense of the harmonious relationship of her form, colour and inner forces.'[9] Humboldt elaborated on this point later, when he wrote about his emotional response to the rapids at Atures and Maipures in his book *Views of Nature* (*Ansichten der Natur*, 1808):

> [I]n the innermost receptive mind, the physical world is reflected, living and true. That which designates the character of a landscape—the profile of the mountains that border the horizon in the hazy distance, the darkness of the fir forests, the roaring forest river that plummets between overhanging cliffs—all of it stands in an ancient and mysterious association with the disposition of human temperament.[10]

Again, there is the same paradox, so striking already in Humboldt's physiological experiments on himself: the thing that might be thought of as the most subjective of measures—his own emotional response—was, in his view, the thing capable of the most objective judgement.

On April 16, they were told that their pirogue had arrived at the top of the Atures rapids, having been carried there by local porters in less than six hours. But while this obstacle had been cleared, it was with some difficulty that Father Zea managed to get hold of some provisions: a few bunches of bananas, some manioc, and a couple of chickens.

They reached the rapids further upstream, at Maipures, just a day later. These presented themselves as an archipelago of rocky islands, effectively clogging the riverbed over a distance of five kilometres, like a series of dams. While porters hauled the pirogue across, Humboldt climbed a small nearby hill to get a view of the natural spectacle:

> Thick fog drifts eternally over the water's surface. Through the steaming cloud from the foam the tops of the tall palm trees emerge. When a ray of the glowing evening sun penetrates the vapours, an optical magic begins. Colourful rainbows appear and disappear from view. The ethereal image fluctuates in the play of the airs.[11]

These sublime scenes of nature, he explained elsewhere, corre-
spond to the highest we experience in the fields of art and literature.[12]

On April 21, they caught up with their pirogue again, which was
waiting for them above the rapids. It was slightly the worse for
wear—bashed about, but without any obvious cracks, and they
thought it would probably hold for the rest of the journey (though it
was not as if they had much of a choice). Father Zea, it turned out,
was in no rush to resume his duties, and continued with them further
upriver, to rejoin his mission station at Atures on the return journey.

By negotiating the great rapids, they had passed yet another dividing line between the more settled coastal regions and the 'wild,
unknown' lands of the interior.[13] They were travelling deeper and
deeper, towards something they couldn't identify, other than to say
that it denoted the opposite of Western civilisation and that which
was known to them.

The unknown seemed to require constant cross-referencing with
the known. On the one hand, they were entering the 'completely
uncharted' forests of Sipapo, home to the fabled Rayas, a headless
people said to eat by putting food straight into an orifice at about the
height of their navels. This belief was widely held, and Humboldt
and Bonpland had been assured by a missionary that he had seen the
Rayas with his own eyes. On the other hand, the mountain range
traversing the forest, the Cerros de Sipapo, was, Humboldt thought,
rather similar to that of the Montserrat in Catalonia.[14] And west of
the Orinoco, where the Vichada River joined, the landscape reminded
Humboldt of a precise stretch of countryside near Bayreuth—the
area between Steinberg and the Chateau of Fantaisie. (The chateau,
with its landscape garden in the sentimental style, was one of the
main settings for the novel *Siebenkäs* by Jean Paul.[15])

From now on, the tributaries they encountered had black waters.
The waters looked 'black as coffee grounds' in the shade, but, when
rippled by a light wind, 'meadow-green, like the Swiss lakes.'[16]
Humboldt and Bonpland swished some around in a glass, where it
reminded them of 'smoky topaz' or 'India ink swirled in water,' and,

in a return to the European point of reference, it seemed to '[surpass] even the waters of the Lakes Como and Maggiore in clarity and the degree to which it reflected the light.'[17] The black water was an all-round improvement: it seemed to attract far fewer mosquitoes and crocodiles than did the tepid Orinoco water; better still, it tasted nice.

In late April, as they approached the mission station San Fernando de Atabapo, they reached the place where the rivers Atabapo and Guaviare join with the Orinoco.[18] Having followed it for such a long time, they now left the Orinoco, drifting almost imperceptibly, or so it felt, across the large expanse of water, and steering their pirogue into the Atabapo. Travelling upriver, they found that the shores were almost completely hidden by dense vegetation. The aim was to get as close as possible to the rivers on the other side of the watershed, which flowed into the Rio Negro, and thereby into the Amazon water system. To this end, they followed a series of ever-smaller river branches. They turned into the Temi, which meandered through large swathes of half-submerged forest; their guides took them along shortcuts along slightly deeper channels before joining the river again. Freshwater dolphins emerged from underneath foliage, squirting water, and at some point the pirogue got stuck between two tree trunks. Turning into the last of these tributaries, the Tuamini, they followed it up to the small mission at San Antonio de Javita, and arranged for their pirogue to be carried across the watershed to the Rio Pimichín, one of the headstreams of the Rio Negro.[19] This was a laborious procedure which took the best part of five days; twenty-three people pulled and dragged the boat through the forest, in places using tree trunks as rollers.

On May 5, the explorers took receipt of their pirogue again, travelled down the Rio Pimichín (which merges with other headstreams), and found that, as predicted, they were coming to the Rio Negro. This was a relief—not least because they now had a clearly defined task ahead of them: to prove that the Casiquiare really was what they thought it was—a link between two huge river systems separated by a watershed.

As exciting as the idea of exploring an undiscovered river was, this was emphatically not what they were doing. The existence of the Casiquiare, as well as the fact that it connected the water systems of the Orinoco with those of the Amazon, was well known locally. It had first been reported by the French naturalist and explorer Charles-Marie de La Condamine in 1745, and had been confirmed, eleven years later, by the Spanish boundary expedition led by José Solano y Bote. What was left for Humboldt was less glamorous: to confirm the connection between the two water systems and to map the Casiquiare's course. Humboldt himself admitted that using the canal to get from one river system to the other was about as remarkable as French skippers using the Orleans Canal to get from the Loire to the Seine.[20] In order to build up his exploration of the Casiquiare as the main purpose of their journey, he emphasised the European opposition to the idea that two major water systems could be connected. But this construction of purpose seems to have happened largely in retrospect—after all, he had arrived on the Casiquiare as a result of a chain of often accidental events. The watershed itself, when they crossed it, was not particularly dramatic, either. There was no impressive mountain ridge separating the waters, but something more like an inclined plane—it was, as Humboldt called it, an 'imperceptible watershed.'[21]

Instead of turning straight into the mouth of the Casiquiare, they overshot it, travelling on a little further, to San Carlos del Rio Negro, the southernmost point of their journey, near the border with the Portuguese colony of Brazil. On the way, they had the opportunity to check if their personal boundaries vis-à-vis the unfamiliar had shifted. This opportunity came in the form of some dough-like, black-and-white speckled cakes, made from roasted, ground-up ants, that they were offered in a small native settlement on a river island. Humboldt asked which crops were grown on the island, and was told that the manioc did poorly; it was good ant country, however, and one could live well off them. Father Zea pronounced the offering a 'most excellent ant paste,' but Humboldt couldn't concur: 'we were still too deeply steeped in European prejudice.' He did taste a little: 'like butter that was slightly off, with bread crumbs kneaded into it.'[22]

What 'civilization' meant, and whether it was the missionaries from Europe who could rightfully claim to embody it, was something that the travellers had recently had an opportunity to think on. Upriver from San Fernando de Atabapo, a curiously shaped granite rock had caught their attention; it was, they were told, the *Piedra de la Madre*, named after a woman from the Guahiba tribe. The story behind it was an appalling one, and it had taken place in that very area. Some years back, one of the missionaries from San Fernando de Atabapo, a predecessor of the present incumbent, had led a 'human hunt.' In this case, the ostensible aim was to win souls for Christianity; according to Humboldt, however, the spiritual element of the operation was not much in evidence. The usual practice consisted in targeting children, with the purpose of turning them into de facto slaves of the Christians in the mission station.

In this particular 'hunt,' a mother and her young children (the older ones were out with their father), were surprised in their hut, and taken by boat to San Fernando. Several times the mother attempted to flee with her children, and each time they were captured and returned. At last, the missionary decided to separate her from her children, and sent her, tied down, by boat up the Atabapo. Still, she somehow managed to free herself, swam through the river, and got on land by climbing a steep rock—the one named after her. However, she was captured again, flogged right there on the rock, and taken further upriver, to the mission station at San Antonio de Javita. Again, she fled, and, against almost impossible odds—a distance of many miles, through seemingly impenetrable forests—arrived, after four days, in San Fernando, where she was found near the hut in which her children were imprisoned. Removed again, this time to a mission station on the upper Orinoco, she finally refused all food and died.

The tale, Humboldt admitted, had touched him deeply—even though he was at pains to point out that he had not told the story because of its human interest, but because it pointed beyond a single case, to 'the misery to be found wherever there are masters and slaves.'[23] The rock of the Guahiba mother was a shameful monument to 'the virtue of the ["uncivilized"], and the barbarism of the civilized.'[24]

They continued right up to the border between Spanish and Portuguese territories. It was reinforced, on the Spanish side, by seventeen soldiers—but, with the great humidity, Humboldt reckoned it probable that none of their guns would be in a state to fire. After the ringing of the Angelus bells, it was announced, with great seriousness, that 'all seemed quiet around the fort.'[25] On May 10, Humboldt and his group travelled back up the Rio Negro and on towards the Casiquiare.

Very sparsely inhabited, the Casiquiare was as close to wild nature as Humboldt had ever seen. The experience, he had to admit, was not always uplifting. The landscape, as far as they could see it from the river, did not differ greatly from that which they had passed through on the Rio Negro. The sky was overcast, with neither sun nor stars visible, and remained so. This was particularly unhelpful because the astronomical fixing of the Casiquiare's course had now emerged as the one area where they could hope to make an original contribution. The high moisture content in the air persisted, and Bonpland's botanical collections rotted by the crateful. Now that they were back in white-water territory, the mosquitoes made a strong showing again, and ants were also making their presence felt: 'until now, we had assumed that they did not climb up the hammock ropes.'[26]

There were tales alleging that cannibalism was rife in the area. A young man had come to their attention; he was good-natured and intelligent, and they had asked him to help them set up their instruments. They considered taking him into their employ, but were taken aback when he told them about his culinary preferences. He explained that, while 'the meat of the Manimondas-monkey was blacker, it still was very similar in taste to human flesh'; he also offered the information that, in both cases, the palms of the hands were much the finest part. While he was appalled, Humboldt still recognised that he brought his own cultural framework to the situation. There was no point remonstrating with the young man; it would be a bit 'as though a Brahmin from the Ganges were travelling in Europe, reprimanding us that we ate animal flesh.'[27]

The fact that everything was saturated with moisture also meant that it was difficult to find wood that was dry enough to burn, though this became increasingly irrelevant as their food supplies dwindled. Humboldt found that eating dried cocoa powder in small quantities worked some way towards suppressing his hunger.

Then, on their last night on the Casiquiare, their dog, Turco, was lost, probably taken by a jaguar. Humboldt and Bonpland had been well aware of the jaguar's presence, as they had heard it howl; the dog had whimpered and crept beneath their hammocks, at which point the howling had seemed to quiet down. The next morning, however, the dog was gone. Humboldt was distraught: perhaps he had gone to sleep and not heard the dog's distress? They waited for a long time, and searched the forest around them, but without success. Turco, who had accompanied them since Caracas, and managed to escape the crocodiles on the Apure, a 'young, gentle, and affectionate animal,' had clearly been killed in the forests around the Casiquiare. 'I merely mention the incident,' Humboldt concluded after much self-recrimination, 'as it throws a light on the cunning of those big spotted cats.'[28]

On May 21, the Casiquiare opened into the Orinoco. Instead of following the Orinoco's course, they first travelled a bit further upstream, to visit the 'loneliest, remotest Christian mission on the upper Orinoco'—La Esmeralda. In spite of its reputation as a sort of penal colony for missionaries, it was quite picturesque. It was surrounded by large water meadows—though its name was not derived from their emerald freshness, but from the bits of coloured quartz that had been found in the vicinity and, erroneously, had been believed to be emeralds. In fact, this mission station didn't even have its own priest: the nearest one was in Santa Bárbara, many miles downstream near San Fernando de Atabapo. This priest made an appearance five or six times a year, and in the meantime, a superannuated soldier stood in for him, teaching the children the words of the rosary, and ringing the church bells every so often.[29]

Despite the misunderstanding about the emeralds, La Esmeralda still possessed one distinction: it was known as the place with the finest preparations of the arrow poison called curare. Humboldt and Bonpland's stay in La Esmeralda coincided with the return from the forest of the men harvesting Brazil nuts, as well as quantities of mavacure vines, the plant from which curare was prepared. Their arrival back in the village was celebrated with a sort of harvest festival, involving the whole village: 'for two days, there were none but drunk Indians to be seen.'[30] It was a collective binge, complete with dancing and feasting. Entering one hut, Humboldt was slightly taken aback by what that included: 'large, fried, smoke-blackened monkeys were stacked up against the wall.' He couldn't help thinking that they looked horribly human-like, and the manner of preparation didn't help, since 'the skinned monkey is bent so that it looks to be in a seated position; often it is positioned in a way where it is supported by its long, thin arms.' Once cooked, things didn't get better: 'the roasted monkeys—especially those with very round heads— looked eerily like children—which is why Europeans, when they have to eat monkeys, prefer to have the arms and legs cut off, and only the torso served up.' But it seems that they tried some, since Humboldt pronounced the meat 'lean and quite dry.' At any rate, Bonpland took an arm and a hand, and added it to his samples.[31]

They also ate small quantities of curare, just to see how it tasted: 'pleasantly bitter,' Humboldt found. It was more useful than one might think, being used locally as a digestive aid, and also as poison for killing animals for the pot: 'there is hardly a chicken eaten on the Orinoco that hasn't been killed with a poison arrow.'[32] They gathered some mavacure vines themselves, and couldn't resist cooking them up in different ways, trying to determine whether the poison needed boiling down, or was present in the uncooked infusion already. Humboldt came close to calamity. When tasting curare, he had been careful to make sure that his mouth was free of any cuts or grazes. But a jar of curare broke where they had stored it, in their laundry, and Humboldt noticed, just as he was about to put a sock on, that it was sticky from the poison. This was unsettling because his foot boasted four open wounds caused by sand fleas.[33]

After a few days, they left La Esmeralda, worn down by the sparseness of the food and the constant onslaught from the mosquitoes. They travelled with the current, and their progress down the Orinoco was fast. They reached Santa Bárbara in only thirty-five hours. There was indeed a priest, who, they were dismayed to find, abused his dual position to draft in extra labourers from his flock at La Esmeralda to help with the building of a two-storey house for his own use. He told his guests with some pride that he was awaiting the arrival, at any moment, of a church lamp from Madrid, which had been paid for by the newly converted. Humboldt noted drily that, this necessity now taken care of, hopefully there might also be moves to supply the locals with clothes, agricultural tools, and a school for their children.[34]

About a month ago they had left San Fernando de Atabapo by travelling south, up the Atabapo; now, after their journey to the Rio Negro and along the Casiquiare, they arrived back at San Fernando from the east, on the Orinoco. It was May 27. They lodged in the house of the superintendent of the missions. Since their earlier stay, he had had time to worry about the way the Spanish missions would appear in any account that Humboldt might present to the court in Madrid on his return. So he had prepared a document, ready for Humboldt to sign, declaring that he had found all the mission stations in good order, and the natives treated leniently. Humboldt managed to make his excuses; after all, he was a Protestant, so his testimony was unlikely to carry much weight. That out of the way, Humboldt launched into a frank criticism of the practices of the church—the despotism of the monks and their exploitation of the native inhabitants. The superintendent listened patiently enough, Humboldt thought, but most probably 'in his heart he was wishing (no doubt in the interest of natural history) that people who pick up plants and investigate rocks, might not so insolently concern themselves with the welfare of the copper-coloured races and the affairs of human society.'[35]

From San Fernando, they once again let themselves be carried by the current. When they got to the rapids at Maipures, they stopped to explore the cave of Ataruipe. Used as a burial vault, it contained hundreds of skeletons stored in carefully woven baskets (called *mapires*), ranging in size from tall adults to newborns. Humboldt opened several of the baskets. The remains didn't seem all that old— a hundred years at most, he reckoned, but owing to the maceration it was impossible to say. He and Bonpland measured some of the skulls, 'to the great annoyance of our guides.'[36] Still, they went further, and removed several skulls from the *mapires*, as well as the skeleton of a child and two adult skeletons. They wrapped and disguised the remains carefully, but they couldn't avoid attracting attention. Perhaps it was the resin in which the bones were covered: although Humboldt and Bonpland couldn't detect any smell, the contents of their cargo seemed to advertise themselves to those with finer sensibilities. Wherever they went, people told them unbidden that the mule that was carrying 'the dead man' would perish.[37] These were bones of crocodiles and manatees, they lied, but nobody was fooled. It was their kinsmen, the people insisted, that Humboldt and Bonpland were carrying away, and nobody was willing to sell them fresh mules.

One of the skulls would eventually make its way to Göttingen, into Blumenbach's anatomical collection. The rest of the human remains that they had taken against so much resistance would not contribute anything to science: they were sunk, together with Juan Gonzales, the young Franciscan they had first met in Caracas, coming to rest somewhere near the African coast.[38]

The explorers were slowly gliding back into a more familiar world. The closer they came to Angostura (Ciudad Bolívar), the fewer mosquitoes, and the more Christian settlements they encountered. In June, they arrived at the great trading post of the Orinoco: 'it is hard to express the pleasure with which we set foot in Angostura.'[39]

Their attire and general appearance was at this stage, by Humboldt's own admission, 'rather below exquisite'—on top of which, they were still bearing, faintly, the black streaks they had acquired at the turtle side of Pararuma.[40] For the first few days, the comforts of Western civilisation seemed lovely; the pinnacle, to Humboldt, seemed the wheat bread they were served at the table of Angostura's governor. However, while Bonpland laboured at putting their collection of plant samples in order (or at least the depressingly small part of it that hadn't been spoilt in the moist atmosphere), his health, shaky since La Esmeralda, finally caved in. It took the best part of a month for him to get better, and Humboldt became seriously alarmed. He sent for a medicinal plant, Angostura bark, as an antifebrile. Bonpland consumed some of it in the form of a watery extract, but the two couldn't resist trying to classify the plant. They identified it as a new species, and when Humboldt sent a sample to Willdenow in Berlin, he asked whether it might be named in honour of Bonpland's recovery (it is still known as *Bonplandia trifoliata*).[41]

After six weeks in Angostura, the idea of travelling once more in a narrow boat along humid, mosquito-infested waters had distinctly lost its charm. A return to the coast across the Llanos, and then a sea voyage in a conventionally sized boat, seemed very desirable. Perhaps, back in Cumaná, they might turn up a ship that would take them to Cuba, or to Mexico? At any rate, they thought, they were done with South America. Once in Mexico, they would sail on to Manila, and then return to Europe via North Africa: 'we sacrificed the Andes of Peru in favour of the so little-known archipelago of the Philippines.'[42] Once again, the course of their journey was much more subject to chance and instinct than to strict scientific planning. Even on first disembarking from the *Pizarro* at Cumaná a year earlier, they had only meant to explore the surrounding countryside for a short period of time—'how far have we strayed from this initial plan!'[43] But then, not all of what Humboldt had set out to find was to be obtained by a scientific schedule. And much of it—in fact, perhaps more than he had been able to hope for—he had already found.

From his earliest youth, Humboldt had felt that he did not quite agree with his surroundings, the environment that he had been born into. The secure place in life that his brother had achieved with apparent ease had not been for him. But until he left Europe, a place where he might belong had mostly existed in his imagination. Now, he was beginning to gain in confidence that such a place actually existed: it was no longer defined purely negatively as being a place as far removed as possible from the constraints of his upbringing, and the family home in Tegel. The proof, as ever, was his body, that fail-safe, irrefutable instrument. He had found his natural environment. His body instinctively harmonised with it—and, even when that was not quite actually the case, he was determined that it be that way. His health, he wrote to Willdenow, had improved steadily as he approached the Americas: 'The tropics are my element, and I have never had such an uninterrupted run of good health as I have had in the past two years.' Conveniently overlooking his recent indisposition (he had been ill on the way back across the Llanos), he drove home his point, claiming that 'never, never, did I even have as much as a headache.'[44]

But it went further than that. Not only had he found the place that was congenial to him, but the relationship was a reciprocal one. He had explored the interior of South America, taking measurements and sending home samples. But, as he had hoped, the tropics had given him something back: they had wrought a change in him. His sensory experience and the scope of his thinking had been widened, in a way that was irrevocable. 'How fortunate you are,' he wrote to Willdenow, 'to *not* see these impenetrable forests on the Rio Negro, these worlds of palm trees—it would seem impossible after that to get used to a pine wood again.'[45] He, on the other hand, *had* walked beneath palm trees, and, as Goethe would write a few years later, he had indeed not done so 'with impunity'—nor had he ever wanted to.[46]

21

'The Highest Habitation
in the World'

❧❧

Humboldt had spent his time on the coast and in the interior (of modern-day Venezuela) not merely as an observer; he had become involved. This was important to him. In November 1800—after he and Bonpland had stayed in Cumaná once more, since late August—he recounted that 'half the town' accompanied them down to the port at Nueva Barcelona, and when they boarded the ship for Havana, it felt, he wrote, 'as though I parted from my own paternal soil.'[1]

The crossing to Cuba was rough and unpleasant. The only vessel that would take them was a small boat trading in salted meat. It was poorly equipped and lurched alarmingly in the high winds. One evening, a fire started in the kitchen and spread on deck, but it was extinguished fairly easily (thanks in part to the weather, which was bad throughout the journey). In the heavy swell, the pervasive smell of the ship's cargo did little for their comfort.

They arrived in Havana on December 19, 1800, after a crossing that had taken twenty-five days. They spent two months in Havana sorting their collections, and were preparing for their onward journey to Veracruz in Mexico towards the end of February 1801; but their plans, so recently decided on, were again thrown into disarray.

The United States newspapers, available in Cuba, reported that Baudin's French expedition had gone ahead after all: his ships, *Géographe* and *Naturaliste*, were believed to make their way towards Cape Horn, and were expected to then have a stop at Lima. For Humboldt and Bonpland it was a tempting thought: having the machinery of a big, state-funded expedition at their disposal would make life a lot easier, and the idea of working among like-minded company, many of whom they knew from their Paris days, added to the attraction. With Baudin, they would be able to sail to the Pacific islands that Georg Forster had seen with Cook—something that they could not hope to accomplish as private citizens. They changed their plans on an impulse: 'when you're young and full of energy, decisions are arrived at quickly.'[2] If they sailed from Cuba to Cartagena (on Colombia's Caribbean coast), and then journeyed southward, they were likely to intercept Baudin at Guayaquil, on the coast of present-day Ecuador.

By the time they arrived in Cartagena in late March, things looked different again. The passage had been terrible: in the strong winds, their ship had capsized and had only been straightened with the utmost difficulty; another time, the sail had to be cut off at the last minute to prevent it from happening again. So they decided to take the land route to Guayaquil—via Honda, Bogotá, and Quito—instead of another voyage by ship. Humboldt wrote letters to 'the citizen Baudin,' and had them forwarded to Lima, Valparaíso, and Buenos Aires, in the hope of apprising him of his plans: Humboldt expected to arrive in Quito during the summer; had he not heard from Baudin by then, he would climb Chimborazo, and then continue onwards, perhaps catching up with him in Lima.[3]

On June 18, as they approached Honda (northwest of Bogotá), they saw the Andes for the first time—masses of ice- and snow-covered granite, rising high above the clouds 'in the blue distance.'[4] Honda was not propitiously located. Mists in the morning were followed by unpleasant, moist warmth when the sunlight heated up the kettle-like valley, before, in the evening, sharp, icy air was blown across from the mountains. It couldn't be healthy. Humboldt thought that most of the inhabitants appeared to be suffering from colds and fevers. In fact, the closer he looked at them, the less encouraged he felt by what he saw. The locals were 'strangely pale,' and they seemed to be afflicted disproportionately by growths and tumours—'among 100 people, there are surely 80 goitres [swollen glands].' Humboldt observed them in a disconcerting variety of shapes and sizes: 'here was a large, taut ball of about eight to ten inches in diameter [. . .] there, a bulge shaped like a sausage, and there again a mass of grape-like knots.'[5] Some goitres were even decorated, with little gold chains and religious icons. There was a saying, which Humboldt reported with appalled fascination, that an inhabitant of Honda was unlikely to drown, being possessed of an exterior swimming bladder. While the strange always attracted him, the pathological was a step too far.

After a week, they left Honda and started on the long climb up to the high plateau of Bogotá. It was arduous, and even their mules struggled; it was just as well that, as Humboldt had reassured his brother, 'by a happy chance my health is as strong as it has ever been.'[6]

Bogotá was the home of José Celestino Mutis, the most celebrated botanist in South America. At almost seventy years of age, he had a reputation for being prickly and difficult to approach. So Humboldt wrote him a letter calculated to be irresistible. Both he and Bonpland, he wrote, had been hoping to make Mutis's acquaintance for ten years, and had undertaken the difficult and dangerous land route via Bogotá with the express purpose of having the chance to do so; furthermore, he announced that he was coming with some plant samples—two newly discovered species of lichen he had seen along the Magdalena River—with which he was almost certain that Mutis was not familiar.[7] It worked almost too well. Before they had even arrived, they received a polite communication that Mutis had prepared a house for them—he had, it emerged later, evicted his sister-in-law—and was ready to show them all his botanical treasures.

It was on their way to Bogotá that Bonpland's illness re-emerged. Humboldt was less patient this time, worried that Mutis's favourable mood might not last. Bonpland, Humboldt remonstrated, had taken 'a mad, cold bath' during their time in Honda, and anyway the fever was mostly a consequence of his being a bit soft.[8] But, in fact, the delay seemed rather to have increased Mutis's enthusiasm for his new admirers. As they passed through the town of Facatativá, at the edge of the high plateau, they were met by two welcome committees—one sent by Mutis, and one by a rival family.

Humboldt, never comfortable with ceremony, was taken aback. He resisted, as well as he could, entreaties that he put on uniform and travel the rest of the way by coach. But eventually he was persuaded, and so ended up entering Bogotá—on July 8—in a coach and six, surrounded by outriders. The windows were filled with spectators; schoolboys ran alongside the coach, pointing at the important personage within. Humboldt, with a keen sense of what was due, did not disappoint. He emerged from the coach barometer in hand, so as to protect his most delicate instrument; Mutis smiled and came forward to embrace the travellers.[9]

Humboldt and Bonpland spent two months as Mutis's guests. They made use of their host's library, one of the best-equipped on the continent, compared their plant samples to his, and climbed the mountains in the vicinity. These were part of the mountain range east of the city, which separated the barren uplands of the Bogotá plain from the humid, lush Orinoco Basin. Both landscapes were visible, seemingly within reach—'as though it would take just a couple of steps to get from Sweden to Africa.'[10] One of the mountains was called Guadeloupe, another one Montserrat. '[W]hen, in January 1799, in Catalonia, I climbed the Montserrat [. . .] what would it have taken to make me believe that, in 1801, I should be standing on top of a different Montserrat [. . .] admiring the cordilleras of the Andes [. . .].'[11]

On September 8, Mutis sent them off with three mules' worth of provisions, and they were on their way to Quito. The Quindío Pass, southwest of Bogotá, was notoriously difficult to negotiate—so much so that travellers tended to resort to *silleros* (porters), who would carry not only luggage but also the travellers themselves across, on chairs tied to their backs. Passengers discussed their *silleros* much like they might discuss a horse.

Humboldt found the whole practice distasteful—'every one of my instincts made it impossible for me to ride on humans.' He also noted an interesting difference in dignity between the porter and his customer: 'the *sillero* walks about extremely straight and stiffly, while the person carried at the back cuts a miserable, helpless figure.'[12] Wondering if the practice ought to be outlawed, he was quickly confronted with the complexity of trying to effect change. In fact, there had been an attempt to improve the path, he was told, but it had met with an outcry by the *silleros*, who were worried about their livelihoods. Anyway, as Humboldt emphasised, after the privations and toil of their journey so far, the pass didn't seem so daunting. Footholds were separated by wide ditches filled with water and mud, making the experience akin to going for a walk on a ladder.

They arrived in Quito in early January 1802, and ended up staying in the area for five months. Quito did not strike Humboldt as picturesque—or perhaps he had simply ceased to become excited about what he had come to recognise to be the generic architecture of Spanish America. The houses in town were 'as they are in Bogotá, in Caracas, in Cartagena, and in Havana.'[13] And there were still traces of the devastation of the great earthquake of 1797, which, in Quito, had killed thousands of people. Beyond the obvious destruction, though, there were more subtle effects. Regular jolts were a constant reminder of the proximity to danger. As a consequence, Humboldt thought, Quito's inhabitants existed in a heightened emotional state. He wrote to his brother that there was an emphasis on sensual pleasure, luxury, and entertainment: the best way to be if one lived at the edge of the abyss.[14] They themselves stayed right in the centre of Quito, on the Plaza Chica, as guests of the Montúfar family, who also owned a hacienda in the Chillos Valley, south of the city.

This is where Carlos Montúfar enters the picture. The twenty-two-year-old son of the family would accompany Humboldt and Bonpland for the rest of the American journey, and come to Europe with them. The arrangement did not go unnoticed. There were rumours that the association was not merely scientific. These rumours could, for the most part, be traced back to Francisco José Caldas. A young botanist who had worked with Mutis, he had nurtured hopes of entering into a closer association with Humboldt and Bonpland. Mostly self-schooled and without an aristocratic background like Montúfar's, he was piqued to see Humboldt prefer the less experienced, younger man. When Montúfar was invited to join Humboldt and Bonpland on their travels, this irritation hardened into embitterment. Caldas wrote to Mutis, complaining that Humboldt had taken on an 'ignorant, unprincipled, and dissolute Adonis.'[15] He went on to point out that Humboldt's conduct in Quito was very much at odds with the impression that Mutis might have gained at Bogotá. The 'Prussian sage,' Caldas alleged, had visited houses of ill repute, surrounded himself with 'obscene young people,' yielded to passion, and generally failed to comport himself with the dignity expected of a scientist.[16]

Caldas's view of Humboldt's time in Quito was clearly coloured by resentment. But his is not the only report that suggests that Humboldt might have encountered the new continent more intimately than the picture of the dispassionate scientist, barometer in hand, implies. Under Montúfar's tutelage, Humboldt was said to have spent several nights in the Casa del la Virgen, remedying his state of being (in Montúfar's judgement) an 'absolute' virgin. Nor was this, it was alleged, the last of it: in due course, there was a child, who was named Alejandro H. Pazmiño, and who was widely believed to be Humboldt's son.[17] While this assumption is, to say the least, controversial, the strength of the rumours suggests that something about Humboldt's way of living during his time in Quito attracted interest.

Another famous European scientist had come to Quito the previous century: Charles-Marie de La Condamine, the leader of the so-called French Geodesic Mission between 1736 and 1743. His aim had been to determine the exact length of a degree of latitude near the equator, from which inferences could be made about the shape of the earth. In the plains of Yaruquí, he had erected small stone pyramids to mark the beginning and end points. When Humboldt paid a visit to the site, he found them mostly destroyed. It turned out that La Condamine had decorated the tops of the structures with images of the fleur-de-lis, and the locals had become nervous that they represented a territorial claim by France.

Apart from this immediate project, La Condamine had generally confined himself to measuring altitude and atmospheric pressure—'he did not go beyond *quantity*,' as Humboldt put it.[18] Humboldt, by contrast, would climb the great, snow-capped volcanoes, the *nevados*, and take note of everything—the rocks, the plants, the consistency of the air at altitude. What mattered was the total impression. Disparate branches of knowledge converged in one mind—his own—and so the subjective, again, asserted itself as the truest representation of objective reality.[19]

It was in mid-March when Humboldt, accompanied by Bonpland and Montúfar, began with Mount Antisana. The ascent was challenging: the wind was fierce, and it was very cold. 'It was hard to keep upright. Hats were carried up into the air as high as the height of a church steeple—but luckily the gusts of wind were such that they fell straight down again.'[20] Ice needles flew through the air, cutting their faces. Still, Humboldt had time to admire the view of a small mountain lake, and the composition of the landscape: the lake was situated in a 'very romantic' position, and some trees created 'a very pleasing effect.'[21]

They stayed on the high plateau (at an elevation of over 4,000 metres) for three days. The altitude got to them. Every small exertion caused them shortness of breath, their eyes were bloodshot, and

Montúfar spat out blood. They could feel the effect on their mood, too. They felt weak and oppressed—'how strange it is, that the extremes in physics and morale touch each other.'[22] Even the cattle that lived at that altitude, they thought, were affected: they were aggressive and ready to charge whenever they felt threatened in their 'tedious living space.' At night, the group stayed in a small squat house nestled into the bleak hillside, 'without doubt the highest habitation in the world.'[23] Nor was it comfortable: their food provisions had not arrived as expected, so they ate some old potatoes they found in a corner of the hut. In the absence of candles, they lit bits of straw, which filled the place with smoke. Outside, 'the wind blew and howled like on the open sea.' They went to bed at seven. Humboldt shared a bed with Montúfar, but this appears to have been purely for practical reasons: 'how long this night seemed to us [. . .] and how uncomfortable.'[24] Montúfar particularly suffered from the cold, and had pains in his chest and abdomen, but refused Humboldt's offers to heat water for his feet.

The next day, Humboldt observed an increased blueness of the sky: the hue was 'darker than it was in Europe, [. . .] the sky bluer, and the air more transparent.' They had transcended a boundary— they were 'above the eternal snow, higher than any mortal had been before us.' It felt uncomfortable, there seemed to be 'too much light,' and the experience was altogether almost too much to take. Perhaps, he now wondered, other people—shepherds in search of their animals, for example—had attained similar heights as they had, or even greater; however, 'I doubt that one can reach *much* higher.'[25]

Four weeks later it was Pichincha, a volcano with two tall peaks that borders Quito. Resting on the mountainside of one of these two peaks, the Rucu Pichincha, the three naturalists lit a fire to determine the boiling point of water at high altitude. The porters who carried the fire-steel and tinder had not yet arrived, so they used the lens of their telescope and bits of *fraylejón*, a shrub with wool-like fibres, to start the fire. It turned out quite well, Humboldt thought, and he rushed to find some snow to melt before the small amount of coal they had brought with them would burn out. Leaning over the coals and dipping his thermometer in the boiling water, he took a reading of 86.2°C (187.16°F). He felt faint. He measured the atmospheric electricity, and took an air sample. By the time he reached the top, he was distinctly unwell. On the descent, he fell behind a little, and then passed out. On having a little wine administered to him, he recovered, and continued the descent on horseback. His description of the event suggests that the view of the surrounding summits was even more exalted as a result of this liminal experience: 'I felt no ill effects. We descended by moonlight. Cotopaxi, the most beautiful cone in the world, and Antisana, looking like a huge edifice transposed into the sky, presented themselves in their entire grandeur.'[26]

They then started on the Cotopaxi—'of such perfection that a lathe worker wouldn't have been able to improve on its curve'—on April 28.[27] It had been snowing the previous night, and with the cone surrounded by deep ravines, they knew that they wouldn't be able to reach it. And even if the ravines were negotiated, the slopes of the peak were so steep, with no rocks to offer protection from the fierce winds, that reaching the crater would be impossible. Humboldt and his companions made do with hunting stags, which were plentiful: 'I observed no difference to European stags.'[28]

Humboldt was ready to leave Quito but, with the Pichincha so close by, it was difficult to resist the attempt to climb its other volcanic peak, the Guagua Pichincha.[29] Bonpland stayed behind, preparing and packing up a llama skeleton before their departure, and Montúfar decided to keep Bonpland company. Humboldt was not sorry—so far, none of the ascents had felt particularly satisfying, but instead had been full of hardship and physical danger, and he preferred not to subject his friends to it.

On May 26, he set off with four noblemen from Quito, one of whom, Don José Ascásubi, had done some hunting in the area and was for that reason designated their guide. The weather was beautiful; but as they got within sight of the steep slope around the crater, reaching it seemed impossible. Humboldt scrabbled up, accompanied by the nobleman Don Urquinaona and one porter, Philip Aldas. Aldas led the way, 'even though he had as little idea of the path as I.'[30] Near the crater, a large amount of snow had piled up. It was not very hard, but they found that it was just about possible to walk on it. But suddenly Aldas slipped into the snow, down to his midriff. He called out to his companions that his feet were dangling in the air—he must have been directly above a crevice, Humboldt realised, only supported by the compacted snow. Humboldt, who was closest, pulled him out, but it was clear that they couldn't continue this way.

Still, he wasn't easily able to accept that they had to turn back after they had come so close to their goal. After all, La Condamine had made it to the crater in 1742. So he told Don Urquinaona to sit on a rock and wait, persuaded Aldas to come along, and together the two of them climbed an overhanging cliff that towered over the crater. This was not without danger: the cliff was steep; there was not much that provided a foothold; and a fall would have been, Humboldt noted (attempting to translate the danger in European terms), 'like one from the gallery of St. Paul's Cathedral.'[31] The smell of sulphur increased. To reach the next rock, they walked across a small patch of snow. This was where Humboldt noticed a bluish light beneath them. He realised with a shudder that they were on top of the crater itself, with nothing between them and the vent but a thin bridge of compacted snow. Humboldt called out to Aldas, threw himself down on the ground, and pulled him back on to the rock by his poncho.[32] From there, they surveyed the extent of the danger they had been in. Humboldt threw a stone towards the blue light—the hole grew larger, and the stone disappeared into the deep. Had the snow not held, Humboldt mused, they would have fallen (about 400 metres, he guessed) right into the vent, 'and nobody in Quito, save for our footprints in the snow, would have been able to tell what had become of us.'[33]

What they had gained at the price of endangering their lives was an experience that went beyond the ordinary: 'no language has words to express what we saw.' He tried to express it nevertheless. The summits of mountains were below them, like so many stalagmites rising from unfathomable depths. But the experience—nature without life, or even the possibility of life—was also deeply troubling: 'I have a feeling of oppression even as I am writing this.'[34]

The next day, there were earth tremors in Quito. Humboldt found that he was expected to take responsibility for this: it was felt that he had interfered with the volcano. Still, he turned towards the Guagua Pichincha one more time, as Montúfar and Bonpland had decided that they did not want to miss this summit after all, and, 'how could I not share the danger with them?'[35] But this excursion was not a success. Bonpland kept fainting, and continuing tremors soon convinced them of the wisdom of returning to Quito. There they were hoping to observe the eclipse of one of Jupiter's moons; but it 'remained invisible, like all the others.'[36] The tremors that had sent them off the mountain, they learned, had not been felt in Quito at all.

The departure from Quito, in June 1802, followed a by now well-established pattern: since the preceding evening, 'everyone had been in tears.' But in Quito, the sadness of their departure had a different quality. Earlier wistful farewells had tended to involve places to which Humboldt's attachment had been more wishful than real. In Quito, however, Humboldt and Bonpland had, over a period of some five months, made a rather deeper—and perhaps more intimate—connection with the place. More than that, Carlos Montúfar was now travelling with them, with the hope of continuing his studies in Madrid, and the prospect of taking this young man so far from his family and all he knew made everybody feel sombre. Breakfast on the day of their departure, Humboldt wrote, was a heavy and depressing occasion.

Travelling south via Latacunga and Ambato, they arrived in Riobamba on June 17. This was the new Riobamba: the old one—

the epicentre of the earthquake of 1797—had been destroyed so comprehensively that it had made more sense to give up on it and start afresh, about nine miles to the east of the original site. The new Riobamba, still in the process of being built, was nestled in a valley between several volcanoes—the Sangay and El Altar ('like an enchanted castle') to the south; the Tungurahua to the north; and, finally, to the west, the Chimborazo (20,702 feet), then believed to be the highest mountain in the world.[37]

It was difficult to approach the Tungurahua because of flooding, so they travelled via the town of Penipe, the location of a famous rope bridge, already documented by La Condamine. It was an attractive construction. Might such a design be of use in the European wars, Humboldt wondered? Or perhaps it would be better employed as a special feature for a garden in the English style? Then again, he felt a bit queasy crossing it, nor 'would it be fair to say that horses easily take to walking across these swinging works of art.'[38] The day they had set aside for the Tungurahua was rainy. They ascended on a narrow ridge of rock with a chasm either side, but when the rain got heavier they abandoned the climb.

The date of their attempt on the Chimborazo—June 23, 1802— marked, Humboldt observed, three years exactly from that of their ascent of the Pico del Teide in Tenerife (though with his appetite for establishing connections, he overlooked the fact that he was out by two days).[39] In all other ways, the day was inauspicious. It was dark and foggy, which prevented the use of their sextant and the artificial horizon. Furthermore, there had been heavy snowfall the night before. The vegetation consisted of a monotonous cover of grasses, and the rocks had a 'grotesque, spongy shape.' Humboldt clearly did not expect to reach the summit. Above the snowline they found a narrow crest, which they ascended. To their left, the mountainside, encrusted with snow, rose with 'terrifying sheerness'; on the right, it was much the same, only with rocks instead of snow. They decided that being dashed by rocks was narrowly preferable to being buried under a blanket of snow, and spent the rest of the ascent leaning to the right.[40]

The gradient became so steep that Humboldt's little group had to hold on with their hands, which soon bled (they did not wear gloves). Their boots filled with snow and water, making their feet numb with cold. All suffered from nausea and vertigo, and bled from their lips and gums. Montúfar was the worst affected. Breathing was an effort. A heavy mist had settled on the mountain, blanketing the summit and obfuscating the way ahead. They carried on like this for another half an hour. Then, for the briefest of time, the mist lifted, and the peak became visible: 'it was a solemn, sublime moment.'[41] Against their better knowledge, they allowed themselves, for an instant, to believe that they might reach the summit after all. Indeed, just then the ridge widened slightly, and for a short while progress became easier—until their path was cut off by a large crevasse. The ridge, they could see, continued on the other side, but there was no way to cross or bypass the chasm. Nor did they try—they were cold and knew that they had reached the limits of their physical endurance: 'the crevasse was our pillars of Heracles.'[42] They took an air sample, and turned around.

Would it have made a difference had they made it to the top? Several aspects both of the event and of Humboldt's account of it suggest that scaling the summit was never quite what was intended. Not reaching the top, in fact, may have been more in keeping with Humboldt's project.

According to conventional Romantic thought, a lofty peak was expected to have a correspondingly lofty effect on the mind. And the short glimpse of the snowy peak, as it appeared in the distance, seemed to achieve just this. The idea of their own bodily presence in that borderland of the possible, on the other hand, was sobering. Beyond its habitable zones, the Chimborazo was 'sombre and depressing.'[43] Its slopes were a seemingly endless incline of rocky debris: there was no living thing up there, 'no insect, not even a condor'—nothing but two species of lichen, duly identified as *Lichen geographicus* and *Lichen pustulatus*.[44]

With plants so conspicuously absent from the higher slopes of the mountain—Humboldt made the point that the Chimborazo had the poorest plant life of all the *nevados*—it is curious that he should have chosen the Chimborazo for his famous illustration of the distribution of South American flora.[45] In this profile view of the mountain, Chimborazo is presented as if in cross-section. All over the exposed rock face, the names of the different plants near the equator are written—according to the height at which they occur—in tiny, almost illegible letters, increasing the impression that the composition serves an aesthetic purpose at least as much as a strictly scientific one.[46]

Humboldt was surprisingly candid about the limited scientific use of climbing great peaks. Of course, it was possible to take barometric altitude readings on a summit, but more reliable results were achieved by trigonometric measurements from the high plateaux that often conveniently surrounded such peaks. And while the Chimborazo had the distinction of supposedly being the highest mountain in the world, Humboldt was keen to play down its singularity. The whole chain of Andean volcanoes, he explained, was really a single volcano with different outlets, the Chimborazo merely happening to be the highest of them.

Predictable conventional narratives always produced a certain wariness in Humboldt. He was certainly not attracted by the idea of an explorer placing his snow-sodden boot on the highest peak of a country or continent, thereby symbolically subjugating it. But failing to reach the peak of the Chimborazo was not merely a form of rebellion against such narratives; it was part of a wider pattern observable throughout his life. The unfinished and the fragmentary, of which the ascent of the Chimborazo is emblematic, are significant aspects of Humboldt's approach. On his return to Europe, he never finished writing up his travels: the *Personal Narrative of a Journey to the Equinoctial Regions of the New Continent* breaks off before Humboldt and Bonpland even reach the Andes proper. His account of the ascent of Chimborazo is contained in volume one of a book entitled *Kleinere Schriften* ('Minor Writings';

there never was a volume two). His life's work, *Cosmos*, was likewise left unfinished.[47] The Romantic preference for the fragment carries within it the acknowledgement that one can never give a full and true representation of reality. At the same time, it points to the presence of a greater whole, one beyond description and therefore out of reach, forever ideal. As Humboldt wrote, 'the seemingly unattainable holds a mysterious attraction.'[48]

Two days after the abandoned ascent, back in Riobamba, the Chimborazo was clearly visible again: it appeared 'in its whole greatness and grandeur.' The weather was a lot better, too; but Humboldt dismissed the idea of making another attempt. 'Without doubt, it would have turned out as fruitless as the first.'[49]

22

'I Don't Want to End with a Tragedy'

❧

Humboldt, Bonpland, and Montúfar left Riobamba towards the end of June. (Some weeks earlier news had reached them that Baudin had decided not to travel via South America after all, but had headed to Australia by way of southern Africa instead.) The damage of the 1797 earthquake was still noticeable everywhere: 'for two weeks now we've seen nothing but bells suspended from trees, owing to the destruction of all churches in the earthquake.'[1] Moving steadily south, they travelled through the market town of Guamote and on to Tixán, where they visited a sulphur mine so inexpertly arranged that 'more sulphur is lost than gained,' Humboldt observed. From there they travelled to the town of Alausí, the location of which, nestled between high mountains, was 'very romantic—though the dense mists, which often don't allow even two feet of visibility, render it melancholy.'[2] After traversing a 'long and boring' high plateau, the Ladera de Cadlud, at Los Paredones they set foot on what was 'classical ground, as far as Peruvian [Inca] architecture is concerned.'[3]

Los Paredones was the location of an Inca structure, now in ruins. From there, the old Inca road led to a second Inca site, Ingapirca, a little further to the south. 'The old Roman roads that I've seen in Italy are not more solid or greater,' Humboldt pronounced later, noting particularly the striking regularity of the rectangular carved stone blocks—all the more remarkable and mysterious for the fact that the Incas did not have iron tools.[4]

The structure at Los Paredones had been shown a certain lack of respect: 'they had closed up the doors, to transform it into cowsheds. That's how in Palmyra, in Heliopolis, in Greece, in Italy, and the West Indies, human greatness had become a plaything of the fates.'[5] At Ingapirca, an oval temple built of stonework and surrounded by various structures was in much better condition. The temple's centrepiece, the 'house of the Inca,' had already been described by La Condamine. In spite of its obvious age, the edifice, Humboldt noted, had a surprisingly familiar aspect: a gabled roof, which had formerly been covered with flat stones. They owed this information to the owner of the hacienda where they were staying, who explained, not without pride, that his ancestors had played a part in destroying the palace, removing many of the stones with their own hands.[6]

The ruins were full of signs and meaning, though the meanings were not easily discerned. The house seems to have had space for two rooms only; might they have been for a high-ranking Inca and his wife? The rooms, however, were not connected. A striking feature of Inca architecture were the blind windows and doors—were they little recesses for household gods, Humboldt wondered. A highly decorated stone, like a step, was set against a wall: 'it's likely that it originally had another purpose, but which?'[7]

A local path led to a large rock carved into the shape of a bench, and with an elaborate ornamental relief. The rock work was so exquisite that it would not have been out of place, thought Humboldt, in the gardens at Wörlitz, the romantic landscape park in Germany. It had space for one person only, but the view it afforded that person, presumably the Inca chief, was highly 'picturesque'—he must have been susceptible to the beauty of nature. Then again, its name, *Inga-Chungana* ('game of the Inca'), seemed to suggest the possibility that the decorations were part of an elaborate game (possibly one involving marbles, though it seemed far from obvious how such a game might have been played).

In a little valley nearby, Humboldt discovered a rock with what seemed to him to be an image of the sun. He described three concentric circles on the face of the rock, in the middle of which traces of a mouth and two eyes seemed discernible: 'it is impossible to deny that this figure depicted the sun in just the way that all people at all times have always represented it.'[8] On closer inspection, he established that the circles themselves were not man-made, but had been formed by a vein of brown iron ore enclosing a patch of white sandstone. Priests, 'always ready to deceive the people,' had probably drawn in eyes and mouth. On the other hand, those features were now difficult to make out. The Spanish, trying to eradicate the un-Christian image, likely tried to undo the facial features: 'it is clear to see that the face in the middle has been destroyed with a chisel.' And while Humboldt included a plate of the rock in his book *Views of the Cordilleras* (*Vues des Cordillères*), with eyes and a smiling mouth, the site today, which is much smaller than Humboldt's illustration seems to imply, suggests nothing beyond a circular discolouration.[9]

On July 4, they arrived in Cuenca—two days before they had been expected, 'and thus, fortunately, evading the triumphal reception that had been prepared for us.'[10] A certain waning in his enthusiasm for the area is palpable. The city was built on a regular plan, but the buildings were 'below average'; Humboldt detected 'no commercial activity' among the inhabitants; there was some weaving of 'coarse' cloth, as well as knitting of socks, but all done 'with immense slowness.'[11] Observing a moon of Jupiter was impossible because of bad weather.

The travellers still had to submit to five days of bullfights that had been arranged in their honour. Two people died in the proceedings—not during the fights, but outside, as the animals were led to the arena. The locals, Humboldt noted laconically, had completely lost their knack for fighting and brutality. What he had in mind here were the dramatic events that had taken place during La Condamine's visit in Cuenca in 1739. Jean Seniergues, the surgeon of La Condamine's expedition, had met a terrible end here. La Condamine, in his account of the affair, had only provided the basics, describing how Seniergues had been dragged from his seat during a bullfight and mauled by an angry mob, dying from his injuries several days later. Humboldt had no hesitation in filling in the background: the 'beautiful lady who had been the object of the dispute,' Manuela de Quesada, had still been alive in Cuenca until very recently. For good measure, he added that there were also two daughters of La Condamine still living in Cuenca—'natural daughters,' he explained somewhat redundantly, who 'still practise their mother's gallant profession.'[12]

In the town of Loja, they compared the bark derived from the local cinchona trees with others they had seen at the different stations of their journey and those collected by Mutis and Georg and Reinhold Forster—'nobody has inspected so many different types of cinchona bark as we have.'[13] Out botanising with Montúfar one night, the two of them sat down, Humboldt's diaries tell us, and gazed into the sky. The stars could be seen with great clarity: 'it was a glorious night. Moon, Venus, Jupiter, and Saturn were very close together.' Trying to retrace their steps, however, they lost their way. Humboldt, using the stars for direction, eventually succeeded in leading them towards the welcoming lights of their house—except, it wasn't their house. Disoriented, and still deliberating whether they should try to spend the night there anyway, they heard Bonpland's voice calling for them. It was 'with great astonishment' that Humboldt learned from him that their house was located 'diametrically opposite' to the one that he had found.[14]

On their way south, on August 1, they crossed into the Spanish viceroyalty of Peru. They came through Baños and Tarqui, sites where La Condamine had taken geodesic measurements. In Baños, Humboldt was delighted to discover that the water inside the natural dams had the alga *ulva thermalis* growing in it—just like in the Bohemian spa town of Karlsbad, frequented by Goethe and Rahel Levin. In Tarqui, the monuments of La Condamine's expedition made (much like the pyramids at Yaruquí) a less well-lasting impression than his more personal legacy in Cuenca: 'there is no trace of the work left, apart from a half-broken stone at a hacienda nearby that indicates the degree of latitude that the savant was trying to determine.'[15]

The journey to Lima was strenuous. The travellers spent many nights sleeping under the stars, where, more often than not, the natural world kept them awake ('the ants, stinging us every so often, allowed us to witness the setting of the stars at our leisure'). At other times they crammed into narrow huts, and here it was their food provisions that turned out to be an unexpected source of disturbance to their night's rest: the guinea pigs' 'constant squeaking is the travellers' scourge in these parts.'[16] A single river, the Huancabamba, had to be crossed twenty-seven times, which was often precarious, especially with all the luggage they carried: 'it is a disagreeable feeling to see the trunk with one's manuscripts, the fruit of much toil, on the back of a swaying mule, as it swims in the middle of the river.'[17]

Near the Marañón River—the Andean headwater of the Amazon—they met some members of the tribe of the Jivaro, a people notorious for their head-hunting and the making of shrunken heads. Humboldt, however, found them to be an attractive and likeable people: 'the most cheerful free Indians I have ever seen.' He took the encounter as a chance to develop his thoughts on people who lived far removed from Western civilisation. In his diaries, he was at pains to make the point that behaviour, far from being innate to a particular people, was rather the result of the situation such a people finds itself in. And the most important factor here was whether a people was subjugated or had the chance to be self-determining: 'what a difference between the free Indio and the one of the missions, who is enslaved by priestly views and oppression!'[18]

The Jivaro whom he met had an astonishing keenness, as well as facility, for learning languages (Humboldt tried German, French, and English on them and attested them to have an almost perfect pronunciation); but, perhaps more surprisingly, they showed 'an equal obsession' for teaching their own language.[19] There was a similar confidence about their dances, which they wanted Humboldt and his companions to learn. The dancing proceeded in pairs, with partners holding on to each other with both hands, and, Humboldt reported, 'once they'd started with one of us, they were not going to let go of him.' This was a relationship of equals: the Jivaro were happy to be observed by the European travellers, but they, in turn, looked back. Humboldt's interest in this reciprocity shows that the principles of sociocultural perspective were self-evident to him. Members of free indigenous tribes were capable of great intellectual or physical feats; yet, when there was no need for exertion, they were also able to do very little: 'they spend two or three months lying in a hammock, where they turn the bananas they are roasting over the fire with their toes, so as to not have to get up out of their hammocks and use their hands.' But why should they exert themselves when they didn't need to? This certainly could not be construed as a sign of 'primitiveness,' unless one was prepared to lay the same charge at the feet of 'our own men of learning, who don't cultivate the earth, never walk anywhere and allow themselves to be waited on.'[20] If Western culture was indeed 'superior,' then this certainly wasn't obvious to the Jivaro: they showed a clear distaste for the travellers' food, with the sauces a particular source of disgust. Humboldt also couldn't help noticing that, unusually, the Jivaro women did very little beyond cooking. Spinning and weaving, for example, were done by the men. Most customs and traditions of all cultures, it appeared, were hard to justify on functional grounds, and thus looked arbitrary. Indeed, it seemed that there was huge scope for doing things differently.

Cajamarca, further south, had been the Inca town where, in 1532, the Spanish conquistadors under Francisco Pizarro had conclusively extinguished Inca rule, capturing Atahualpa, the Inca ruler, by stealth and the use of firepower and horses. The room in which Atahualpa had been imprisoned could still be seen. A mark on the wall indicated the point to which Pizarro had demanded that Atahualpa fill it with gold to buy his freedom. Remarkably, the Incas managed to provide the incredible ransom, but Pizarro had Atahualpa executed anyway. There was a stone that, it was said, was still stained with Atahualpa's blood. Humboldt had a closer look, and even washed the stone, determining that the brown discolourations were veins in the stone, probably a silicate called hornblende. In any case, he noted, Atahualpa had not been decapitated, but strangled.

A dwelling in Cajamarca was inhabited by one Silvester Astorpilco and his family, thought to be the nearest living descendants of Atahualpa. They lived in utter destitution, a fact that struck Humboldt as particularly poignant. The son of the family, 'a young man of seventeen years, with attractive features,' spoke of his belief that the Inca had buried their treasure underneath the house.[21] He related the story of a female ancestor who was said to have seen the treasure. Her husband had led her, blindfolded, down into the chambers beneath. When he removed the cloth from her eyes, she saw trees made of gold wire, with birds of solid gold sitting on the branches. An old wives' tale, of course, Humboldt wrote in his diary—only to note, a few lines down, that the existence of the golden trees could not be altogether dismissed. He delicately enquired of the boy whether he was not sometimes tempted to dig beneath the house for the treasure, and felt rebuked by the young man's understanding of the realities of his situation: they had some land to cultivate, which allowed them a meagre but peaceful existence; if they owned trees and birds made of solid gold, they would be hated and persecuted.

In mid-September, they left Cajamarca and began their slow descent towards the coast. They were hungry for their first glimpse of the Pacific. It took longer than they had thought: there was always one more mountain range impeding their view. It was generally a bit like that, Humboldt reflected, in life as in science: 'blessed is he who knows his limitations, and doesn't mistake the clouds for the horizon that he is looking for.' The Pacific, when they finally saw it from near the village of Huangamarca, provided just what Humboldt desired. Here was a sight that was foreign and familiar at the same time, and, almost best of all, reassuringly out of reach: 'On the back of the Andes, surrounded by what is left of a sage and industrious people, our eyes searched for those blessed isles [of the South Sea], where there is still the purity of manners, the strength of character, which the Europeans have destroyed here.' He thought of those whom he had known and admired, and who had fed the flame of this longing—Banks, Bougainville, and Forster—but he knew that, even if he set sail for the blessed isles, they were unlikely to yield what he was looking for: 'how small and straight the real world is, compared to the one that human beings create in the depth of feeling.'[22]

Towards the end of September, they arrived in Trujillo, on the coast. Most of the streets were unpaved and bordered by white-washed walls, which formed the façade of the houses within: 'one has to be used to Peruvian towns to find Trujillo attractive.'[23] Just outside Trujillo they visited the site of Chan Chan, the ruins of a great city built by the Chimú people (who were conquered by the Inca in the 1400s).

Their onward journey along the coast proceeded by sedan chair, necessitated by the heavy winds blowing in from the sea. Mounted on mules, they rattled the travellers about, inducing nausea—it was like being in 'the cabin of a bad ship.' Humboldt tried to distract himself by reading and looking out to sea—walking, in his mind, 'from one island to another.'[24] In this way, they covered the 300 miles to Lima, the southernmost part of their journey, arriving in the capital of the viceroyalty of Peru on October 23, 1802.

On Christmas Eve, Humboldt, Bonpland, and Montúfar left Lima. They boarded the frigate *La Castora*, to sail all the way back north along the coast to Guayaquil (Ecuador). Humboldt had noticed the relatively low temperature of the coastal waters in Lima: 'Peru's extraordinarily cold temperature arises from the coldness of the sea.'[25] Continual measuring of the water temperature established the existence of the cold current that flows northwards along much of the western coast of South America; it was later named the Humboldt Current. Humboldt was well aware that Peruvian fishermen had long known of the current. He never claimed credit for having discovered it, nor did he himself ever refer to it by the name that has become one of his best-known legacies.

Less than two weeks later, they arrived at Guayaquil. The atmosphere was humid, the vegetation lush, and the Guayas River carried floating islands of plants and foliage—it was very picturesque, Humboldt wrote. On the day of their arrival, January 4, 1803, the distant Cotopaxi erupted, its roar audible at all hours of the day and night. Humboldt and Montúfar set off to see it up close, even though 'everybody told us that we would surely die en route, the mountains were so impenetrable.' As they travelled up the Guayas in the direction of Quito, the roar accompanied them but did not increase as they approached: the source of the noise must be subterranean, they reckoned. It was not a comfortable journey: they ran out of food because their provisions had rotted in the heat, and a snake entered their canoe—though it was expelled before Humboldt and Montúfar could effect a more precise classification than that it was probably poisonous. Just as they prepared for the most perilous part of the trip, entering the high Andes, a messenger overtook them: the *Orue*, a brigantine bound for Acapulco, was due to leave earlier than expected, on February 18. So they turned back towards Guayaquil. They were glad to have done so, since the eruption, it turned out, had amounted to no more than the expulsion of some ash. On February 17, a day earlier than expected, they were on the *Orue*, heading for Mexico. The Pacific was full of life—it was as though the sea was paved with fish. Pods of dolphins passed by, 'resembling herds of swine.' There was a plethora of birds, too: pelicans, gulls, sea swallows, so that 'the sea looked like a huge pond covered in birds.'[26]

They reached Acapulco in late March, and travelled on to Mexico City. Humboldt was about ready to go home. The idea of sailing to the Philippines was abandoned—it would, he now felt, be an immense sea journey for the sake of seeing Manila and not much more.[27] In a letter to Willdenow, he looked forward to 'embracing you all again'; in Mexico, he felt isolated, 'cut off from the rest of the world, as if on the moon.'[28] If he could, he would get back to Europe before the end of the year—but the most straightforward route, across the Atlantic from Mexico's east coast, was looking problematic: there was news of an outbreak of yellow fever in the port of Veracruz, as well as in Havana. By the autumn, crossing the Atlantic during the stormy season was notoriously dangerous. (After all, it was a shipwreck that brought disaster on Paul and Virginia.) 'I don't want to end with a tragedy,' he wrote.[29]

The time when Humboldt was prepared to risk everything had passed. His remaining stay in the Americas was relatively safe. Most of his time was spent in Mexico City, and especially in the government archives there. Mexico City was the capital of the viceroyalty of New Spain—the Spanish possessions north of the Isthmus of Panama—and its archives, to which Humboldt's Spanish passport gained him admission, contained information that he couldn't bear to leave unrecorded. There were occasional excursions, particularly to Mexico's volcanic belt. He measured the height of Mexico's most famous volcano, Popocatépetl. Visible from Mexico City, it had been continually active for centuries. El Jorullo, on the other hand, had been nothing but an indentation in a farmer's field until 1759, when, in a series of eruptions spanning a five-month period, it grew to over 1,300 metres. There were no reliable eyewitness accounts of the eruptions, and Humboldt was probably the first scientist to see the volcano.

By February 1804, the yellow fever was over, and in early March the travellers sailed from Veracruz to Havana, where the American consul, Vincent F. Gray, delivered the invitation to visit the United States.

Humboldt's recent stay in New Spain, together with the geographic and economic information he had collated in Mexico City, was of great interest to the American government—particularly in light of the Louisiana Purchase in 1803. By buying from France a huge swathe of land west of the Mississippi, President Jefferson had managed to double the size of the country. The United States now shared a long border, still disputed in parts, with Spain.

Humboldt, for his part, was always alive to the possibility of a potentially useful connection or an interesting experience. On a practical level, too, the change of route had advantages: travelling across the Atlantic from Philadelphia would mean that he could sail directly to France, whereas from Spanish Cuba, he would have had to travel via Spain, which might have embroiled him in political complications he wished to avoid.[30]

When Humboldt and his fellow travellers arrived in Philadelphia in mid-May, they were welcomed into the American Philosophical Society and shown the natural history collection of the painter and naturalist Charles Willson Peale, which housed the bones of a mastodon that had been found in New York. Humboldt, Bonpland, and Montúfar travelled on to Washington, and in early June were received in the White House for a 'very elegant dinner.'[31] Peale recorded that the talk was not of politics, but of natural history.

In late June, Humboldt and his companions said their goodbyes. They boarded their ship, sailed down the Delaware River, and out onto the Atlantic.

23

The Mind Made Visible

᠅

On August 3, 1804, Humboldt arrived in Bordeaux. After more than five years, he was back in Europe. Not only was he transformed—'healthier, stronger, and more keen to work than ever'—but he was also laden with treasure of all sorts. There were thirty boxes of samples, as well as botanical, astronomical, and geological data. But that was not all: 'I have collected in all directions,' he wrote, 'and have gathered psychological treasure, too.' He had gained a deep knowledge of the countries he had seen, by allowing himself to become deeply entangled with them. He would point out proof of that entanglement, like a badge of honour, until the end of his life, rarely failing to point out, for example, that his all-but-illegible writing was the consequence of chilly nights spent on the banks of the Orinoco. His findings were so manifold, he announced, that 'I will need years to publish my great work.'[1]

News of Humboldt's return reached Caroline, his sister-in-law, who was staying in Paris before joining her husband in Rome, where he was serving as the Prussian envoy to the Vatican. Even though Wilhelm's life so far had followed rather more conventional lines than his brother's, he enthused in a letter to Caroline:

[W]hen I sit with my coffee on the black sofa in Rome of a Saturday evening, it does strike me that we really have done something for the Humboldt family glory. First they were sitting for God knows how long in furthest Pomerania, and now here we are—in Philadelphia, in Paris, [. . .] and in Rome.[2]

Caroline, on the other hand, felt that Alexander's commitment to Germany was not sufficiently evident. Wilhelm had quoted a letter he'd had from Alexander, to the effect that he would be content never to see the spires of Berlin again, and concluded—correctly— that once Alexander had spent some time in Paris, he might not be sufficiently motivated to move back to Prussia. Perhaps it would be a good idea, Caroline suggested, for Wilhelm to write his brother 'a serious letter about his hanging on to his German identity.'[3] Wilhelm agreed that appearances mattered: 'From his letter I can see that he is neglecting Berlin. This is in no way wise. In the eyes of the world, one has to honour one's fatherland, even though it be a sandy desert.'[4]

On August 27, Alexander arrived in Paris. Caroline reported that he was looking much less copper-coloured (*'cuivré'*) than she had been led to believe from his letters. The difference in Alexander's and Caroline's perceptions of his skin quite possibly reflected a difference in their expectations. He felt himself to be so deeply changed that it would be strange if this change didn't show itself outwardly. Caroline, however, merely observed that he was looking well and had become 'much fatter.'[5] But then she and Wilhelm had changed too, of course. As of 1803, they had made a new life for themselves in Rome. Since Alexander had said good-bye to them in Paris in the autumn of 1798, they had also had three more children, Adelheid, Gabriele, and Louise. Wilhelm wondered whether Alexander would sense the more subtle change: 'progress in the realm of inner experience has a way of escaping his notice,' he wrote to his wife.[6]

'He seems pleased to find me [in Paris],' Caroline wrote back. Alexander tended to have breakfast with her and, when he did not go out, he spent his evenings with her and her children. Bonpland and Montúfar were not invited: 'I drew the line at having his travel companions for supper, but Alexander is putting up with this.'[7] He had arrived in time for Napoleon's coronation. '[Alexander] is spending a great deal of money on his clothes,' Caroline reported to Wilhelm, mentioning that there was 'an embroidered velvet cloak'; Alexander explained, on the reverse of the letter, how 'after such a journey it won't do to look as though one had gone to the dogs.'[8]

In October, Caroline and Wilhelm's daughter Louise, just eight weeks old when Alexander had arrived in Paris, died shortly after being vaccinated. (Their oldest son, Wilhelm, had died unexpectedly the year before.) Alexander was sympathetic, of course—he had played with his newborn niece and taken enough of an interest to express the opinion, welcome or not, that 'Mathilde' would be a much better name for her. But at the little girl's death, Caroline couldn't help feeling that her brother-in-law's 'affectionate utterances' were 'more a demonstration of sentiment than real emotion.'[9] Perhaps the presence of the freshly returned explorer, in high spirits and not entirely averse to being celebrated, was not quite what she needed at the time. Alexander was busy having his drawings engraved in copper by local artists, submitting his astronomical observations to the Bureau des Longitudes ('they are finding them very, very exact'), and giving a series of talks at the Académie des sciences, where the renowned scientists Claude-Louis Berthollet and Pierre-Simon Laplace were in an auditorium that was, he reported, 'crammed full whenever I read.'[10]

On Christmas Day, Caroline and her children left for Rome. Alexander followed at the end of April 1805. He arrived at the Prussian residence, the Palazzo Tomati, with a new friend in tow, the twenty-seven-year-old chemist Joseph Louis Gay-Lussac. Caroline wasn't altogether keen. 'I think we'll give him the top floor,' she suggested to her husband, in what was clearly an exercise in damage limitation. 'As he'll be much engaged with doing chemistry, it'll be good to have him near the kitchen. Perhaps would it even be an idea to get the little kitchen up and running, so he can go about his business at least in a makeshift sort of way?'[11]

Alexander's thoughts had been turning towards the preparation of his scientific results for publication. In January 1805, Johann

Friedrich Cotta, publisher of both Schiller and Goethe, had been in touch with a view to publishing an account of the American journey. Alexander responded that he should be delighted to enter into business with somebody who was 'the friend of his friends,' referencing Cotta's two most prominent authors. There was also a previous, tenuous connection that existed through Alexander's contribution of 'The Life Force' to Schiller's journal *The Horae*, which was published by Cotta. Schiller did not repay Alexander's confidence: he advised, when Cotta consulted him, that Alexander was not much of a writer, and indeed that 'his journey may have easily been more interesting than the description of the same was likely to turn out.'[12] Alexander, naturally unaware of this, announced to Cotta that he planned to dedicate the work to Schiller—but Schiller died not long after, in May 1805, and that put an end to that.

When Alexander had first intimated to Caroline that writing up the results of his journey might take years rather than months, even she could see that this was ambitious: 'he'll need five to six years at the very least.'[13] Soon, Alexander estimated that he'd need two years just to order his material. The more he worked on his task, the bigger it became, and, over the years that followed, it became increasingly clear that the work was in essence impossible to complete. In Rome, he started on a more self-contained project, a small treatise on the distribution of plants across the globe—a topic on which he had already talked at the Académie des sciences in Paris. The resulting *Essay on the Geography of Plants* (*Ideen zu einer Geographie der Pflanzen*) was published in 1807 (simultaneously in French and in German).

Among the boxes Alexander von Humboldt had brought back with him was also some material that he had collected especially for his brother: descriptions of American languages, several books of grammar, everything he had been able to lay his hands on. He had also collated lists of words throughout his travels—those from the Chaima language were particularly extensive. He had in mind that, in the publication of the results of his journey, Wilhelm should produce the section on languages. The idea seemed natural enough: Wilhelm had taken up the study of several languages, though he had abandoned each in turn. In Rome, he had been preoccupied with Greek and Latin, but had got distracted by his fascination with the Basque language; in 1803, he had announced that his work on Basque was about to be finished (but it never was). By the time Alexander arrived in Rome, Wilhelm had, serendipitously, become interested in South American languages. This was the result of an encounter with the Jesuit Lorenzo Hervás y Panduro, who had extensive collections of material on American languages.

While Wilhelm thus seemed perfectly primed, he turned out to be deeply unsuited to the task—because, in effect, his approach to the study of languages was not altogether unlike that of Alexander to the study of nature. Instead of applying himself to a single language, or group of languages, Wilhelm was interested in connections and comparisons. Just as Alexander was convinced that there was little point in observing and cataloguing phenomena if one didn't then use the results to find hidden, underlying connections and structures, for Wilhelm, language pointed beyond itself: it held the key to a people's deepest and most distinctive attributes—the soul of a nation. While Wilhelm worked for a while, on and off, on a chapter that sought to amalgamate Alexander's material with that of Hervás, he finally gave up for good in 1826, after which he went on to develop interests in Egyptian, Chinese, and Sanskrit.

Also staying at the Palazzo Tomati at the time was August Wilhelm Schlegel, who was trailing Germaine de Staël-Holstein as a tutor of her children, and possibly also as her lover. Napoleon had not cared for Madame de Staël's criticism of him; besides having her books pulped, he also banned her physically from coming within 30 miles of Paris. The consolidation of his power, which had culminated in his recent coronation, had made it advisable for Madame de Staël to remove herself from France for a while. Wilhelm von Humboldt was unenthusiastic to see her: 'at every opportunity, come she must,' he complained to his wife.[14]

As mentioned, August Wilhelm Schlegel had married Caroline Böhmer after her disastrous involvement in the failed Mainz Republic. However, in Jena, where Schlegel had obtained a professorship in 1798, Caroline had fallen in love with the university's other recent acquisition, the philosopher Friedrich Schelling. (Through the intercession of Goethe, who had been taken with Schelling's ideas of a joint, organic structure underlying both nature and the self, he had been appointed extraordinary professor of philosophy at Jena in 1798, at only twenty-three years of age.)

In 1803, the Schlegels divorced, and Caroline went on to marry Schelling. Schlegel entered into a short-lived liaison with Sophie Bernardi, a writer and the sister of the Romantic poet Ludwig Tieck. She soon left him for another man, though, and Schlegel's legacy from the affair consisted mostly of repeated pleas for financial assistance from Sophie.

His employment by Madame de Staël, which saved him from money worries and conveniently took him out of the reach of his former entanglements, was a welcome safe haven. Wilhelm, who would have preferred to host an unencumbered Schlegel in Rome, complained to Goethe that his friend 'had, through his dealings with de Staël, gained less in versatility than he had lost in activity.'[15] Still, that didn't stop Schlegel and Alexander from applying a geological eye to the treasures of antiquity, establishing, for example, that the lions on the Capitoline Hill were made neither of basalt nor porphyry, as had been widely assumed, but were instead made of 'hornblende with enclosures of feldspar.'[16] This allowed the inference that the stone for the lions had originated in Egypt, as opposed to being Greek or Roman, as Goethe (who liked to think of classical forms as having arisen in their original setting) had preferred to think.

Friedrich Schelling also got in touch with Alexander von Humboldt around this time. He had heard that Humboldt was potentially well disposed towards his new system of *Naturphilosophie* (philosophy of nature), and was hoping that the support of his newly famous friend-of-friends might help his own standing. His theory, he wrote, had been much misunderstood; *Naturphilosophie* had been accused of spurning the empirical. No natural scientist, however, he protested, had yet taken the trouble to understand his system as an integrated whole.[17]

Nature philosophy attempted to draw laws for the natural sciences from a priori principles. Schelling picked up on Kant's refusal to deal with biology, whose status as a science the latter had denied, declaring it an area unfit for philosophical investigation. The Romantic view of biology was different, and contrasted sharply with Newton's mechanistic understanding of nature (from which Goethe had instinctively recoiled): nature was recognised as a living entity with agency of its own, rather than a passive object. Biology had, for the Romantics, risen from a non-science to the status of the most relevant of the sciences. Nature was equivalent to the self, and was thus governed by the same laws and forces. With both constructed along organic lines, the study both of nature and of the self would, eventually, reveal the same truths. This merging of objective nature and subjective self constituted the core of the Romantic project. As for naturalists, aesthetic understanding was not, in the Romantic view, a hindrance, but rather a valuable asset for revealing the secrets of both nature and one's own self.[18]

Humboldt was interested in principle: 'what should be more apt to attract my attention than a revolution of those sciences to which I have devoted my whole life?'[19] He sensed that Schelling might be getting at something that he himself had been grasping at for years: 'Vacillating between theories based on excitability ["animal electricity"] and those based on chemistry, I've always intuited that there must be something better and higher, something that all of this can be traced back to.'[20] It was Schelling who had claimed that there was a unity between nature and the self, saying, 'As long as I myself am identical with nature, I understand what living nature is as well as I understand myself.'[21] A particularly ringing statement by Schelling—'Nature should be Mind made visible'[22]—similarly seemed to justify treating the self as the most reliable measure of nature. If all empirical observations pointed to an underlying principle, then it should, hypothetically, also be possible to move in the opposite direction, by drawing inferences from this principle to shed light on empirical reality. However, Humboldt cautioned against overstretching this latter point by forgoing empirical observation, since (for now) the underlying principle remained essentially indefinable. People should not 'practise chemistry by resorting to the power of their brains, as opposed to getting their hands wet.'[23] Still, Humboldt's cautiously positive answer was enthusiastically received, and a friend duly congratulated Schelling for having 'won this man for us.'[24]

In July 1805, Alexander was off to Naples with Gay-Lussac, to see Vesuvius at last ('but the cost!' sighed Wilhelm).[25] They were there during the great earthquake of July 26, which destroyed large parts of Naples; Wilhelm thought that their escape was almost miraculous, but Alexander's account registers hardly any surprise. Vesuvius itself was as a hill compared to the majesty of Cotopaxi—'like an asteroid appears next to Saturn.'[26]

Kunth, the brothers' old tutor, had been writing intermittently, mostly through Wilhelm, remonstrating with Alexander for neglecting his finances, as well as squandering goodwill from Berlin. Knowing that Kunth was right, Alexander returned to Berlin in November 1805. Things went smoothly: he was appointed royal chamberlain, elected a member of the Berlin Academy of Sciences, and allocated a yearly salary of 2,500 thalers. His almost immediate response was to develop a skin complaint, a measles-like outbreak. Otherwise, his first winter in Berlin was spent pretending he was elsewhere, writing down his observations on crocodiles and sending them to the zoologist Georges Cuvier in Paris, and telling people that he'd be off again soon—though he couldn't decide between the North Pole and Central Asia.[27]

In October 1806, Napoleon's victory in the twin battles of Jena and Auerstedt resulted in the comprehensive defeat of Prussia, the occupation of Berlin, the flight of King Friedrich Wilhelm III to East Prussia, and the effective trapping, for the time being, of

Humboldt in Berlin. Among the many who had died in battle was Prince Louis Ferdinand of Prussia, who had been the most illustrious member of Rahel Levin's circle, and the lover of Pauline Wiesel— who herself was a friend of both Rahel and Humboldt. Prince Louis had been killed in a preliminary engagement with the enemy— trying to intercept Napoleon's army on the way to Berlin—at Saalfeld (known to Humboldt from his days as mining inspector).

With the French occupation, and Prussia's fortunes so radically changed, Rahel Levin tried to keep her mind on matters close at hand. 'We have mild weather, and that puts everyone in a better mood: saves firewood, and is a blessing for the poor,' she mused.[28] 'We are living very cheerfully this winter, mainly because we don't know whether it will be our last cheerful one.'[29] But there was no escaping the fact that the atmosphere had turned, with feelings of nationalism and antisemitism on the rise. Rahel considered going to Paris, and perhaps on to Amsterdam if necessary; Humboldt, who spent most evenings at her house, often reading to her assorted guests, suggested (unrealistically, of course) that they should all go and live in the Canaries. Meanwhile, all present (including Pauline Wiesel) had made the switch from tea—formerly the 'only refreshment' Rahel had prided herself on serving at her salons—to beer.[30]

To his publisher, Cotta, Humboldt wrote, 'why didn't I stay on the Orinoco, or on the high ridge of the Andes!'[31] But since he had committed himself, for the time being, to a 'sadly isolated life' in Berlin, he settled down to write his book *Views of Nature* (*Ansichten der Natur*).[32] This is a thoughtfully conceived selection of the most memorable and vivid scenes of his travels, free of scientific observation, for the common reader. To Cotta, he explained that he wanted to deliver a book in the vein of Bernardin de Saint-Pierre's *Paul and Virginia*. Of course, *Views of Nature* is not a love story, nor even fiction, and still it is not the sort of book one would expect from arguably the foremost scientist of his day. Humboldt's involvement with the Romantics had not only retained its grip on him, but the Romantic influence had been transmuted into something new. The interest closest to his heart was the interplay of nature with the human aesthetic and moral imagination. In the foreword to *Views of Nature*, Humboldt wrote about the importance of appealing to 'feelings and fancy,' and about the connection between nature and 'the moral disposition of Humanity.'[33] To this end, he invited his readers to follow him 'into the thickets of the forest, into the immeasurable steppes, and out upon the spine of the Andes range.'[34] With Prussia having turned into a much smaller, less important, and more oppressive place, his audience was more than ready to let itself be carried away by Humboldt's vivid descriptions of countries that seemed further out of reach than ever. *Views of Nature* was a great popular success, and it remained Humboldt's own favourite book among all his works—he kept updating and publishing it in new editions into his eightieth year.

In November 1807, Humboldt was chosen to assist Prince Wilhelm, a younger brother of King Friedrich Wilhelm III, on a mission to Paris, to try and negotiate relief from the punitive payments Prussia was obliged to pay according to the terms of the Treaty of Tilsit. Prince Wilhelm returned home, without much success, after a few months; Humboldt stayed on for another twenty years. He would not return to live in Berlin until 1827.

In Paris, Humboldt moved addresses with some frequency, often living with specialists drafted in to help with a particular field. With Gay-Lussac, who was commissioned to help with the chemical aspects of the publications, he shared a damp apartment in the École polytechnique. Later, he cohabited with a young German botanist, Carl Sigismund Kunth, the nephew of his old tutor. But Humboldt's closest friend and collaborator in Paris was the mathematician and astronomer François Arago, who was sixteen years his junior. Arago helped with the analysis of Humboldt's astronomical findings. His personality and scientific approach were both congenial to Humboldt. Arago placed great value on a personal engagement with science. He had been involved in the project of measuring the meridian line through France, and, when he wrote about the experience in his

History of My Youth (1854), he related several instances where he had almost died: like Humboldt, he believed that it was impossible to engage with research without laying one's own body on the line if necessary. Arago's position as director of the Bureau des longitudes, and his involvement with the Académie des sciences and the Observatoire de Paris (whose director he later became), put Humboldt in the center of Parisian scientific life.

Humboldt had planned to first provide a narrative of his travels for the general reader, before presenting the scientific results in a series of volumes, each one dedicated to a different discipline. In the event, the first volume of *Personal Narrative of a Journey to the Equinoctial Regions of the New Continent* wasn't published until 1814; the scientific publications appeared, for a while, in quick succession. After the *Essay on the Geography of Plants* in 1807, there followed papers on the cinchona forests of South America (also in 1807); on the respiration of fishes, and on the Casiquiare canal as a connection between the Orinoco and the Amazon (both in 1809). Bonpland, it had been agreed, would look after the botanical content of the publications. This worked well in the beginning, with Bonpland delivering his contributions to the *Essay on the Geography of Plants* without any problems. By 1810, however, things had deteriorated. 'I plead with you again, my dear Bonpland,' Humboldt was reduced to writing, 'to help bring to a conclusion a matter that is of great importance for the sciences [. . .]. I ask you to deliver manuscripts; for your assurances won't further the matter.'[35]

It had become clear that Bonpland's enthusiasm and reliability in the field was not matched by a comparable zeal when he was placed behind a desk. In any case, the time he could spend behind a desk was limited, as he had a new job: he had been appointed gardener to the French empress Joséphine—in fact, this had been achieved with the help of a recommendation from Humboldt. It was an absorbing and fulfilling occupation, especially after Napoleon divorced Joséphine in 1810, which saw her retreat to the Château de Malmaison, and Bonpland elevated to scientific manager of Malmaison and another chateau, Navarre in Normandy. In Malmaison's grand and ambitious gardens, he grew a number of plants from seeds that he had brought back from the Americas. It was partly thanks to his work that Malmaison and Navarre became the foremost centres for cultivation of rare plants in France.

After it had become clear that it was futile to expect more contributions from Bonpland, Humboldt's old friend and teacher Willdenow stepped in, but he died shortly after, in 1812, and Carl Sigismund Kunth took over.

The project of publishing the scientific findings of Humboldt's great journey had a way of slowly and inexorably eating up his finances. He was singularly unsuited to the idea of making a profit. While refusing on principle to take advances for his publications, he paid generous wages to draughtsmen and engravers, drawing heavily on what was left of his inheritance. By 1809, Wilhelm estimated that his brother owed around 16,000 thalers. Alexander's combined income from his position of Prussian chamberlain and member of the Académie des sciences in Paris amounted to only about 5,000 thalers per year, so his way of life was often met with incomprehension by those with more practical natures. His sister-in-law, Caroline, was certainly unimpressed with the order of his priorities: 'Where, then, is the great bounty that is supposed to spring from his works? I fear that his so-called friends in Paris will come to cost him dear. We know his good nature. He will eat dry bread, so that they can have roast.'[36] While Caroline was clearly preoccupied with money and respectability, her brother-in-law did not reject either on principle. But neither did such considerations seem important enough for him to compromise the way he lived his life.

24

A Different Life

❧❦

In the summer of 1813, Caroline von Humboldt opened a letter from Alexander. It announced a gift for her and Wilhelm, and indeed for the whole family—an heirloom. She would like it, her brother-in-law felt sure: 'the present is my picture, life-size.' It would be executed by Carl von Steuben, a young man with whom, he explained, he was now spending time 'every day.' The portrait would show him leaning on a low group of basalt columns, pen and paper in hand, 'in a very simple and natural attitude.' The likeness was extraordinary—'as if stolen from the mirror.' After all, 'I'm growing older all the time, and, if I want to have myself painted among snowy mountain-tops, it won't do to let more time pass.'

Wilhelm reacted with composure. He told Caroline that, 'even though it's only by Steuben [. . .] it'll at least give some sort of impression of Alexander; and we do love him very much, and will always like his image.' The likeness, he admitted, when they eventually received the painting, was not particularly striking. Still, he thought the colouring was nice, and if a greater verisimilitude had been achieved, such a portrait 'would indeed be commendable.'[1]

Alexander's preference, of course, would have been to be among the mountains, snowy or otherwise, in person. But while the pull of the distant never loosened its grip, it was not any particular place that drew him. The most important feature of any destination, once again, was simply that it was far from Europe—and, more specifically, far from Berlin. In January 1812, Alexander had proposed a Siberian research trip to the Russian government, conceived to last six to eight years. Wilhelm, on the other hand, was under the impression that his brother was shortly going to set off to Tibet. However, that same year, Alexander was also taking lessons in Persian. A letter to a friend describes what feels like an almost desperate grasp at the map: 'I'd like to spend a year in Benares; if I can't get to Bukhara or Tibet, I could then go on to the Indian peninsula, the coasts of Malacca, the isle of Ceylon, Java, or the Philippines.'[2] To Goethe, he wrote, simply, that he longed for 'the wide and the blue.'[3]

But Alexander von Humboldt was being pulled, at the same time, towards Berlin. Karl August von Hardenberg had already, in 1810, offered him the directorship of the cultural and scientific institutions of Berlin, with the prospect of becoming minister—an offer that Alexander had declined. But in Paris, after the fall of the First Empire in 1814, Humboldt found himself uncomfortably between camps. While allied troops occupied the city, he had negotiated with the Prussian commanders to prevent soldiers from being billeted at the Muséum national d'histoire naturelle; more controversially, he also argued that columns taken by Napoleon from Cologne Cathedral should stay in the Louvre rather than be returned, which earned him accusations of being unpatriotic. It would have been a good moment to show his allegiance to Germany—or this, at any rate, is what Wilhelm and Caroline thought. But receiving letters from Germany, and more so being a Prussian in Paris, was fraught with the suspicion of others, and Alexander found himself, as he'd written to Caroline, 'as isolated as on the Orinoco.'[4] But when Hardenberg made another attempt to get him back into the Prussian civil service, this time as Prussian envoy to Paris, Humboldt turned that down, too.

In the autumn of 1817, Wilhelm accepted a position as Prussian envoy to London. Alexander, who had been elected a Fellow of the Royal Society only the year before, took the chance to visit him almost straight away, in November. He didn't, however, stay in the ambassadorial residence. Wilhelm, slightly piqued, wrote to Caroline that a room had already been prepared, but, 'you know his passion for always having a person around who, for the moment, is his favourite. Now he's got an astronomer, Arago; he refuses to be separated from him; to host both of them, while physically possible, would have been very inconvenient for me.' In Wilhelm's view, his brother had aged greatly, and had put on weight, too. What was particularly regrettable, however, was how '[Alexander] has ceased being German and, in almost every detail, has become Parisian.'[5] During Alexander's time in London, he tried to obtain a travel permit to India; however, this proved harder than he had expected. But the weather was mild and the skies clear, and so he and Arago ended up spending much of their time at the Royal Observatory at Greenwich.

To get a truthful idea of a person, Alexander von Humboldt wrote to his brother a little while later, it was necessary to know their 'landscape, the background'—their own particular habitat.[6] While Alexander's 'background' was still not satisfactorily resolved, others seemed to know theirs. August Wilhelm Schlegel, free again after the death of his patron, Madame de Staël, in 1817, had absented himself—albeit only in his mind—to India, and immersed himself in the study of Sanskrit. One of the fruits of his labours was a treatise on the elephant in mythology, literature, art, and sculpture. He sent a copy to Alexander, who went on to refer to it, in a historical section of the second volume of *Cosmos*.[7]

The fate of Carlos Montúfar (who had come with Humboldt to Europe in 1804) had been short and glittering. In 1810, Montúfar had returned to South America, where he joined the independence movement. He took over the defence of the newly-declared Republic of Quito; however, the city fell to the Spanish and he had to flee, spending time hiding in the Chillos Valley. He was captured, managed to escape, and joined Simón Bolívar's army as assistant general. His side was defeated by Spanish forces in the battle of Cuchilla del Tambo in 1816, he was captured again (alongside his old rival Francisco José Caldas), and executed.

Bonpland's thoughts, after Joséphine died in 1814, also turned to the Americas, and he began announcing his intention of returning there. He was unable to depart immediately—there were finances to sort out and connections to be made. But there was also the matter of his wife, Adeline, who, apparently, was still married to somebody else, and had to wait for her divorce to become official. (Relatively little is known about Adeline, and about the exact circumstances of her marriage to Bonpland.) So when Bonpland arrived in Buenos Aires in February 1817, it was with Adeline, her daughter Emma, two assistants, 200 books destined for a botanical library (this never came to pass), and more than 2,000 living plants—different kinds of pasture grasses, vegetables, medicinal plants, and samples of every sour-fruit tree native to France. Just before his departure, in November 1816, he had written to Humboldt, 'If I do not succeed, I shall stay there buried on some hill or other, or in a beautiful valley.'[8] And indeed, he would never return to France.

In 1820, after working as a professor and having tried several business ventures in Buenos Aires (with varying success), Bonpland settled in the province of Corrientes, not far from Paraguay, with the idea of commercially growing yerba mate. It was while he was trying to establish a settlement that he fell foul of José Gaspar de Francia, the dictator of Paraguay—who saw him as an unwelcome interloper whose commercial success threatened Paraguay's economy. In 1821, Francia's soldiers attacked the settlement, massacred the indigenous population, and captured Bonpland. He would remain a prisoner for almost a decade, even though, over the years, there were various efforts to set him free. At Humboldt's instigation, Simón Bolívar wrote to Francia, with the hope of seeing 'this best of men and most celebrated of travellers' given his freedom. Humboldt also tried to send messages to Francia, but to no avail.

Even though Bonpland suffered repressive measures (in 1822, for example, Francia had all his books and instruments seized), for a prisoner, he was given some liberties. Making the best of his circumstances, he grew tobacco, ran a distillery, a carpentry shop and a forge, eventually employing forty-five people. In 1829, Francia, mysteriously, decided to give Bonpland his freedom; however it was not until early 1831 that he was actually released. By the time of Bonpland's death, in 1858, aged eighty-four, he had been remarried, and there were reports of several 'natural children,' all of whom Bonpland acknowledged.

For Humboldt, towards the end of 1818, it looked as though the door to the world was opening again after all: King Friedrich Wilhelm III promised to fund a scientific journey to India. Details had been agreed. Humboldt was to purchase all the scientific instruments he thought necessary, and hand them over to the state on his return. However, the East India Company withheld permission, and the plan came to nothing. In 1823, there was a new project: Mexico had achieved independence from Spain in 1821. Now would be the perfect time for a research institute in Mexico City, to open the country up to scientific investigation. Such a project held the additional attraction that it would 'not exclude a journey to the Philippines and Bengal'; indeed, such a detour would be 'a very short trip.'[9] The financing of all this, however, remained hazy, and, in the autumn of 1824, Caroline wrote to Wilhelm: 'between ourselves, I don't really believe in this second journey of his.'[10]

Three years later, the gravitational force of Berlin finally won out: the king personally recalled his errant chamberlain.[11] This was very much *not* what Humboldt wanted. The writer and diplomat Karl August Varnhagen von Ense, who had married Rahel Levin during Humboldt's years in Paris, became one of his closest confidants in Berlin. Varnhagen immediately saw that, as far as Europe was concerned, Paris was Humboldt's ideal habitat: 'Paris is the right place for him, and he will be sure to return there.'[12] But Humboldt was dependent on his salary as a chamberlain, which, by way of sweetening the pill, had been doubled to 5,000 thalers annually. In a particularly accommodating arrangement, he was also given leave to spend four months a year in Paris.

In the spring of 1827, Humboldt travelled to Berlin by the long route, via London, where he spent time at Greenwich and Kew, was invited to a dinner given by the British statesman George Canning, and descended (accompanied by the engineer Isambard Kingdom Brunel) to the bottom of the Thames in a diving bell.[13] The new Prussian ambassador in London was Heinrich von Bülow, who was married to Wilhelm and Caroline's daughter Gabriele.

Alexander von Humboldt, now fifty-seven years old, arrived in Berlin in May 1827. He moved into rooms in the centre of Berlin, on what is today's Museumsinsel. The address, Hinter dem Neuen Packhof 4, was far from glamorous—the place had been an industrial area, and warehouses and arsenals were only slowly making way for homes. Humboldt lived up some stairs, where he shared his household with Johann and Emilie Seifert, a married couple who looked after him and would do so for the rest of his life.

In November, Humboldt held a series of lectures on physical geography at the University of Berlin. They proved so popular that he felt compelled to look for a bigger venue, which he found in the new concert hall, the Singakademie. The aim of the lectures he gave between December 1827 and April 1828, as in the case of his book *Views of Nature*, was to share the impressions made on him by the natural world of the Americas with as wide an audience as possible. (It was August Wilhelm Schlegel, also in Berlin, who had pioneered the popularisation of academic subjects by means of the public lecture.[14]) The notion that most people, while perhaps unable to comprehend the finer points of Humboldt's scientific findings, would still be able to grasp their essence through their emotional response, was essentially a Romantic one. The wide dissemination of ideas presupposes the existence of a common underlying understanding that is universal to all people, and Humboldt was proud of the diversity of his listeners—which included men and women, and, as he put it, 'king and bricklayer.'[15] The poet Karl von Holtci, who was in the audience in the Singakademie, wrote to Goethe: 'Such an audience has, I think, never been gathered before the lectern of a man of learning. The king, the whole of the court, the highest members of the administration and the military plus their ladies, all the scholars, the important artists, the whole belle monde.'[16] It was not just the evocative descriptions of a strange and distant natural world but also the scientific aspects of the lectures that caught the public imagination: a lady who had been in the audience, so the story went, asked her tailor to make the sleeves of her new dress 'twice the width of the star Sirius.'

A special commemorative coin was minted to mark the occasion, featuring a relief portrait of Humboldt by the artist Friedrich Tieck on one side, and allegorical representations of nature, fashioned by the sculptor Christian Daniel Rauch, on the other. After an honour such as this, Humboldt quipped, there was really nothing left to do but to die.[17] Humboldt did not oblige quite yet, however. Instead, he travelled to Russia.

The Russian journey, in 1829, came about quite unexpectedly. The Russian finance minister Georg von Cancrin was in need of mineralogical advice. In the Urals, large deposits of alluvial platinum had been discovered, and Cancrin was wondering about its commercial potential—in particular, he thought that it might be turned into a new coinage. Humboldt was sceptical, but went anyway. Now that Russia was a distinct possibility, the idea of seeing the Urals grew on him.

Russia would be a return to travelling in a minor key, a far cry from his departure for the Americas thirty years earlier. Then he was able to travel freely, follow his inclinations, throw over his plans at short notice, and put his life in danger if he so wished. Now he was in his sixtieth year, and conscious that, as a representative of the government, he would be constrained by protocol and a tight schedule.

Just before he was due to leave, in March 1829, Caroline died. Alexander had been with her and Wilhelm only two days before, when she had been on her deathbed, but he thought she was showing signs of rallying, or so he had told Rahel Levin Varnhagen. Now, Alexander worried about his brother, alone in Tegel, and talked his journey to Russia down, referring to it as a 'summer trip.'[18]

He was off in April. The roads became worse the further they moved east, with their carriage often sinking wheel-deep into the icy puddles. Humboldt was obliged to take a more passive part than he would have liked, and was often confined to his carriage for lengthy periods of time. Generally, he was just a little bit too well looked after: 'there is a constant greeting, riding, and driving ahead by the police and officials, there are Cossack guards! But unfortunately there is not a moment to be by oneself; not a step, without being led by the arm, just like a sick person!'[19] And, later, 'I am being suffocated with civilities.'[20] From Petersburg, and then from Moscow, he wrote of his longing for fresh air and mountains. Siberia, when they got there, was geologically interesting, but disappointing in terms of plant and animal life. 'A Siberian journey,' he wrote, 'is not lovely in the way that a South American one is; but you feel you have done something useful, and have covered a lot of ground.'[21] He was back in Berlin in late December, after a journey lasting some eight months.

Even though the king's condition that Humboldt be no more than four months per year in Paris had been removed, he was spending more time in Berlin, mainly to be near Wilhelm. In March 1832, Goethe died. Rahel Levin Varnhagen, one of the great poet's earliest and most steadfast admirers, had once been instrumental in bolstering his popularity in Berlin, by the expedient of publishing a selection of letters (expressing admiration for Goethe) she had exchanged with her husband, Varnhagen. Now, Varnhagen asked Wilhelm for help with editing a book about Goethe. But neither Varnhagen nor Rahel were particularly well that winter: 'I hear with some pain,' wrote Alexander, 'that you and your brilliant friend [that is, Rahel] possess only a small bit of health between you, which you, ever polite, are taking turns to lend to each other.'[22] Rahel was in fact seriously ill, and died shortly after, in March 1833. Alexander wrote to Varnhagen that 'the world will seem bleak to you for a long time.'[23]

Just a few months before, Alexander von Humboldt's publisher, Johann Friedrich Cotta, had died too. Perhaps these losses suggested to him that it might be time to concentrate on the book he considered the synthesis of all that he had done. The aim of *Cosmos*, 'my life's work,' as Humboldt called it, was to pull together everything that mattered to him about his approach to science.[24] The book's deepest concern was to be the investigation of common forces and structures underlying different phenomena—it was to emphasise that phenomena should not be looked at in isolation. A mass of different observations would be brought together, to establish a reliable picture of the state of knowledge of different branches of science. Connections were then to be made between different sorts of observations; for example, to establish how plants were distributed across the globe according to such factors as distance from the equator, or altitude. And beyond that, on an even higher level, there was Humboldt's overarching aim: to unite scientific enquiry with aesthetic and emotional perception. *Cosmos* was going to 'represent nature as one great whole, moved and animated by internal forces.'[25] His vision was lofty: the work would take in 'the remotest nebulous spots, and the revolving double stars in the regions of space.'[26] Presenting his schedule to Varnhagen, in late 1833, he still thought that two volumes would be sufficient to cover all that he wanted to say.[27]

The duties of a chamberlain and trusted friend of the Prussian king were not conducive to finishing *Cosmos* quickly, however. The rhythm of Humboldt's life was dictated by the pleasure of Friedrich Wilhelm III, and Humboldt moved as though 'by the swing of an eternal pendulum'—joining the king during a 'boring stay in Potsdam' at the summer residence of Charlottenhof, when not following him to Paretz, 'a private possession of the king's in a boring part of the Havel country.'[28] Retreating to Humboldt's own rooms in the royal residence was a rare privilege.

On April 8, 1835, Wilhelm von Humboldt died. According to Alexander's telling of the event, he did so in what must pass for an exemplary fashion. A few days before his death, only intermittently conscious, he expressed his joy at soon being reunited with Caroline. On the day itself, he declaimed some verses from the *Iliad*, before dying in the evening. Alexander felt exposed and lonely, the leftover brother. He began almost immediately to prepare three of his brother's unfinished manuscripts on linguistics for publication. There was also an exchange of letters by Wilhelm, which eventually appeared as 'Letters to a Woman Friend.' They chronicle the curious friendship between Wilhelm and Charlotte Diede, whom he had once met when very young, just for a day. Their fates had diverged after the encounter, but when Wilhelm was ambassador in Rome, she had applied to him for financial assistance, which he gave. Thereafter, they maintained a correspondence for thirty years. Alexander thought it was all perfectly innocuous: 'all in all, I suppressed less than three to four pages' worth—cakes, domestic detail, a few rants by Diede against the duke of Brunswick.'[29]

When King Friedrich Wilhelm III died in 1840—giving Humboldt, in his own weary assessment, an 'increasing familiarity with death'—it did not improve his working conditions.[30] The successor on the throne, Friedrich Wilhelm IV, liked Humboldt's company and made him a privy councillor; but he did not, it seems, greatly value Humboldt's scientific contributions. Varnhagen put it brutally: 'he [Humboldt] is well aware that it is only his name that gives him any standing with the king, and that he is far outranked in his influence by others.'[31] Humboldt agreed that being in the king's favour was of little or no use. Favourites, he observed, 'can do nothing beyond detecting conceits and foibles, and nurturing those with self-sacrificial devotion—but should they want something that went into a different direction, they would fall out of favour straight away.'[32]

In 1841, Humboldt was asked to read Schelling's essay on nature and art to the king, but he was not confident that much was achieved by the exercise: 'the lecture made the same sort of impression on the king as some lovely music would have done.'[33] By that time, Humboldt himself was done with Schelling. In 1834, he had tried to obtain a position for the philosopher at the University of Berlin (by now known as Friedrich-Wilhelms-Universität) but the friendship had cooled, mostly because his misgivings about Schelling's disregard for empirical evidence had increased.

The rooms in Berlin's Oranienburger Straße into which Humboldt moved in 1842, together with Johann and Emilie Seifert and their children, were his last address. It had been chosen primarily for economical reasons, and he was not hugely enamoured of it, at least not at first. As he told Varnhagen with distaste, he had moved 'into vulgar rooms in the Siberian quarter, the Oranienburger Straße!'[34] Later, the Mendelssohn family, his old friends, bought the house, because they were worried at his steadily worsening financial situation, and wanted to relieve him of the expense of the rent. Varnhagen, who visited, found that Humboldt lived in something like a small tropical environment of his own. His study in Oranienburger Straße was heated to a temperature Varnhagen found 'intolerable'; the room also appears to have harboured a live chameleon.[35] Humboldt's private rooms in Charlottenhof, too, seemed to not quite be in Prussia: pieces of fabric were pinned up in folds across the bed, re-creating the impression of the inside of a tent.[36] He took to signing his letters 'Old Man of the Hills,' or 'Vecchio della Montagna,' signalling a certain detachment from his surroundings, and a kinship to a different realm.[37]

When Humboldt was ill in early 1844, people were quick to jump to conclusions. Carl Gustav Carus, the painter and physiologist, dispatched a letter to the sculptor Christian Daniel Rauch, asking him to take possession of Humboldt's skull. Rauch took the letter to Humboldt, who replied that, while for the moment he still had use for his skull himself, he would be happy to be of service at a later point. But there was a sense of Humboldt's time running out. 'I am about to celebrate, alas, my seventy-fifth birthday,' he wrote later that year. 'I say "alas" because in 1789 I believed the world would have seen the solution of a few more problems. I have seen much, but compared to what I wanted, only very little.'[38]

The first volume of *Cosmos* appeared in 1845, and in 1847 a second volume followed. Two years later, now working on the third volume (which would be published in 1851), Humboldt was convinced that this would now be the last.[39] The material seemed to grow, however, and in 1852, it was clear that a fourth volume would be needed ('or I would have had to cover earth and the heavens in one volume, which would have been impossible'). Then, in 1857, the fourth volume burst its bounds, and Humboldt suggested dividing it into two instalments. It was 'a screw without end.'[40] Johann Georg Cotta, who had succeeded his father at the Cotta publishing house, in 1858 decided instead to simply publish the fourth volume with the material that was ready, limiting it to a discussion of geognosis (which dealt with the material composition of the earth). The fifth volume of *Cosmos*, of which only ninety-five pages had been written by the time of Humboldt's death in 1859, came nowhere near to completing his plan. What was missing was not a minor matter; it was, in effect, the most interesting, and perhaps most difficult part of the whole work: his discussion of the living parts of the planet, which was to culminate with a discussion of the human population.

In 1850, Humboldt recoiled from a piece of 'dreadful news' that he had just received: 'the erection of a bust!!' If it should come to pass, he said, it would 'distress me so much that it would stop me from working for months.'[41] He meant this only half in jest: he had always felt it vital to be wholly and bodily present in what he was engaged in, to get his fingers dirty or, as he put it in his charge against the nature philosophers (foremost among them Schelling), at least wet. The idea of becoming an empty husk on a pedestal was intolerable to him. His wariness was not entirely without basis. He was increasingly assailed with petitions from all sides, which often betrayed the petitioners' complete lack of engagement with Humboldt's background or personality: people asked him where best to emigrate, which place to colonise, or sent him unsolicited advice on how to strengthen his religious faith.[42] He had become an institution, and his reputation, more often than not, stood between him and the world around him.

There were also indignities. When, at the request of King Friedrich Wilhelm, Humboldt read excerpts from his writings, the other dinner guests regularly talked over him. His voice could be monotonous, 'and, not infrequently, those who were not interested in the sciences, would fall asleep. If that happened, the king tended to be greatly amused. Humboldt would take it badly though.'[43]

By the summer of 1852, friends noticed a certain unsteadiness in Humboldt's walk, and a general slowing down, but Humboldt robustly protested that he was still able to work through the night, 'without a noticeable lessening of strength,' and could stand on his feet for eight hours or more, if necessary.[44]

In 1856, Humboldt suffered from a dermatological complaint, 'enough to make me want to shed my skin.' It was a continuous itchiness that reminded him of nothing so much as of the mosquitoes that had so afflicted him in South America. A return to the Orinoco was possible only in ironical, absurd reflections. He happened to receive, just then, a letter from one M. Foster, 'excessively Christian,' who enquired whether Humboldt believed that mosquitoes possessed souls. 'So they will bother me up there, too,' Humboldt wrote, 'all these animal souls I knew on the Orinoco—there they will all be, and singing hymns of praise, too.'[45]

At the end of that year, his niece Adelheid died; she had been four years old when he returned from the Americas. 'I bury my whole kind,' he told Varnhagen.[46] But when Varnhagen died, in the autumn of 1858, it was a shock that he did not expect: 'He, called away before me!' Humboldt wrote to Varnhagen's niece Ludmilla Assing.[47]

There was a sense that he was done. Early in 1859, he placed an advertisement in the *Vossische Zeitung*, asking, with respect, that people refrain from using him as an 'address-*comptoir*' for 'publications concerning matters I know nothing about; manuscripts for appraisal; plans for emigration or colonisation; submission of models, machines and natural produce; inquiries about aerostatics; augmentation of autographical collections; offers to look after, distract and amuse me etc.' He expressed the hope that this 'cry for help' might not be misinterpreted as a lack of feeling on his part.[48]

Alexander von Humboldt died on May 6, 1859. Some months earlier, he had received a letter from Nebraska: it was an inquiry concerning the whereabouts of the swallows in wintertime. 'A floating enquiry, surely,' Varnhagen had ventured, and Humboldt admitted that he didn't know. But to admit as much, he said, would be telling.[49]

25

'Love and Cheerfulness'

The image of Humboldt spending his last years as an increasingly lonely old man, plagued by the iniquities of old age, with his friends and family falling away one by one, does not provide the whole picture.

For thirty-two years, after his return from Paris in 1827, Humboldt lived in a shared household with the Seifert family.[1] Johann Gustav Seifert had married Emilie Caroline Thiede in October 1827, by which time he was already listed in the church register as being in Humboldt's service. Emilie (called Mila) then also entered Humboldt's employ, as his cook. Two years later, Seifert accompanied Humboldt on his Russian journey. The Seiferts went on to have five children. Two of these, it has been claimed, Caroline and Agnes, were not Johann's, but Humboldt's. What evidence there is for such an assertion must by necessity be circumstantial—but, taken as a whole, it amounts to more than can easily be dismissed.[2]

Rumours to this effect began to circulate as early as 1859, the year of Humboldt's death.[3] The most striking piece of evidence is a letter concerning Balduin Möllhausen, a traveller and writer of adventure novels about America, who married Caroline Seifert in 1855. (Möllhausen had spent several years in the American West, and befriended Humboldt in Berlin.) The letter, from Möllhausen's grandson, provides a deposition of some oral testimony entrusted by Möllhausen to his grandson. According to this document, Humboldt took Möllhausen aside and told him that his bride-to-be, as well as her younger sister Agnes, were not Johann's daughters but instead his own.[4] A copy of this letter still exists in the Möllhausen family, as do several items from Humboldt's estate.[5]

While there is nothing in Humboldt's correspondence to indicate such a relationship with comparable clarity, there are some remarks that catch the attention. When Humboldt explained to Cotta, his publisher, that he wished to leave all his material goods to the Seifert family, his choice of words seems to volunteer more information than strictly necessary: he specified the heirs as 'my servant Seifert and the many children that were sired in my house.'[6] At the christening of Caroline's first child, named Alexander, Humboldt wrote to Varnhagen to tell him that he had attended the occasion 'in a patriarchal capacity.' In the same letter, he also emphasised Caroline's beauty and talked, at some length, about Möllhausen's exploits in America and his favourable employment prospects back in Berlin.[7] To Caroline, he wrote about his joy at having 'been granted the good fortune of witnessing this celebration!'[8]

Humboldt was concerned to guarantee the financial security of the Seifert family in the event of his death, and he went to great lengths to make their position as unassailable as possible. As early as 1841, he had told his publisher that, should he die before completing *Cosmos*, Cotta should pay a sum of money to Seifert.[9] Wills in which Humboldt left all his estate to Seifert were lodged in 1841, and updated in 1854 and 1857. In 1853, he added a codicil: 'it would be quite unnecessary that anything should be sealed after [Humboldt's] death, as everything in the house was left to his servant and his family.'[10] Just five days after adding this codicil, he drew up a petition to the king (framed as a 'last favour') in which he requested that, on his death, what remained of his debt to the Mendelssohn banking house be written off ('I hope it will not exceed one year's income'). That way the Seiferts' inheritance would not be swallowed up by the repayment of the debt from his estate.[11]

The careful and thorough manner in which Humboldt proceeded suggests that he was aware that Seifert's position was precarious, and that the inheritance might easily be contested.[12] He went to the trouble of writing a letter to Seifert (who, after all, lived under the same roof as him), to confirm that a sum of money that he had given him was rightfully his. In the same letter, he reiterated that he was leaving 'all my material goods' to Seifert—'and, after your death, to your heirs.' He then went on, as a precaution, to itemise these goods: 'gold medals, chronometers and clocks, books, maps.' This was in March 1855, shortly after Caroline Seifert's wedding to Möllhausen; perhaps this event added urgency to Humboldt's intention to render the Seiferts' legacy as incontestable as possible.

Whether Caroline and Agnes were Humboldt's daughters or not may remain impossible to prove. But Humboldt did for sure treat the Seiferts as if they were his family, and referred to them as such. Again writing to Cotta, he described Seifert as 'living in my family.'[13] This was no isolated occurrence: to Möllhausen, he wrote of 'the family which I now think of, patriarchally, as my own'; in a letter of recommendation for Möllhausen, he not only stated that he took 'a lively and deep-rooted interest' in the young man's fate, but also that the latter was 'living in my family'; in another letter, to George Catlin, the American artist, he used the words 'ma famille' when referring to the Seiferts.[14] When he announced the impending marriage of Caroline Seifert and Möllhausen to Cotta, he introduced the communication as 'something from my innermost domestic life'—giving an indication of where he felt the centre of his life was. [15]

Looking beyond his death, Humboldt procured a post for Seifert as a castellan with the king, and for Möllhausen a position as custodian of the royal libraries. He also wrote to August von Hedemann, his niece Adelheid's widower, to request a burial place at Tegel for Seifert and his family.[16] When she was a very old woman, Caroline Seifert remembered how, as a child, she would perch on the ladder in Humboldt's study and read, while he went about his work. In the last weeks of Humboldt's life, it was Caroline who nursed him, and who was at his bedside when he died.[17] In her autograph book, he had written: 'think of me, when I'm gone, with love and cheerfulness.'[18]

Were Caroline and Agnes his daughters, or were they not? Was Humboldt gay, or straight, or both, or neither? Were Johann and Emilie Seifert his servants, or his family? Perhaps none of these questions is all that important. But what is relevant, surely, is that they are part of Humboldt's calm yet persistent refusal to submit to definitions. His natural inclination always tended towards the undefined, the unfinished, and the open. Refusing to commit to an established, predictable way of life meant, at the same time, to allow for the possibility of a different way of living—one that, perhaps, chafed less and felt truer to the person he was.

Alexander von Humboldt winks at us across two centuries, always keeping a bit of himself in reserve, refusing to live up to what might be expected of him by his society—and perhaps even by those who would come after him.

Acknowledgements

This book has taken an unfeasibly long period of time to write, and I have accrued a correspondingly huge number of debts of gratitude along the way.

In particular, I'd like to thank:

My parents, Hanna and Volker Meinhardt, for their unstinting and unquestioning support, always.

My daughters, Iona and Mary Imlah, to whom I'm grateful for more than I can say; in this case, though, for their patience and understanding.

Stig Abell and all at the *TLS*, in particular Catharine Morris, Jim Campbell and Rupert Shortt, for advice, support and encouragement whenever it was most needed.

Michael Dwyer and everybody at Hurst, as well as Jan-Erik Guerth at BlueBridge. Also, Hurst's two readers, for their insightful suggestions, as well as for saving me from embarrassing errors.

Maureen Allen, for kindness and generosity.

Jennie Erin Smith, for coming to South America with me, and for demonstrating what style and brilliance look like.

Hildegard Maier and the German choir, for nourishing my spirit with music, wine and cheese.

Those whose friendship, help and encouragement have accompanied me through long tracts of this seemingly interminable project: Vera Chalidze, Stephanie Homer, Janet Kroll, Friederike Lüpke, Julia and Ferdinand Mount, Nicola Penfold, Mandana Seyfeddinipur, Helen Simpson, Haf Stephens, Peter Stothard, Jane Wellesley, Mags Young and Meike Ziervogel.

Michael Rosen, for advice, and for happiness.

I wish I were able to thank Mick Imlah, whose presence lit up my life from when I first met him, in 1996, until 2009.

List of Illustrations

The young Humboldt, copper engraving by Charles Victor Normand (born 1814) after painting, 1795, by François Gérard (1770–1837), later colouring © akg-images.

The chateau at Tegel, coloured steel engraving by Johann Poppel, c. 1850, after L. Rohbock © akg-images.

The interior of the crater of Pico del Teide, Tenerife. Etching by P. Parboni after J. G. Gmelin after Alexander von Humboldt. © Wellcome Library, London.

Passionflower (Passiflora ligularis), collected by Humboldt and Bonpland in 1799, Herbarium of Paris (Herbier de Paris), Herbier Ancien, Laboratoire de Phanérogamie, Paris, Natural History Museum © akg-images.

Golden-backed uakari, Cacajao melanocephalus (Cacajao monkey, Simia melano-cephala), after a drawing by Alexander von Humboldt, handcoloured copperplate engraving from Edward Griffith's The Animal Kingdom by the Baron Cuvier, London, Whittaker, 1824 © Florilegius/Science & Society Picture Library.

Sketch of the Orinoco basin: Orinoco-Casiquiare-Amazon River-System, drawn by Humboldt in 1799. © Wellcome Library, London.

The rope bridge near Penipe, engraved by Bouquet of Paris, from *Vues des Cordillères, et monumens des peuples indigènes de l'Amerique*, Paris: Schoell, creation date 1810, Science Museum Library, Wroughton: Special Collections © Science Museum/ Science & Society Picture Library.

Inti-Guaicu, the 'Sun Rock', engraved by Dutterhoffer of Stuttgart, from *Vues des Cordillères*, Science Museum Library, Wroughton: Special Collections © Science Museum/Science & Society Picture Library.

A raft on the Guayas river, aquatint by Marchais/Bouquet after a sketch by Humboldt from his travel writing "*Vues des Cordillères*", Paris 1810–15 © akg-images.

The house Humboldt thought of as the highest habitation in the world, on the slopes of the Antisana. Author's photograph.

An engraving of Cotopaxi based on a drawing by Humboldt, aquatint by F. Arnold after G. Gmelin after A. von Humboldt © Wellcome Collection.

Cross section through South America based on the Chimborazo, engraving (1805) by Lorenz Adolf Schönberger and Pierre François Turpin after a drawing by Humboldt © akg-images.

'Evening lectures with King Frederick William IV of Prussia', with Alexander von Humboldt, Friedrich Karl von Savigny, Prince William (the future emperor), wood-cut, c. 1870, after a drawing by Rudolf Oppenheim, magazine illustration, Berlin, Sammlung Archiv für Kunst und Geschichte © akg-images.

Notes

INTRODUCTION

1. Letter from Thomas Jefferson to Charles Vidua, 6 August 1825, Founders Online, National Archives (archives.org).
2. Charles Darwin, *Life and Letters, Volume One*, London: John Murray, 1887, p. 336.
3. Edgar Allen Poe's poem is 'Eureka'; Byron refers to Humboldt in the fourth Canto of 'Don Juan'; and Goethe's reference is in *The Elective Affinities* (*Die Wahlverwandtschaften*; see my chapter 'Chemical Attractions' for details).
4. David Knight points out that Goethe, in a natural philosophy that was 'resonant with Romanticism,' was not looking for genealogy, but for an underlying unity in different life forms: 'Goethe was not seeking an explanation of how plants came to be the way they are, but an understanding.' 'Romanticism and the Sciences,' in Andrew Cunningham and Nicholas Jardine (eds), *Romanticism and the Sciences*, Cambridge: Cambridge University Press, 1990, p. 16.
5. Charles Darwin, *The Works of Charles Darwin, vol. 29*, Paul H. Barrett and R. B. Freeman (eds), New York: New York University Press, 1989, p. 133.
6. Humboldt's word is *Totaleindruck*, which I translate as 'total impression.' Alexander von Humboldt, *Ansichten der Natur*. Wilhelm Bölsche (ed.), Leipzig: Philip Reclam Junior, 1920, p. 223.
7. Alexander von Humboldt, *Aus meinem Leben: Autobiographische Bekenntnisse*, Kurt-R. Biermann (ed.), Jena: Urania, 1987, p. 39.
8. Johann Wolfgang von Goethe, *Die Wahlverwandtschaften*, Stuttgart: Reclam, 1956, pp. 183–4.

1. 'A CITIZEN OF THE WORLD'

1. Alexander von Humboldt, *Reise auf dem Río Magdalena, durch die Anden und Mexico, Part Two: Übersetzung, Anmerkungen, Register*, Margot Faak (ed. and trans.), Berlin: Akademie Verlag, 1990, p. 301.
2. Ibid.
3. Humboldt, *Río Magdalena II*, p. 302.
4. Ibid.
5. Letter to Jean Baptiste Joseph Delambre, 25 November 1804, in E. T. Hamy (ed.) *Lettres Américaines d'Alexandre de Humboldt*, Paris: Librairie Orientale et Américaine, 1904, p. 147; translation by Douglas Botting.
6. Humboldt to Jefferson, 24 May 1804, quoted in Helmut de Terra, 'Alexander von Humboldt's correspondence with Jefferson, Madison, and Gallatin,' in *Proceedings of the American Philosophical Society*, Vol. 103, No. 6, 15 Dec. 1959. I have made slight adjustments to the translation.
7. Humboldt, *Río Magdalena II*, p. 306.
8. From Margaret Bayard Smith's Commonplace Book, in the Manuscript Division of the Library of Congress, quoted by Hermann R. Friis, 'Baron Alexander von Humboldt's Visit to Washington, D. C., June 1 through June 13, 1804,' Records of the Columbia Historical Society, Washington, D.C., Vol. 60/62, 1960/1962, p. 22.
9. Friis p. 27.
10. From Katherine S. Anthony: Dolley Madison: Her Life and Times, Garden City, 1949, p. 148; quoted in Friis pp. 23–4.
11. Margaret Bayard Smith's husband, Samuel Harrison Smith, was the founder of Washington's most important newspaper, the *National Intelligencer*. Mrs. Smith is here quoted from a letter she wrote to Mary Ann Smith, dated 10 June 1804, in the Papers of Margaret Bayard Smith, vol. 8, folios 67147–67148, Mss. Div., LC., 3 pp. ALS, and reported in Friis.
12. From Margaret Bayard Smith's manuscript 'The President's House forty years ago,' in her Commonplace Book, pp. 15-16, among the Margaret Bayard Smith Papers in the Mss. Div., LC., quoted in Friis.

2. THE VIEW FROM TEGEL

1. While it is still not entirely certain whether Humboldt was born at Jägerstrasse 22 or in Tegel, the consensus now seems to tend towards Tegel; this is supported by Christine und

Ulrich von Heinz in their book *Wilhelm von Humboldt in Tegel: Ein Bildprogramm als Bildungsprogramm*, Munich and Berlin: Deutscher Kunstverlag, 2001, pp. 13 and 71.

2. Letter to Carl Freiesleben, 6 June 1792; in Alexander von Humboldt, *Die Jugendbriefe Alexander von Humboldts, 1787–1799*, Ilse Jahn and Fritz G. Lange (eds), Berlin: Akademie Verlag, 1973, pp. 191–2.

3. Anton Friedrich Büsching, quoted in Rudolf Borch (ed.), *Alexander von Humboldt: Sein Leben in Selbstzeugnissen, Briefen und Berichten*, Berlin: Verlag des Druckhauses Tempelhof, 1948, p. 12.

4. Ibid.

5. Alexander von Humboldt, *Aus meinem Leben: Autobiographische Bekenntnisse*, Kurt-R. Biermann (ed.), Jena: Urania, 1987, p. 38.

6. Quoted in Borch, *Alexander von Humboldt*, p. 23.

3. AN ENDLESS HORIZON

1. Alexander von Humboldt, *Cosmos: A Sketch of the Physical Description of the Universe*, vol. 2, E. C. Otté (trans.), London: Johns Hopkins University Press, 1997, p. 20.

2. Letter to Joachim Heinrich Campe, 27 Feb. 1781, in Rudolf Borch (ed.), *Alexander von Humboldt: Sein Leben in Selbstzeugnissen, Briefen und Berichten*, Berlin: Verlag des Druckhauses Tempelhof, 1948, p. 17.

3. Letter from Wilhelm von Humboldt to Caroline von Dacheröden, 22 May 1789, Anna Sydow (ed.), *Wilhelm und Caroline von Humboldt in ihren Briefen: Briefe aus der Brautzeit, 1787–1791*, Berlin: Mittler, 1918, p. 38.

4. Karl August Varnhagen von Ense, *Denkwürdigkeiten und Vermischte Schriften*, vol. 1, Mannheim: Heinrich Voss, 1837, p. 496.

5. Johann Wolfgang von Goethe, *Faust II*, Walpurgisnacht scene, the first line translated by me, the others following the translation by Juliet Sutherland et al

6. Nicolai suffered from a nervous complaint, under the influence of which he reported that he saw ghosts.

7. Alexander von Humboldt would later remark of Nicolai that he talked as though he owned the leasehold on common sense. See Alexander von Humboldt, *Die Jugendbriefe Alexander von Humboldts, 1787–1799*, Ilse Jahn and Fritz G. Lange (eds), Berlin: Akademie Verlag, 1973, p. 63.

8. Friedrich and Paul Goldschmidt, *Das Leben des Staatsrath Kunth*, Heidelberg: Springer, 1881, p. 17.

9. Quoted in Karl Bruhns, *Alexander von Humboldt, vol. 1* (Jane and Caroline Lassell trans.), London: Longmans, 1873, pp. 20–1.

10. Letter from Wilhelm von Humboldt to Caroline von Dacheröden, 6 June 1791, in Sydow (ed.), *Wilhelm und Caroline von Humboldt in ihren Briefen*, p. 479.

11. Borch (ed.), *Alexander von Humboldt*, p. 23.

12. The woman he married had previously been the third wife of the Romantic poet and dramatist Zacharias Werner.

13. Carl Freiesleben, in a talk given at Freiberg on 27 Dec. 1826, and printed in the magazine *Zeitgenossen, vol. 2*, Leipzig: Brockhaus, 1830, p. 66.

14. Hanno Beck, *Alexander von Humboldt, vol. 1: Von der Bildungsreise zur Forschungsreise*, Wiesbaden: Franz Steiner Verlag, 1959, p. 10.

15. Heim was later appointed Prussian 'Geheimrat' (privy councillor).

16. Borch (ed.), *Alexander von Humboldt*, p. 19.

17. In Alexander von Humboldt, *Aus meinem Leben: Autobiographische Bekenntnisse*, Kurt-R. Biermann (ed.), Jena: Urania, 1987, p. 32.

18. Ibid., p. 64.

19. Karl Bruhns, *Life of Alexander von Humboldt, vol. 1*, Jane and Caroline Lassell (trans.), London: Longmans, 1873, p. 45.

4. THE DISCOVERY OF WARMER CLIMES

1. Letter to Ephraim Beer, Nov. (no precise date) 1787, in Alexander von Humboldt, *Die Jugendbriefe Alexander von Humboldts, 1787–1799*, Ilse Jahn and Fritz G. Lange (eds), Berlin: Akademie Verlag, 1973, p. 4.

2. Letter to Ephraim Beer, 14 Oct. 1787, in ibid., p. 3.

3. J. Fürst (ed.), *Henriette Herz: Ihr Leben und ihre Erinnerungen*, Berlin: Wilhelm Hertz, 1850, p. 93.

4. See Alexander von Humboldt, *Briefe von Alexander von Humboldt an Varnhagen von Ense*, Leipzig: Brockhaus, 1860, p. 123.

5. Letter from Rahel Levin to David Veit, 2 Apr. 1793, in Barbara Hahn (ed.), *Rahel: Ein Buch des Andenkens, vol. 2*, Göttingen: Wallstein, 2012, pp. 23 and 25.
6. Fürst (ed.), *Henriette Herz*, p. 79.
7. Ibid., p. 91.
8. Letter to Henriette Herz, 4 Sept. 1788, in Humboldt, *Jugendbriefe*, pp. 25–6.
9. Henriette Herz refers to the *Menuet à la Reine*. See Hanno Beck, *Alexander von Humboldt, vol. 1: Von der Bildungsreise zur Forschungsreise*, Wiesbaden: Franz Steiner Verlag, 1959, p. 143.
10. In Rudolf Borch (ed.), *Alexander von Humboldt: Sein Leben in Selbstzeugnissen, Briefen und Berichten*, Berlin: Verlag des Druckhauses Tempelhof, 1948, p. 24.
11. Letter to Ephraim Beer, Nov. 1787 (no precise date), in Humboldt, *Jugendbriefe*, p. 4.
12. Letter from Wilhelm von Humboldt to Ephraim Beer, autumn of 1787 (not precisely dated), in Theodor Kappstein (ed.), *Wilhelm von Humboldt im Verkehr mit seinen Freunden: Eine Auslese seiner Briefe*, Berlin: Borngräber, 1917, p. 16.
13. Leopold Krug, *Betrachtungen über den Nationalreichtum des preussischen Staats*, Berlin: Unger, 1805, p. 6; my translation.
14. Letter to Ephraim Beer, Nov. 1787, Humboldt, *Jugendbriefe*, p. 4.
15. In Borch (ed.), *Alexander von Humboldt*, p. 28.
16. Letter to David Friedländer, 19 Dec. 1787, in Humboldt, *Jugendbriefe*, p. 6.
17. In Borch (ed.), *Alexander von Humboldt*, pp. 28–9.
18. Letter to Wilhelm Gabriel Wegener, 26 June 1788, Humboldt, *Jugendbriefe*, p. 17.
19. Letter to Wegener, 10 May 1788, ibid., p. 8.
20. Letter to Wegener, 23 Sep. 1790, ibid., p. 107.
21. Robert Mitchell discusses the Romantic fascination with plants in the chapter 'Cryptogams' in his book *Experimental Life: Vitalism in Romantic Science and Literature*, Baltimore: Johns Hopkins University Press, 2013; and even though he refers to plants in general, his argument applies particularly forcefully to cryptogams.
22. Alexander von Humboldt, *Aus meinem Leben: Autobiographische Bekenntnisse*, Kurt-R. Biermann (ed.), Jena: Urania, 1987, p. 34.
23. Ibid.
24. Letter to Wegener, 25 Feb. 1789, Humboldt, *Jugendbriefe*, p. 40.
25. Letter to Wegener, 10 May 1788, ibid., p. 8.
26. Letter to Wegener, 12 June 1788, ibid., pp. 10–11.
27. Alexander von Humboldt, *Cosmos: A Sketch of the Physical Description of the Universe, vol. 2*, E. C. Otté (trans.), London: Johns Hopkins University Press, 1997, p. 20, with 'Hodge' corrected to 'Hodges'; Warren Hastings and the painter William Hodges had met in Calcutta, when Hastings was governor-general of Bengal. The two became good friends.

5. 'FIRST STEP INTO THE WORLD'

1. Letter to Wilhelm Gabriel Wegener, 24 Feb. 1789, in Alexander von Humboldt, *Die Jugendbriefe Alexander von Humboldts, 1787–1799*, Ilse Jahn and Fritz G. Lange (eds), Berlin: Akademie Verlag, 1973, p. 40.
2. Letter to Wegener, 15 June 1790, ibid., p. 93.
3. Letter to Wegener, 24 Feb. 1789, ibid., p. 40.
4. Letter to Wegener, between 28 Apr. and 3 May 1789, ibid., p. 52.
5. Johann Wolfgang von Goethe, *Aus meinem Leben: Dichtung und Wahrheit, Book 13*, p. 111.
6. Goethe, in a letter to Duke Karl August, 13 Sep. 1826; in Bettina's letters to the admired poet, she styles herself as the 'child' of the heavily edited correspondence that she named *Goethes Briefwechsel mit einem Kinde* ('Goethe's correspondence with a child'), published 1835, when Goethe was safely dead.
7. Letter from Caroline von Dacheröden to Wilhelm von Humboldt, 9 Apr. 1789, Anna Sydow (ed.), *Wilhelm und Caroline von Humboldt in ihren Briefen: Briefe aus der Brautzeit, 1787–1791*, Berlin: Mittler, 1918, p. 33.
8. Letter to Wegener, 27 Mar. 1789, in Humboldt, *Jugendbriefe*, p. 48.
9. Roger Paulin, *The Life of August Wilhelm Schlegel: Cosmopolitan of Art and Literature*, London: Open Books, 2016, p. 182.
10. Letter to Wegener, between 28 Apr. and 3 May 1789, in Humboldt, *Jugendbriefe*, p. 53.
11. Ibid.
12. Ibid., p. 54.
13. Letter to Wegener, 27 Mar. 1789, ibid., p. 47.
14. Robert J. Richards, *The Romantic Conception of Life: Science and Philosophy in the Age of Goethe*, Chicago: University of Chicago Press, 2002, p. 218.
15. Ibid.

16. Letter to Wegener, 28 Apr. 1789, in Humboldt, *Jugendbriefe*, p. 55.
17. For a discussion of cameralism, and Beckmann's contribution, see Andre Wakefield, *The Disordered Police State: German Cameralism as Science and Practice*, Chicago: University of Chicago Press, 2009.
18. Letter to Wegener, 17 Aug. 1789, in Humboldt, *Jugendbriefe*, p. 70.
19. Heinrich Heine, *Die Harzreise*, Hamburg: Hoffmann und Campe, 1824, p. 8.
20. Letter to Wegener, 17 Aug. 1789, in Humboldt, *Jugendbriefe*, p. 68.
21. Sydow (ed.), *Briefe aus der Brautzeit*, p. 87.
22. Letter to Wegener, 17 Aug. 1789, in Humboldt, *Jugendbriefe*, p. 68.
23. This is related in the introduction, by Klaus Harpprecht, to the 2007 edition of Georg Forster's *Reise um die Welt*, Frankfurt: Eichborn Verlag, 2007, p. 21.
24. *A Voyage Round the World* was published first in English, in 1777, as *A Voyage Round the World in His Britannic Majesty's Sloop* Resolution, *Commanded by Capt. James Cook, during the Years, 1772, 3, 4, and 5*, so as to forestall the official account by James Cook. Forster provided his own translation for the German edition, published in 1778–80.
25. Humboldt, *Jugendbriefe*, p. 80.
26. Ibid., p. 83.
27. Ibid., p. 84.
28. James Hutton's *Theory of the Earth* had been published, in essay form, in 1788 (it would appear as a book, expanded and in two volumes, in 1795).
29. Some Neptunists claimed to have found fossils in basalt; Charles Lyell finally established the volcanic origin of basalt in his *Principles of Geology* (1830–3).
30. Letter to Joachim Heinrich Campe, 17 Mar. 1790, Humboldt, *Jugendbriefe*, pp. 88–9.
31. Humboldt, *Aus meinem Leben*, p. 39.
32. Humboldt, *Jugendbriefe*, p. 97.
33. Cited in Hanno Beck, *Alexander von Humboldt, vol. 1: Von der Bildungsreise zur Forschungsreise*, Wiesbaden: Franz Steiner Verlag, 1959, p. 26
34. Georg Forster, *Ansichten von Niederrhein: Von Brabant, Flandern, Holland, England und Frankreich, im April, Mai und Junius 1790* (first pub. 1791–4), Gerhard Steiner (ed.), Frankfurt: Insel, 1989, pp. 558–9. (*Ansichten von Niederrhein* was originally published in three parts. The first two parts appeared in 1790; the third part, which contains the notes on the English leg of the journey quoted here, was published after Forster's death by Ludwig Ferdinand Huber, by then married to Therese).
35. Letter to Friedrich Heinrich Jacobi, 3 Jan. 1791, in Humboldt, *Jugendbriefe*, p. 118.
36. Letter to Dietrich Karsten, 7 Sep. 1790, in Humboldt, *Jugendbriefe*, p. 103
37. Cited in Albert Leitzmann, *Georg und Therese Forster und die Brüder Humboldt*, Bonn: Röhrscheid, 1936, pp. 167–8; my translation.
38. Cited in Forster, *Ansichten vom Niederrhein*, p. 600.
39. Goethe's letter to Samuel Thomas von Sömmerring, 17 Feb. 1794, in Johann Wolfgang von Goethe, *Briefe 1792–1796*, Weimar: Böhlau, p. 141.
40. Alexander von Humboldt, *Kosmos: Entwurf einer physischen Weltbeschreibung, vol. 2*, Stuttgart: Cotta, 1847, p. 72; my translation.
41. Letter from Wilhelm to Caroline von Humboldt, 2 Apr. 1790, in Humboldt, *Jugendbriefe*, p. 90.
42. Humboldt, *Jugendbriefe*, p. 67.
43. Alexander von Humboldt, *Cosmos: A Sketch of the Physical Description of the Universe, vol. 2*, E. C. Otté (trans.), London: Johns Hopkins University Press, 1997, p. 80.
44. Alexander von Humboldt, *Aus meinem Leben: Autobiographische Bekenntnisse*, Kurt-R. Biermann (ed.), Jena: Urania, 1987, p. 34.
45. Letter to Wegener, 27 Mar. 1789, Humboldt, *Jugendbriefe*, p. 47.

6. HAMBURG, AN INTERLUDE

1. Alexander von Humboldt, *Aus meinem Leben: Autobiographische Bekenntnisse*, Kurt-R. Biermann (ed.), Jena: Urania, 1987, p. 39.
2. Letter to Abraham Gottlob Werner, 25 July 1790, in Alexander von Humboldt, *Die Jugendbriefe Alexander von Humboldts, 1787–1799*, Ilse Jahn and Fritz G. Lange (eds), Berlin: Akademie Verlag, 1973, p. 99.
3. Letter to Paul Christian Wattenbach, 18 Feb. 1792, ibid., p. 170.
4. Letter to Wilhelm Gabriel Wegener, 23 Sep. 1790, ibid., p. 107.
5. Ibid., p. 106.
6. Rudolf Borch (ed.), *Alexander von Humboldt: Sein Leben in Selbstzeugnissen, Briefen und Berichten*, Berlin: Verlag des Druckhauses Tempelhof, 1948, p. 64.

7. Letter to Friedrich Heinrich Jacobi, 3 Jan. 1791, Humboldt, *Jugendbriefe*, p. 118.
8. Letter to the anatomy professor Samuel Thomas von Sömmerring, 28 Jan. 1791, ibid., p. 122.
9. Letter to Archibald Maclean, 6 Nov. 1791, Humboldt, *Jugendbriefe*, p. 156.
10. Letter to Paul Usteri, 27 June 1790, ibid., p. 97.
11. Letter to Wegener, 23 Sep. 1790, ibid., pp. 106–7.
12. Letter to Sir Joseph Banks, 18 Sep. 1790, ibid., p. 111.
13. Reply from Banks, 17 Nov. 1790, ibid., p. 111.
14. Letter to Wegener, 23 Sep. 1790, ibid., p. 106.
15. Letters to Wattenbach, 18 Feb. 1792, and to Maclean, 6 Nov. 1791, ibid., p. 170 and p. 156.
16. Letter to Wattenbach, 7 May 1791, ibid., p. 136.
17. Letter to Paul Usteri, 22 Sep. 1791, ibid., p. 151.
18. Letter to Johann Albert Heinrich Reimarus, 1 June 1791, ibid., p. 140.
19. Letter to Friedrich Anton Freiherr von Heinitz, 14 May 1791, ibid., p. 137.
20. Reply from Heinitz, 31 May 1791, ibid., p. 138.
21. Wilhelm von Humboldt, *Briefe 1781 bis Juni 1791*, Berlin: De Gruyter, p. 406; the letter to Friedrich Wilhelm II was dated 19 May 1791.
22. Ibid., pp. 415–6.
23. Alexander had left early on 3 June 1791; Wilhelm writes to Caroline that he is writing in the evening of the same day. In Anna Sydow (ed.), *Wilhelm und Caroline von Humboldt in ihren Briefen: Briefe aus der Brautzeit, 1787–1791*, Berlin: Mittler, 1918, p. 477.
24. Borch, (ed.), *Alexander von Humboldt*, p. 74.
25. Letter from Wilhelm to Caroline, 26 June 1790, Sydow (ed.), *Wilhelm und Caroline von Humboldt in ihren Briefen*, p. 182. Naturally, Caroline protested, but unfortunately the excised part of the letter does not survive.
26. Letter to Jacobi, 5 April 1791, Humboldt, *Jugendbriefe*, p. 134.

7. THE COMPENSATIONS OF MINING

1. Letter to Carl Freiesleben, 14 June 1791, in Alexander von Humboldt, *Die Jugendbriefe Alexander von Humboldts, 1787–1799*, Ilse Jahn and Fritz G. Lange (eds), Berlin: Akademie Verlag, 1973, p. 141.
2. Humboldt, *Jugendbriefe*, p. 155, quoted in original English; in a later letter, of 6 Nov. 1791, he explained that the 'Obereinfahrer' was the second most important position, the 'Oberbergmeister' being the most important.
3. Letter to Archibald Maclean, 14 Oct. 1791, Humboldt, *Jugendbriefe*, p. 155.
4. In Heinrich Heine, *Die Harzreise*, Hamburg: Hoffmann und Campe, 1824, pp. 22–4; my translation. The mine Heine visited was not in Freiberg; it was the Carolina mine, near Clausthal in the Harz mountains, and, as he quipped, 'the dirtiest and most unpleasant Carolina I ever had the pleasure to meet.'
5. Letter to Johann Leopold Neumann, 23 June 1791, in Humboldt, *Jugendbriefe*, p. 155.
6. Anna Sydow (ed.), *Wilhelm und Caroline von Humboldt in ihren Briefen: Briefe aus der Brautzeit, 1787–1791*, Berlin: Mittler, 1918, p. 65.
7. Letter to Maclean, 14 Oct. 1791, Humboldt, *Jugendbriefe*, p. 153.
8. Letter to Dietrich Karsten, 25 Aug. 1791, ibid., p. 144.
9. Letter to Maclean, 6 Nov. 1791, ibid., p. 159.
10. Ibid., p. 158.
11. Ibid., p. 159.
12. Letter to Karsten, 25 Aug. 1791, ibid., pp. 144–5.
13. Letter to Maclean, 14 Oct. 1791, ibid., p. 154.
14. Del Río would move on to become Lavoisier's assistant. He later discovered element 23, vanadium, and went on to Mexico, where he met Humboldt again.
15. Letter to Karsten, 26 Nov. 1791, *Jugendbriefe*, p. 159; and letter to Paul Usteri, 10 Jan. 1791, Humboldt, *Jugendbriefe*, p. 165.
16. This is described in more detail in the letter to Paul Usteri of 10 Jan. 1791, in ibid., p. 165.
17. Extracts had been printed in the *Botanical Magazine* in Zurich in 1792; the full title of the book, published in 1793, was *Florae Fribergensis specimen plantas cryptogamicas praesertim subterraneas exhibens*.
18. Johann Peter Hebel, 'Unverhofftes Wiedersehen,' in *Schatzkästlein des rheinischen Hausfreundes*, 1811, pp. 292–4; E. T. A. Hoffmann, 'Die Bergwerke zu Falun,' in *Die Serapionsbrüder*, 1819, pp. 171–97; Friedrich Rückert, 'Die goldene Hochzeit'; Achim von Arnim: 'Des ersten Bergmann's ewige Jugend,' in *Armut, Reichtum, Schuld und Buße der Gräfin Dolores*, 1810. A more comprehensive discussion of the mining motif in German

Romanticism can be found in Theodore Ziolkowski, *German Romanticism and Its Institutions*, Princeton: Princeton University Press, 1990.

19. Schubert wrote about Falun in a book called *Aspects of the Nightside of the Natural Sciences* (1808). See Jeremy Adler, *Eine fast magische Anziehungskraft: Goethe's 'Wahlverwandtschaften' und die Chemie seiner Zeit*, Munich: Beck, 1987, pp. 196–7.
20. From Robert J. Richards, *The Romantic Conception of Life: Science and Philosophy in the Age of Goethe*, Chicago: University of Chicago Press, 2002. An oblique echo of some of these events is found in *Heinrich von Ofterdingen*.
21. Novalis, *Werke*, Gerhard Schulz (ed.), Munich: Beck, 2013, p. 7.
22. Humboldt, *Jugendbriefe*, p. 173, p. 180.

8. THE LIFE OF THE CIVIL SERVANT

1. Alexander von Humboldt, *Die Jugendbriefe Alexander von Humboldts, 1787–1799*, Ilse Jahn and Fritz G. Lange (eds), Berlin: Akademie Verlag, 1973, p. 267.
2. Hanno Beck, *Alexander von Humboldt, vol. 1: Von der Bildungsreise zur Forschungsreise*, Wiesbaden: Franz Steiner Verlag, 1959, p. 248.
3. Letter to Carl Freiesleben, 7 Mar. 1792, Humboldt, *Jugendbriefe*, p. 175.
4. Ibid.
5. Ibid.
6. Letter to Carl Freiesleben, 19 Mar. 1792, ibid., p. 179.
7. Ibid.
8. Ibid.
9. Their very names seeming to imply freedom, the first, freedom of the mountains, the latter, a life of freedom.
10. Letter to Freiesleben, 19 Mar. 1792, Humboldt, *Jugendbriefe*, p. 179.
11. Letter to Freiesleben, 11 May 1792, ibid., pp. 186–7.
12. Elizabeth Craven wrote a number of plays and several accounts of her travels.
13. Humboldt, *Jugendbriefe*, p. 201.
14. Caroline Wilhelmine Marie von Humboldt was born on 16 May 1792.
15. Letter to Freiesleben, 6 July 1792, Humboldt, *Jugendbriefe*, p. 202.
16. Letter to Freiesleben, 11 July 1792, ibid., pp. 203–4.
17. Letter to Freiesleben, 11 July 1792, ibid., p. 204.
18. Letter to the Royal Saline Department in Berlin, 28 Nov. 1793, ibid., p. 287.
19. Letter to Freiesleben, 11 July 1792, ibid., p. 204.
20. Letter to Freiesleben, 27 Aug. 1792, ibid., p. 209.
21. Ibid., p. 209.
22. Letter to Freiesleben, 2 Nov. 1792, ibid., p. 222.
23. Ibid., p. 222.
24. Ibid.
25. Letter to Archibald Maclean, 9 Feb. 1793, ibid., pp. 234–5.
26. Caroline had been 'guided towards "the German"' by Becker, writes Beck in his biography (*Alexander von Humboldt, vol. 1*, p. 30). Becker was the founding editor of a magazine, the *Deutsche Zeitung für die Jugend*, later, in 1796, renamed *Nationalzeitung für die Deutschen*.
27. The report had been given to Hardenberg already in Sep. 1792; it was only now that Humboldt received a copy from Hardenberg's office that he was able to pass on.
28. Letter from the Mining Department in Berlin, Humboldt, *Jugendbriefe*, p. 247.
29. Letter to Maclean, 9 Feb. 1793, ibid., p. 233.
30. Alexander von Humboldt, *Kosmos: Entwurf einer physischen Weltbeschreibung, vol. 2*, Stuttgart: Cotta, 1847; my translation; p. 458.
31. Letter to Freiesleben, 10 June 1793, Humboldt, *Jugendbriefe*, p. 251.
32. Letter to Freiesleben, 6 Sep. 1792, ibid., p. 212.
33. Letter to Freiesleben, 10 June 1793, Humboldt, *Jugendbriefe*, p. 251.
34. Letter to Karl August Graf von Hardenberg, 1 Dec. 1793, ibid., p. 289.
35. The 'Royal' was more by way of dedication than by authorisation.
36. Letter to Friedrich Wilhelm Graf von Reden, 17 Jan. 1794, Humboldt, *Jugendbriefe*, p. 309.
37. Letter to Freiesleben, 20 Jan. 1794, ibid., p. 312.
38. Humboldt's letter denying the request was dated 1 Oct. 1793. See Humboldt, *Jugendbriefe*, p. 276.
39. Letter to Freiesleben, 20 Jan. 1794, ibid., p. 310.
40. Ibid.
41. Letter to Freiesleben, 2 Apr. 1794, ibid., p. 335.

9. CHEMICAL ATTRACTIONS

1. The *Ansichten vom Niederrhein* that was published in Forster's lifetime ends before the Channel crossing; Forster's descriptions of England were published posthumously.
2. Goethe's account of that evening in Mainz dates from more than two decades later, from his *Campagne in Frankreich*, 1822. Cited in Klaus Harpprecht's introductory essay in Georg Forster, *Reise um die Welt* (first pub. 1778–80), Frankfurt: Eichborn, 2007, p. 32.
3. Mike Mitchell, introduction to his translation of Johann Wolfgang von Goethe, *The German Refugees* (first pub. 1795), Sawtry: Dedalus, 2006, p. 14.
4. Wilhelm and Caroline von Humboldt had moved to Jena in Feb. 1794, and Alexander came to visit them soon after. Goethe, though based in Weimar, visited Jena frequently, to oversee his duties at the botanical garden there, attached to the university.
5. Alexander von Humboldt: *Versuche über die gereizte Muskel- und Nervenfaser, vol. 1*, Berlin: Rottmann, 1797, p. 1.
6. See also the letter from Goethe to Humboldt, 18 June 1895, where he expresses his astonishment at what 'a mere breath' can do; Humboldt, *Jugendbriefe*, p. 435.
7. Humboldt, *Versuche über die gereizte Muskel- und Nervenfaser, vol. 1*, p. 3.
8. Rudolf Borch (ed.), *Alexander von Humboldt: Sein Leben in Selbstzeugnissen, Briefen und Berichten*, Berlin: Verlag des Druckhauses Tempelhof, 1948, p. 91.
9. Humboldt wrote to Markus Herz that 'Wilhelm is completely at home in the world of cadavers. He has bought a whole beggar-man for himself and (according to Goethe), all but lives on human brains.' Letter to Markus Herz, 15 June 1794, in Humboldt, *Jugendbriefe*, p. 433.
10. For a more detailed discussion, see Nicholas Boyle, *Goethe: The Poet and the Age, vol. 2: Revolution and Renunciation, 1790–1803*, Oxford: Clarendon Press, 2000; also Dennis L. Sepper, 'Goethe, colour and the science of seeing,' in Andrew Cunningham and Nicholas Jardine (eds), *Romanticism and the Sciences*, Cambridge: Cambridge University Press, pp. 189–98.
11. Johann Wolfgang von Goethe, *Elective Affinities* (David Constantine trans.), Oxford: Oxford University Press, 1994, p. 169. Goethe sent Humboldt a copy of the *Elective Affinities*, together with a letter, on 5 Oct. 1809; he made the point of calling to Humboldt's attention the scene where he is evoked by Ottilie: 'your name,' Goethe told him, 'is uttered by fair lips.' See *Das Allgemeine und das Einzelne: Johann Wolfgang von Goethe und Alexander von Humboldt im Gespräch*, Ilse Jahn and Andreas Klippert (eds), Halle: Acta Historica Leopoldina, no. 38, 2003, p. 17.
12. Jeremy Adler, *Eine fast magische Anziehungskraft: Goethe's 'Wahlverwandtschaften' und die Chemie seiner Zeit*, Munich: Beck, 1987, p. 23.
13. Johann Wolfgang von Goethe, *Die Wahlverwandtschaften*, Stuttgart: Reclam, 1956, pp. 183–4. The first part of the Ottilie quotation follows the translation by David Constantine; this second part is my translation.
14. Johann Wolfgang von Goethe, *Sämtliche Werke nach Epochen seines Schaffens, vol. 12*, Karl Richter et al (eds), Munich: Hanser, 1985–1998, p. 86.
15. Wilhelm's diary entry of 22 July 1794 notes that 'the Schillers and Goethe dined with us.' In Wilhelm von Humboldt, *Tagebücher, Vol. 1: 1788–1798*, Albert Leitzmann (ed.), Berlin: Behr's, 1916, p. 249.
16. Humboldt, *Jugendbriefe*, pp. 346–7.
17. 'The Life Force, or The Rhodian Genius,' Alexander von Humboldt, *Views of Nature*, translated by E. C. Otté and Henry G. Bohn, Chicago: University of Chicago Press, 2014.
18. For the idea that Humboldt influenced Goethe's *The Elective Affinities*, see also Dorothea Kuhn in Jahn and Klippert (eds), *Das Allgemeine und das Einzelne*, p. 17.
19. Bettina von Arnim, letter to Goethe, 9 Nov. 1809, in Bettina von Arnim, *Goethe's Briefwechsel mit einem Kinde, vol. 2*, Berlin: Dümmler, 1835, p. 136.
20. Goethe, *Elective Affinities*, p. 35.
21. Letter to Reinhard von Haeften, 19 Dec. 1794, Humboldt, *Jugendbriefe*, p. 388.

10. EXPOSED NERVES

1. Letter to Carl Freiesleben, 2 Apr. 1794, Alexander von Humboldt, *Die Jugendbriefe Alexander von Humboldts, 1787–1799*, Ilse Jahn and Fritz G. Lange (eds), Berlin: Akademie Verlag, 1973, p. 334.
2. Letter to Freiesleben, 21 Nov. 1794, ibid., pp. 378–9.
3. See Christian Suckow, *Der Oberbergrat privat: Freundschaften Alexander von Humboldt's in seinen fränkischen Jahren*, Pamphlet no. 6 of Berliner Manuskripte zur Alexander-von-Humboldt-Forschung, 2003.
4. Letter to Reinhard von Haeften, 19 Dec. 1794, Humboldt, *Jugendbriefe*, p. 388.

5. The results of these experiments were eventually published as *Versuch über die gereizte Muskel- und Nervenfaser* (1797). Humboldt had been experimenting on and off since 1792, carrying his equipment with him as he travelled between mines in Ansbach and Bayreuth.
6. Letter to the mathematician Johann Samuel Traugott Gehler, 18 Apr. 1795, Humboldt, *Jugendbriefe*, p. 418.
7. Alexander von Humboldt, *Versuche über die gereizte Muskel- und Nervenfaser, Volume One*, 1797, pp. 203–4.
8. Ibid., pp. 327–8.
9. Letter to Friedrich Anton Freiherr von Heinitz, 27 Feb. 1795, Humboldt, *Jugendbriefe*, p. 400.
10. Letter to Johann Wolfgang von Goethe, 16 July 1795, ibid., p. 449.
11. Letter to Freiesleben, 4 July 1795, ibid., p. 442.
12. Letter to Freiesleben, 5 Sep. 1796, ibid., p. 525.
13. Letter to Freiesleben, 14 July 1795, ibid., p. 444.
14. He described the experimental set-up in a letter to Johann Friedrich Blumenbach, 26 Aug. 1795, ibid., p. 454.
15. Letter to Freiesleben, 2 Sep. 1795, ibid., p. 456.
16. Saussure's *Voyages dans les Alpes* appeared in four volumes from 1779 to 1796.
17. In Hanno Beck, *Alexander von Humboldt, vol. 1: Von der Bildungsreise zur Forschungsreise*, Wiesbaden: Franz Steiner Verlag, 1959, p. 74.
18. Letter to Christiane von Waldenfels, soon to be von Haeften, no exact date but written towards the end of Oct. 1795, Humboldt, *Jugendbriefe*, p. 462. There are echoes here, too, of Friedrich Gottlieb Klopstock's ode 'Der Zürchersee,' where the poet proposes to build 'huts of friendship,' in which to live 'forever, forever!'
19. Letter to Freiesleben, 2 Dec. 1795, ibid., p. 473.
20. Letter to Freiesleben, 14 Dec. 1795, ibid., p. 475.
21. Letter to Blumenbach, 17 Nov. 1795, ibid., p. 471.
22. Letter to Haeften, written between 1 and 4 Jan. 1796; ibid., pp. 477–9.
23. Letter to Henriette Herz, 4 Apr. 1796, with a postscript dated May, ibid., pp. 501–2.

11. THE LOOSENING OF TIES
1. Letter to Carl Freiesleben, 15 Sep. 1796, Alexander von Humboldt, *Die Jugendbriefe Alexander von Humboldts, 1787–1799*, Ilse Jahn and Fritz G. Lange (eds), Berlin: Akademie Verlag, 1973, p. 525.
2. Letter to Freiesleben, 7 Apr. 1796, ibid., p. 503.
3. Letter to Freiesleben, 14 July 1795, ibid., p. 475.
4. Goethe recorded his famous remark about thirty years later, in *Kampagne in Frankreich*, 1792; he is unlikely to have uttered exactly those words.
5. Letter to Freiesleben, 2 Aug. 1796, Humboldt, *Jugendbriefe*, p. 520.
6. Letter to Freiesleben, 17 July 1796, ibid., p. 514.
7. Letter to Freiesleben, 2 Aug. 1796, ibid., p. 520.
8. Letter to Freiesleben, 22 Aug. 1796, ibid., p. 521.
9. Louis Desaix died less than four years later, after a glittering military career, when he was shot with a musket in the decisive moments of the Battle of Marengo.
10. Letter to Freiesleben, 2 Aug. 1796, Humboldt, *Jugendbriefe*, p. 521.
11. Letter to Freiesleben, 15 Sep. 1796, ibid., p. 525; also see p. 528.
12. Letter to Freiesleben, 2 Oct. 1796, ibid., p. 528.
13. Letter to Freiesleben, 21 Nov. 1794, ibid., p. 378.
14. Christian Friedrich Gödeking, 1770–1851, later director of the mint in Berlin.
15. Humboldt, *Jugendbriefe*, p. 540; the minister referred to is Heinitz.
16. Letter to Freiesleben, written after 14 Nov. 1796, ibid., p. 545.
17. Letter to Freiesleben, written before and on 25 Nov. 1796, ibid., p. 551.

12. GOETHE'S 'CARAVAN'
1. Bärbel Ruben, *Marie Elisabeth von Humboldt (1741–1796): Spurensuche in Falkenberg*, Berliner Manuskripte zur Alexander-von-Humboldt-Forschung, vol. 17, Berlin: Alexander-von-Humboldt-Forschungsstelle, 2008, p. 10.
2. Letter to Karl Ludwig Willdenow, 20 Dec. 1796, Alexander von Humboldt, *Die Jugendbriefe Alexander von Humboldts, 1787–1799*, Ilse Jahn and Fritz G. Lange (eds), Berlin: Akademie Verlag, 1973, p. 560.
3. Letter to Johann Wolfgang von Goethe, 4 May 1797, ibid., p. 577.
4. Letter to Carl Freiesleben, 18 Apr. 1797, ibid., p. 574.
5. Letter to Friedrich von Schuckmann, 14 May 1797, ibid., p. 579.

6. Letter from Goethe to Humboldt, 14 Mar. 1797, ibid., p. 573.
7. Letter from Goethe to Friedrich Schiller, 26 April 1797, in Rudolf Borch (ed.), *Alexander von Humboldt: Sein Leben in Selbstzeugnissen, Briefen und Berichten*, Berlin: Verlag des Druckhauses Tempelhof, 1948, p. 92.
8. *Versuche über die gereizte Muskel- und Nervenfaser* (*Experiments on stimulated muscle and nerve fibres*) was published, in two volumes, in 1797.
9. Borch (ed.), *Alexander von Humboldt*, p. 91.
10. Letter to Freiesleben, 18 Apr. 1797, Humboldt, *Jugendbriefe*, p. 574.
11. Borch (ed.), *Alexander von Humboldt*, p. 93.
12. Ibid., p. 94.
13. Friedrich Gustav Alexander von Haeften was born on 1 Jan. 1794; the Haeftens married on 10 Oct. 1795.
14. Letter to Freiesleben, 10 July 1797, Humboldt, *Jugendbriefe*, p. 587.
15. Douglas Botting, *Humboldt and the Cosmos*, London: Sphere, 1973, p. 51.
16. Humboldt, *Jugendbriefe*, p. 589.
17. Ibid., p. 590.
18. Letter to Freiesleben, 14 and 16 Oct. 1797, ibid., p. 593.
19. Borch (ed.), *Alexander von Humboldt*, p. 99.
20. Ibid., p. 100.
21. Letter to Freiesleben, 14 Oct. 1797, Humboldt, *Jugendbriefe*, p. 592.
22. Ibid., p. 593.
23. Letter to Freiesleben, 22 Apr. 1798, ibid., p. 629.
24. Ibid.
25. Letter to Christian Günther Graf von Bernstorff, 25 Feb. 1798, ibid., p. 612.
26. Letter to Christian von Loder, 1 Apr. 1798, ibid., p. 617.
27. Letter to Freiesleben, 22 Apr. 1798, ibid., p. 629.
28. Ibid.
29. Letter to Bernstorff, 25 Feb. 1798, ibid., p. 612
30. Letter to Willdenow, 20 Apr. 1789, ibid., p. 661.
31. Borch (ed.), *Alexander von Humboldt*, p. 103.
32. Alexander von Humboldt, *Reise in die Äquinoktial-Gegenden des Neuen Kontinents, vol. 1* (Ottmar Ette ed.), Frankfurt: Insel, 1999, p. 47.
33. Borch (ed.), *Alexander von Humboldt*, p. 103.
34. Ibid.
35. Ibid., p. 104.
36. Letter to Willdenow, 20 Apr. 1799, Humboldt, *Jugendbriefe*, p. 662.
37. Letter to Freiesleben, 4 June 1799, ibid., p. 680.

13. DEPARTURES

1. Alexander von Humboldt, *Reise in die Äquinoktial-Gegenden des Neuen Kontinents, vol. 1*, Ottmar Ette (ed.), Frankfurt: Insel, 1999, p. 48. The translations from the German are primarily my own; where Jason Wilson's translation seems preferable, I used his, either a whole paragraph, or single words or phrases (from: *Alexander von Humboldt: Personal Narrative of a Journey to the Equinoctial Regions of the New Continent*, abridged and translated by Jason Wilson, London: Penguin Classics, 1995).
2. Ibid.
3. Alexander von Humboldt, *Reise durch Venezuela: Auswahl aus den amerikanischen Reisetagebüchern*, Margaret Faak (ed.), Berlin: Akademie Verlag, 2000, p. 43. The translations from this book are my own.
4. Ibid. The baby was Theodor, whom he had helped look after in Jena.
5. Ibid., p. 44.
6. Humboldt, *Reise in die Äquinoktial-Gegenden*, p. 49.
7. Humboldt, *Reise durch Venezuela*, p. 45; the word *éboulloir* seems to have been used exclusively by Humboldt—he may be referring to a kettle, *bouilloire*.
8. Humboldt, *Reise in die Äquinoktial-Gegenden*, p. 49.
9. Ibid., p. 50.
10. Humboldt, *Reise durch Venezuela*, p. 49.
11. Ibid., p. 54.
12. Ibid.
13. Ragusa was a small republic in today's Croatia, which came to an end in 1808 after it was conquered by Napoleon.
14. Humboldt, *Reise durch Venezuela*, p. 55.

15. Ibid.
16. Ibid.
17. Ibid.
18. Letter to Wilhelm von Humboldt, after 25 Jan. 1799, in Alexander von Humboldt, *Die Jugendbriefe Alexander von Humboldts, 1787–1799*, Ilse Jahn and Fritz G. Lange (eds), Berlin: Akademie Verlag, 1973, pp. 647–8.
19. Ibid., p. 648.
20. Ibid.
21. Letter to Reinhard and Christiane von Haeften, 28 Feb. 1799, ibid., p. 649.
22. Karl August Varnhagen, in *Rahel: Ein Buch des Andenkens für ihre Freunde, vol. 6*, Barbara Hahn (ed.), Göttingen: Wallstein Verlag, 2011, pp. 344–5.
23. Humboldt, *Reise in die Äquinoktial-Gegenden*, p. 52.
24. Alexander von Humboldt, *Aus meinem Leben: Autobiographische Bekenntnisse*, Kurt-R. Biermann (ed.), Jena: Urania, 1987, p. 28.
25. Humboldt, *Reise in die Äquinoktial-Gegenden*, p. 52.
26. Ibid., pp. 53–4.
27. Ibid., p. 62.
28. Humboldt, *Reise durch Venezuela*, p. 58.

14. ACROSS THE ATLANTIC

1. Alexander von Humboldt, *Reise durch Venezuela: Auswahl aus den amerikanischen Reisetagebüchern*, Margaret Faak (ed.), Berlin: Akademie Verlag, 2000, p. 59.
2. Ibid., p. 60.
3. Alexander von Humboldt, *Reise in die Äquinoktial-Gegenden des Neuen Kontinents, vol. 1*, Ottmar Ette (ed.), Frankfurt: Insel, 1999, p. 66.
4. Humboldt, *Reise durch Venezuela*, p. 61.
5. Ibid., p. 65.
6. Humboldt, *Journey through Venezuela*, p. 67.
7. Humboldt, *Reise in die Äquinoktial-Gegenden*, p. 86.
8. Humboldt, *Reise in die Äquinoktial-Gegenden*, p. 91.
9. Ibid., pp. 76–7.
10. All these observations, save for the barrels of wine (where Humboldt uses a later source), are reported in Jacques-Henri Bernardin de Saint-Pierre's *Études de la nature*, 1784. (Bernardin de Saint-Pierre is also the author of *Paul and Virginia*.)
11. Humboldt, *Reise in die Äquinoktial-Gegenden*, p. 87. Lanzarote had been devastated by a volcanic eruption that lasted from September 1730 until 1736.
12. Ibid., p. 88.
13. 'Gunahani' is the name of the island of the 'New World' that was first spotted by Columbus.
14. Humboldt, *Journey through Venezuela*, p. 75.
15. Ibid.
16. Ibid., p. 81.
17. Humboldt, *Reise in die Äquinoktial-Gegenden*, p. 103.
18. Ibid., p. 108.
19. Ibid., p. 107.
20. Ibid., p. 114.
21. Ibid., p. 118.
22. Ibid., p. 119.
23. Ibid., p. 118.
24. Ibid., p. 119.
25. Ibid., p. 123.
26. Ibid., p. 132; *gofio* is still eaten in the Canaries, often stirred into coffee.
27. 'An Account of a Journey from the Port of Oratava in the Island of Tenerife to the Top of the Pike in That Island, in August Last; With Observations Thereon by Mr. J. Edens' (1 Jan. 1753), *Philosophical Transactions of the Royal Society, vol. 29*, pp. 317–325.
28. Humboldt, *Reise in die Äquinoktial-Gegenden*, p. 132.
29. Ibid., p. 133.
30. Humboldt estimates the height of the Pitón to be 'hardly 90 toises' (about 175 metres). The height difference between La Rambleta and the summit is 168 metres—Humboldt's estimate was not far out.
31. Humboldt, *Reise in die Äquinoktial-Gegenden*, p. 144.
32. Alexander von Humboldt, *Reise in die Äquinoktial-Gegenden des Neuen Kontinents, Vol. 1*, Ottmar Ette (ed.), Frankfurt: Insel, 1999, p. 146; my translation.

33. Humboldt refers to a detail in *Julie, or the New Heloise* later, when travelling in today's Venezuela. See my chapter 'Taking Rousseau to America' for details.
34. Humboldt, *Reise in die Äquinoktial-Gegenden*, p. 150.
35. Ibid., p. 151.
36. Jean-Jacques Rousseau, *Julie, or the New Heloise* (Philip Stewart and Jean Vaché trans.), Hanover, New Hampshire: Dartmouth College Press, 1997, p. 64.
37. Humboldt, *Reise in die Äquinoktial-Gegenden*, pp. 152–3.
38. Ibid., p. 155.
39. Ibid., p. 156.
40. Ibid.

15. DECISIONS AND TYPHOID FEVER

1. Letter to Wilhelm von Humboldt, 20 June 1799, in Rudolf Borch (ed.), *Alexander von Humboldt: Sein Leben in Selbstzeugnissen, Briefen und Berichten*, Berlin: Verlag des Druckhauses Tempelhof, 1948, p. 119.
2. Alexander von Humboldt, *Reise in die Äquinoktial-Gegenden des Neuen Kontinents, vol. 1*, Ottmar Ette (ed.), Frankfurt: Insel, 1999, p. 196.
3. Ibid., p. 198; *Paul and Virginia*, by Jacques-Henri Bernardin de Saint-Pierre, was first published in 1788, when Humboldt was nineteen years old; it shaped the way the Romantic generation viewed the tropics. Humboldt refers to it frequently.
4. Alexander von Humboldt, *Reise durch Venezuela: Auswahl aus den amerikanischen Reisetagebüchern*, Margaret Faak (ed.), Berlin: Akademie Verlag, 2000, p. 102; Fredrik Hasselqvist was a Swedish explorer, one of Linnaeus's flock of students.
5. Ibid., p. 104.
6. Ibid., p. 101.
7. Humboldt, *Reise in die Äquinoktial-Gegenden*, p. 195.
8. Ibid., p. 188.
9. Ibid., p. 201.
10. Humboldt, *Reise durch Venezuela*, p. 111.
11. Ibid., p. 110.
12. Ibid., p. 111.
13. Ibid.
14. Humboldt, *Reise in die Äquinoktial-Gegenden*, p. 207.
15. Ibid., p. 206.
16. Ibid., p. 208.
17. Ibid.
18. Humboldt, *Reise durch Venezuela*, p. 112.
19. Ibid., p. 113.
20. Humboldt, *Reise in die Äquinoktial-Gegenden*, p. 214.
21. Ibid., p. 216.
22. Ibid., p. 217.

16. A NEW WORLD

1. Alexander von Humboldt, *Reise in die Äquinoktial-Gegenden des Neuen Kontinents, vol. 1*, Ottmar Ette (ed.), Frankfurt: Insel, 1999, p. 463.
2. Letter to Wilhelm von Humboldt, 16 July 1799, Alexander von Humboldt, *Briefe aus Amerika, 1799–1804*, Ulrike Moheit (ed.), Berlin: Akademie Verlag, 1993, p. 42.
3. Ibid.
4. Humboldt, *Reise in die Äquinoktial-Gegenden*, p. 218.
5. Ibid., p. 219.
6. Ibid., p. 220.
7. Ibid., p. 221.
8. Ibid., p. 222.
9. Ibid., p. 226.
10. Ibid., p. 244.
11. Ibid., p. 241.
12. Ibid., p. 242.
13. Ibid., p. 249.
14. Ibid., p. 253. Humboldt's 'Tacunga' is today's Latacunga.
15. Humboldt cites here 'Jefferys's map published in 1794'—a mere five years earlier. However, Thomas Jefferys, the royal cartographer, died in 1771, so Humboldt most likely was referring to a map published in a collection after Jefferys's death.

16. Ibid., p. 256.
17. Ibid., p. 236.
18. Ibid., p. 260.
19. Ibid., p. 261.
20. Ibid., p. 265.
21. Ibid., p. 282.
22. Ibid., p. 283.

17. 'THE AMERICAN ALPS'

1. Rudolf Borch (ed.), *Alexander von Humboldt: Sein Leben in Selbstzeugnissen, Briefen und Berichten*, Berlin: Verlag des Druckhauses Tempelhof, 1948, p. 123.
2. An instrument used for measuring the inclination, or dip, of the magnetic field of the Earth.
3. Humboldt took more than forty scientific instruments with him—all of them the most sophisticated of their time. Even though they were as portable as was possible, together they still represented a staggering load to carry.
4. Alexander von Humboldt, *Reise in die Äquinoktial-Gegenden des Neuen Kontinents*, vol. 1, Ottmar Ette (ed.), Frankfurt: Insel, 1999, p. 294.
5. Ibid., p. 297.
6. Ibid., p. 302.
7. Ibid., pp. 304–5.
8. Alexander von Humboldt, *Reise durch Venezuela: Auswahl aus den amerikanischen Reisetagebüchern*, Margaret Faak (ed.), Berlin: Akademie Verlag, 2000, p. 139.
9. Humboldt, *Reise in die Äquinoktial-Gegenden*, p. 309.
10. Today, the village is called Arenal.
11. They did eventually encounter Lozano on their return to Cumaná.
12. Humboldt cites here the Jesuit historian Francisco Javier Clavijero and his work *Storia antica del Messico*, 1781.
13. Humboldt, *Reise in die Äquinoktial-Gegenden*, p. 313.
14. Ibid., p. 346.
15. Humboldt, *Reise durch Venezuela*, p. 155.
16. Humboldt, *Reise in die Äquinoktial-Gegenden*, p. 350.
17. Ibid.
18. Ibid., p. 351.
19. Humboldt, *Reise durch Venezuela*, p. 155.
20. Humboldt, *Reise in die Äquinoktial-Gegenden*, p. 352.
21. Ibid.
22. Ibid., p. 362.
23. Humboldt, *Reise durch Venezuela*, p. 156.
24. Ibid., p. 156.
25. On 24 June.
26. Humboldt, *Reise in die Äquinoktial-Gegenden*, p. 357.
27. Humboldt, *Reise durch Venezuela*, p. 156.
28. See also description of *Steatornis caripensis* in Humboldt, *Recueil d'observations de zoologie et d'anatomie comparée*, vol. 2, Paris: Smith & Gide, 1833.
29. Humboldt, *Reise in die Äquinoktial-Gegenden*, p. 363.
30. Ibid., p. 365.
31. Humboldt, *Reise durch Venezuela*, p. 158.
32. Humboldt, *Reise in die Äquinoktial-Gegenden*, p. 368.
33. Ibid., p. 369.
34. A type of Venezuelan howler monkey, of the genus *Alouatta*.
35. Humboldt, *Reise in die Äquinoktial-Gegenden*, p. 373.
36. Ibid., p. 375.
37. Ibid., p. 389.
38. Humboldt, *Reise durch Venezuela*, p. 166.
39. Humboldt, *Reise in die Äquinoktial-Gegenden*, p. 444; Humboldt's calling the attacker a 'Zambo' was not derogatory (unlike the English term 'Sambo,' which is a slur).
40. Ibid., p. 445.
41. Ibid., p. 448.

18. TAKING ROUSSEAU TO AMERICA

1. Alexander von Humboldt, *Reise in die Äquinoktial-Gegenden des Neuen Kontinents*, vol. 1, Ottmar Ette (ed.), Frankfurt: Insel, 1999, p. 462.

2. While there is nothing to contradict this claim, he insisted, in a similar vein, that he never got ill while in the tropics, even though he did on several occasions; ibid., p. 472.
3. Ibid., pp. 476 and 488.
4. Ibid., p. 535.
5. Humboldt, *Reise in die Äquinoktial-Gegenden*, pp. 630–2.
6. Ibid., p. 632.
7. Ibid., p. 633.
8. Ibid., p. 712.
9. Ibid., p. 714.
10. Ibid., p. 748.
11. Ibid., p. 753.

19. VERY FAR FROM PRUSSIA

1. What Humboldt called an 'electrometer' is really an electroscope. Two metal plates, when exposed to electricity, become charged and attract the globules.
2. Alexander von Humboldt, *Reise in die Äquinoktial-Gegenden des Neuen Kontinents, vol. 1*, Ottmar Ette (ed.), Frankfurt: Insel, 1999, p. 768.
3. Ibid., p. 774.
4. Alexander von Humboldt, *Reise durch Venezuela: Auswahl aus den amerikanischen Reisetagebüchern*, Margaret Faak (ed.), Berlin: Akademie Verlag, 2000, p. 239.
5. Ibid., p. 240.
6. Humboldt, *Reise in die Äquinoktialregionen, vol. 2*, p. 780; see also Alexander von Humboldt, *Views of Nature*, E. C. Otté and Henry G. Bohn (trans.), Chicago: University of Chicago Press, 2014, pp. 145–6.
7. Humboldt, *Reise durch Venezuela*, p. 243.
8. Humboldt, *Reise in die Äquinoktialregionen*, pp. 783–5.
9. Humboldt, *Reise durch Venezuela*, p. 243.
10. Humboldt, *Reise in die Äquinoktialregionen*, p. 785.
11. Humboldt, *Reise durch Venezuela*, p. 244; also, Humboldt, *Reise in die Äquinoktialregionen*, p. 786.
12. Humboldt, *Reise in die Äquinoktialregionen.*, p. 789.
13. Ibid., p. 790.
14. Ibid., p. 797.
15. Ibid., p. 804.
16. Ibid., p. 805.
17. Ibid., p. 806.
18. Ibid., p. 816. Garrick Mallery, in *Picture-Writing of the American Indians, vol. 1* (1972) refers to this rock as Tepumereme, a word signifying 'painted rocks' in the language of the nearest tribe.
19. Humboldt, *Reise in die Äquinoktialregionen*, p. 818.
20. Ibid., p. 825.
21. Ibid.
22. Ibid., p. 825.
23. Humboldt, *Reise durch Venezuela*, p. 258.
24. Humboldt, *Reise in die Äquinoktialregionen*, p. 831.
25. Ibid., p. 836.
26. Ibid.
27. Ibid., p. 837.
28. Ibid., p. 840.
29. Ibid., p. 840
30. Ibid., p. 870. There are faint echoes, in Humboldt's rejection of the idea of an interpreter, or mediator, of the pernicious role played in Goethe's *Elective Affinities* by Mittler, whose meddling becomes the instrument of catastrophe.
31. Ibid., p. 848.

20. ACROSS THE WATERSHED

1. Alexander von Humboldt, *Reise in die Äquinoktial-Gegenden des Neuen Kontinents, vol. 1*, Ottmar Ette (ed.), Frankfurt: Insel, 1999, p. 861.
2. Ibid., p. 856.
3. Humboldt explains that the terminology is misleading, with the label 'titi' used locally for monkeys of three different types. He clarifies that he is talking of a squirrel monkey (*Simia sciurea*), even though this is not strictly a titi monkey; ibid., p. 853.
4. Ibid.

5. Ibid.
6. Ibid., pp. 862–3.
7. Ibid., pp. 931, 935, 936.
8. Ibid., p. 892.
9. Ibid., p. 911.
10. Alexander von Humboldt, *Views of Nature*, E. C. Otté and Henry G. Bohn (trans.), Chicago: University of Chicago Press, 2014, p. 117.
11. Ibid., p. 126.
12. Humboldt, *Reise in die Äquinoktial-Gegenden*, p. 964.
13. Ibid.
14. Ibid., pp. 987–8.
15. Jean Paul was a frequent visitor of Henriette Herz's salon.
16. Humboldt, *Reise in die Äquinoktial-Gegenden*, p. 994.
17. Alexander von Humboldt, *Reise durch Venezuela: Auswahl aus den amerikanischen Reisetagebüchern*, Margaret Faak (ed.), Berlin: Akademie Verlag, 2000, p. 285.
18. After the Guaviare and the Atabapo join, the resulting river, for the length of about two miles before it flows into the Orinoco, is called Atabapo; in Humboldt's opinion, it was however the Atabapo that flowed into the Guaviare.
19. The Tuamini is not marked on modern maps, and may just be a stretch of the Temi. San Antonio de Javita, similarly, cannot be traced, but is probably today's Yavita.
20. Humboldt, *Reise in die Äquinoktial-Gegenden*, p. 1,166.
21. Ibid. About the Casiquiare exploration being the 'main purpose' of the journey, p. 1,055; about the watershed being 'imperceptible,' p. 1,078.
22. Ibid., p. 1,097.
23. Ibid., p. 1,026.
24. Ibid., p. 1,023.
25. Ibid., p. 1,099.
26. Ibid., p. 1,145.
27. Ibid., p. 1,140.
28. Ibid., p. 1,153.
29. Ibid., p. 1,173.
30. Ibid., p. 1,181.
31. Ibid., pp. 1,192–5.
32. Ibid., p. 1,187.
33. Humboldt, *Reise durch Venezuela*, pp. 337–8.
34. Humboldt, *Reise in die Äquinoktial-Gegenden*, p. 1,240.
35. Ibid., p. 1,245.
36. Ibid., p. 1,253.
37. Ibid., p. 1,255.
38. They met him again in Nueva Barcelona in July 1800; since he was planning to travel to Spain, he accompanied Humboldt and Bonpland as far as Cuba, and took a substantial part of their collections with him.
39. Ibid., p. 1,293.
40. Ibid., p. 1,294; p. 848.
41. Though it is more commonly known as *Angostura trifoliate*.
42. Humboldt, *Reise in die Äquinoktial-Gegenden*, p. 1,392.
43. Humboldt, *Reise durch Venezuela*, p. 391.
44. Letter to Karl Ludwig Willdenow from Havana, 21 Feb. 1801, in Alexander von Humboldt, *Briefe aus Amerika, 1799–1804*, Ulrike Moheit (ed.), Berlin: Akademie Verlag, 1993, p. 126.
45. Ibid., p. 128.
46. Johann Wolfgang von Goethe, *Die Wahlverwandtschaften*, Stuttgart: Reclam, 1956, pp. 183–4.

21. 'THE HIGHEST HABITATION IN THE WORLD'

1. Alexander von Humboldt, *Reise durch Venezuela: Auswahl aus den amerikanischen Reisetagebüchern*, Margaret Faak (ed.), Berlin: Akademie Verlag, 2000, pp. 393 and 391.
2. Alexander von Humboldt, *Reise auf dem Río Magdalena, durch die Anden und Mexico, Part One: Texte*, Margot Faak (ed. and trans.), Berlin: Akademie Verlag, 1986, p. 178.
3. Alexander von Humboldt, *Briefe aus Amerika, 1799–1804*, Ulrike Moheit (ed.), Berlin: Akademie Verlag, 1993, p. 137; the letter never reached Baudin.
4. Humboldt: *Río Magdalena I*, p. 79.
5. Ibid., p. 80.

6. Letter to Wilhelm von Humboldt, 21 Sep. 1801, Humboldt, *Briefe aus Amerika*, p. 147.
7. Humboldt, *Río Magdalena I*, p. 90.
8. Ibid.
9. Ibid., p. 93.
10. Alexander von Humboldt, *Reise auf dem Río Magdalena, durch die Anden und Mexico, Part Two: Übersetzung, Anmerkungen, Register*, Margot Faak (ed. and trans.), Berlin: Akademie Verlag, 1990, p. 38.
11. Ibid., p. 41.
12. Humboldt, *Río Magdalena I*, p. 133.
13. Humboldt, *Río Magdalena II*, pp. 50–1.
14. Letter to Wilhelm, 25 Nov. 1802, Humboldt, *Briefe aus Amerika*, p. 209.
15. Guadalupe Soasti Toscano, *El Commisionado Regio Carlos Montúfar y Larrea: Sedicioso, insurgente y rebelde*, Quito: Fonsal, 2009, p. 223.
16. Ibid., p. 27.
17. These claims are reported in Fernando Jurado, *Calles de Quito*, Quito: Banco Central del Ecuador, 1989.
18. Humboldt: *Río Magdalena II*, p. 55.
19. Chenxi Tang, discussing Humboldt's striving to gain a 'total impression,' points out that the overcoming of the division between subject and object is one of the aims of early Romantic philosophy. *The Geographic Imagination of Modernity*, Stanford: Stanford University Press, 2008, see esp. pp. 84 and 197.
20. Humboldt: *Río Magdalena II*, p. 57.
21. Ibid.
22. Ibid., p. 65.
23. Ibid., p. 61.
24. Ibid., p. 62.
25. Ibid., p. 64.
26. Ibid., p. 75.
27. Ibid., p. 81.
28. Ibid., p. 84.
29. Humboldt appears to consistently confuse the two summits of the Pichincha.
30. Humboldt, *Río Magdalena II*, p. 86.
31. Ibid., p. 87.
32. Ibid., p. 88.
33. Ibid.
34. Ibid.
35. Ibid., p. 90.
36. Ibid., p. 91.
37. Ibid., p. 111.
38. Ibid., p. 98.
39. They climbed the Pico del Teide on 21 June 1799.
40. Humboldt, *Rio Magdalena II*, p. 105.
41. Ibid., p. 106.
42. Ibid.
43. Ibid., p. 107
44. Ibid., p. 108
45. 'But unfortunately the Chimborazo is, of all the *nevados* that we visited, the one poorest in plant life [. . .] nothing but grasses [. . .] a feeble vegetation, not in keeping with the beauty of the colossus.' Ibid.
46. Oliver Lubrich and Ottmar Ette, in *Über einen Versuch den Gipfel des Chimborazo zu ersteigen*, Berlin: Eichborn, 2006, remark that the impression is not unlike '*Schneegestöber*,' a flurry of snow.
47. Humboldt published four volumes of *Cosmos* in his lifetime; the fifth one appeared posthumously and was compiled from his notes.
48. Alexander von Humboldt, 'Über zwei Versuche, den Chimborazo zu besteigen,' in Lubrich and Ette, *Über einen Versuch*, p. 132.
49. Ibid., p. 146.

22. 'I DON'T WANT TO END WITH A TRAGEDY'

1. Alexander von Humboldt, *Reise auf dem Río Magdalena, durch die Anden und Mexico, Part Two: Übersetzung, Anmerkungen, Register*, Margot Faak (ed. and trans.), Berlin: Akademie Verlag, 1990, p. 112.

2. Ibid., pp. 113–14.
3. Ibid., p. 116.
4. Ibid.
5. Ibid.
6. Ibid., p. 118.
7. Ibid., p. 119.
8. Ibid., p. 120.
9. Ibid., p. 120.
10. Ibid., p. 121.
11. Ibid.
12. Ibid., pp. 121–2.
13. Ibid., p. 126.
14. Ibid., pp. 131–2.
15. Ibid., p. 123.
16. Ibid., p. 134.
17. Ibid., p. 139.
18. Ibid., p. 146.
19. Ibid.
20. Ibid., p. 146.
21. Ibid., p. 159.
22. Ibid., p. 162.
23. Ibid., p. 164.
24. Ibid., p. 167.
25. Ibid., p. 174.
26. Ibid., p. 194.
27. Letter to Wilhelm von Humboldt, 25 Nov. 1802, Alexander von Humboldt, *Briefe aus Amerika, 1799–1804*, Ulrike Moheit (ed.), Berlin: Akademie Verlag, 1993, p. 213.
28. Letter to Karl Ludwig Willdenow, ibid., pp. 229–30.
29. Ibid., p. 230.
30. Thus argues Gerhard Casper in 'A Young Man from "ultima Thule" Visits Jefferson: Alexander von Humboldt in Philadelphia and Washington,' *Proceedings of the American Philosophical Society* Vol. 155, No. 3 (Sep. 2011), pp. 247–62.
31. From Peale's diaries; cited in Sandra Rebok, *Humboldt and Jefferson: A Transatlantic Friendship of the Enlightenment*, Charlottesville: University of Virginia Press, 2014, p. 23.

23. THE MIND MADE VISIBLE

1. Letters to Wilhelm von Humboldt (10 June 1804) and Carl Freiesleben (1 Aug. 1804), in Rudolf Borch (ed.), *Alexander von Humboldt: Sein Leben in Selbstzeugnissen, Briefen und Berichten*, Berlin: Verlag des Druckhauses Tempelhof, 1948, pp. 155, 157.
2. Letter from Wilhelm to Caroline von Humboldt, 22 Aug., 1804, in Anna Sydow (ed.), *Wilhelm und Caroline von Humboldt in ihren Briefen, vol. 2: Von der Vermählung bis zu Humboldts Scheiden aus Rom, 1791–1808*, Berlin: Mittler, 1907, p. 229.
3. Letter from Wilhelm to Caroline, 6 June 1804, and from Caroline to Wilhelm, 22 Aug., 1804; Wilhelm, it seems, wrote the suggested letter, and Caroline reported that Alexander 'made faces' when he read it (letter from Caroline to Wilhelm, 12 Sept. 1804). All in ibid., pp. 182, 226, 249.
4. Letter from Wilhelm to Caroline, 29 Aug. 1804, ibid., p. 232.
5. Letter from Caroline to Wilhelm, 28 Aug. 1804, ibid., p. 231.
6. Letter from Wilhelm to Caroline, 29 Aug. 1804, ibid., p. 232.
7. Letter from Caroline to Wilhelm, 3 Sep., ibid., p. 238.
8. Letter from Caroline to Wilhelm, 14 Oct. 1804, ibid., p. 264; for Humboldt's contribution, see Borch (ed.), *Alexander von Humboldt*, p. 163.
9. Letter from Caroline to Wilhelm, 4 Nov. 1804, ibid., p. 274; in a later letter dated 17 Dec. 1804, Caroline writes: 'I can't talk about Wilhelm and Louise to Alexander, he doesn't understand,' p. 287.
10. Letter from Alexander to Wilhelm, 14 Oct. 1804, ibid., p. 266.
11. Letter from Caroline to Wilhelm, 4 Nov. 1804, ibid., p. 274.
12. Alexander von Humboldt, *Alexander von Humboldt und Cotta: Briefwechsel*, Ulrike Leitner (ed.), Berlin: Akademie Verlag, 2009, p. 14; also letter from Humboldt to Cotta, 24 Jan. 1805, p. 64.
13. Borch (ed.), *Alexander von Humboldt*, p. 158.
14. Letter from Wilhelm to Caroline, 23 Jan. 1805, Sydow (ed.), *Von der Vermählung*, p. 296.

15. Letter to Goethe, 5 June 1805, in *Neue Mitteilungen aus Johann Wolfgang von Goethe's hand-schriflichen Nachlasse, dritter Teil: Goethe's Briefwechsel mit den Gebrüdern von Humboldt*, Leipzig: Brockhaus, 1876, p. 228.
16. Roger Paulin, *The Life of August Wilhelm Schlegel: Cosmopolitan of Art and Literature*, London: Open Books, 2016, pp. 253–4.
17. Petra Werner, *Übereinstimmung oder Gegensatz? Zum widersprüchlichen Verhältnis zwischen A. v. Humboldt and F. W. Schelling*, Berliner Manuskripte zur Alexander-von-Humboldt-Forschung, Heft 15, p. 6.
18. Robert J. Richards also points out that the very titles of Schelling's publications point to the incomplete and unfinished nature of his project—in Richard's words, 'indeed, a Romantic adventure.' In Robert J. Richards, *The Romantic Conception of Life: Science and Philosophy in the Age of Goethe*, Chicago: University of Chicago Press, 2002, p. 127.
19. Werner, *Übereinstimmung oder Gegensatz?* p. 6.
20. Ibid., p. 7.
21. Friedrich Schelling, *Ideen zu einer Philosophie der Natur als Einleitung in das Studium dieser Wissenschaft*, 1797; cited in Richards, *The Romantic Conception of Life*, p. 134.
22. Cited in John Tresch, *The Romantic Machine*, Chicago: University of Chicago Press, 2012, p. 30.
23. Letter from Humboldt to Schelling, 10 February 1806, quoted in Werner, *Übereinstimmung oder Gegensatz?* p. 7.
24. Letter from K. J. H. Windischmann to Schelling, 24 Mar. 1806, ibid., p. 8.
25. Borch (ed.), *Alexander von Humboldt*, p. 170.
26. Ibid., p. 171.
27. Ibid., p. 172.
28. Letter from Rahel Varnhagen to Regina Frohberg, 21 Nov. 1806, Barbara Hahn (ed.), *Rahel: Ein Buch des Andenkens, vol. 1*, Göttingen: Wallstein, 2012, p. 469.
29. Hahn, *Rahel, vol. 1*, p. 500.
30. Ibid., p. 495.
31. Letter to Cotta, 14 Feb. 1806, in *Alexander von Humboldt und Cotta: Briefwechsel*, p. 78.
32. Letter to Karoline von Wohlzogen, 14 May 1806, in Borch (ed.), *Alexander von Humboldt*, p. 176.
33. Alexander von Humboldt, *Views of Nature*, E. C. Otté and Henry G. Bohn (trans.), Chicago: University of Chicago Press, 2014, p. 25.
34. Ibid.
35. Letter to Bonpland, 7 Sep. 1810, Borch (ed.), *Alexander von Humboldt*, p. 202.
36. Letter from Caroline to Wilhelm, 12 Apr. 1809, Anna Sydow (ed.), *Wilhelm und Caroline von Humboldt in ihren Briefen, vol. 3: Weltbürgertum und preußischer Staatsdienst, 1808–1810*, Berlin: Mittler, 1909, p. 131.

24. A DIFFERENT LIFE
1. Rudolf Borch (ed.), *Alexander von Humboldt: Sein Leben in Selbstzeugnissen, Briefen und Berichten*, Berlin: Verlag des Druckhauses Tempelhof, 1948, pp. 212–14.
2. Ibid., p. 207.
3. Letter to Johann Wolfgang von Goethe, 3 Jan. 1810, ibid., p. 197.
4. Letter to Caroline von Humboldt, 24 Aug. 1813, Alexander and Wilhelm von Humboldt, *Briefe Alexander's von Humboldt an seinen Bruder Wilhelm*, Humboldt family (eds), Stuttgart: Cotta, 1880, p. 221.
5. Letters to Caroline, 1 Nov. and 3 Dec. 1817, Anna Sydow (ed.), *Wilhelm und Caroline von Humboldt in ihren Briefen, vol. 6: Im Kampf mit Hardenberg, 1817–1819*, Berlin: Mittler, 1913, pp. 30, 31, 42 and 64.
6. Borch (ed.), *Alexander von Humboldt*, p. 228.
7. Schlegel's interest, it has been pointed out, was Romantic in nature: to go back in time and find the common origins of mythology, language, and nature. Schlegel himself owned two small decorative bronze elephants, of which he was proud. See Roger Paulin, *The Life of August Wilhelm Schlegel: Cosmopolitan of Art and Literature*, London: Open Books, 2016, p. 494.
8. Stephen Bell, *A Life in Shadow: Aimé Bonpland in Southern South America, 1817–1858*, Stanford: Stanford University Press, 2010, p. 23. For a comprehensive account of Bonpland's later life, the reader may wish to turn to Bell's *A Life in Shadow*. Much of the information on Bonpland in this chapter is taken from this book.
9. Letter to Wilhelm von Humboldt, 17 Oct. 1822, quoted in Hanno Beck, *Alexander von Humboldt, vol. 2: Vom Reisewerk zum 'Kosmos'*, Wiesbaden: Franz Steiner Verlag, 1961, p. 60.

10. Letter from Caroline to Wilhelm von Humboldt, 12 Sept. 1824, in Anna Sydow (ed.), *Wilhelm und Caroline von Humboldt in ihren Briefen, vol, 7: Reife Seelen, 1820–1835*, Berlin: Mittler, 1916, p. 222.

11. The letter the king supposedly wrote to Humboldt was first cited by Karl Bruhns, who cautions that it has never been substantiated. Karl Bruhns, *Life of Alexander von Humboldt, Vol. 2*, Jane and Caroline Lassell (trans.), London: Longmans, 1873, pp. 94–5.

12. Cited in Hanno Beck, *Alexander von Humboldt, vol. 2: Vom Reisewerk zum 'Kosmos'*, Wiesbaden: Franz Steiner Verlag, 1961, p. 77.

13. George Canning, when British foreign secretary, had supported the Spanish colonies towards independence.

14. Schlegel had preceded Humboldt in using the Singakademie, for his own course of lectures.

15. Borch, ed., *Alexander von Humboldt*, p. 241.

16. Ibid., p. 242.

17. Ibid., p. 246.

18. Letter to Christiane von Vernejoul, Haeften's widow, 28 Mar. 1829, ibid., p. 260.

19. Letter to Wilhelm, 9/21 June 1829, ibid., p. 268.

20. Letter to Wilhelm, 28 Nov. 1829, ibid., p. 279.

21. Letter to Wilhelm, 9/21 June 1829, ibid., p. 269.

22. Letter to Karl August Varnhagen von Ense, 3 Feb. 1833, Alexander von Humboldt, *Briefe von Alexander von Humboldt an Varnhagen von Ense aus den Jahren 1827 bis 1858*, Leipzig: Brockhaus, 1860, p. 13; Wilhelm von Humboldt had declined the invitation, citing his work on a book on Sanskrit and related languages.

23. Borch (ed.), *Alexander von Humboldt*, p. 292.

24. Ibid., p. 299.

25. Alexander von Humboldt, *Cosmos: A Sketch of the Physical Description of the Universe, vol. 1*, E. C. Otté (trans.), London: Johns Hopkins University Press, 1997, p. 7.

26. Ibid., p. 10.

27. Borch (ed.), *Alexander von Humboldt*, p. 299ff.

28. Letter to Varnhagen, 10 May 1837 and 15 Aug, 1853, Humboldt, *Briefe an Varnhagen*, pp. 39 and 270.

29. Letter to Varnhagen, 27 March 1847, Humboldt, *Briefe an Varnhagen*, p. 236.

30. Borch (ed.), *Alexander von Humboldt*, p. 316.

31. Letter to Varnhagen, 3 Dec. 1841, Humboldt, *Briefe an Varnhagen*, p. 102.

32. Letter to Varnhagen, 24 June 1842, ibid., p. 124.

33. Letter to Varnhagen, 22 Apr. 1841, ibid., p. 87.

34. Letter to Varnhagen, 24 June 1842, ibid., p. 120.

35. Borch (ed.), *Alexander von Humboldt*, p. 373.

36. Borch (ed.), *Alexander von Humboldt*, p. 315.

37. Kurt Biermann has uncovered a further meaning behind Humboldt's allusion to his time in the Andes. While he signed himself 'Old Man of the Hills' from at least 1854, it was in 1857 that he was attacked as a 'soul assassin' for his lack of reference to divine agency in *Cosmos*. Originally published in the 'Mitteilungen,' *AvH-Magazin*, no. 60, December 1992, pp. 71–3, 2008.

38. Letter to Varnhagen, 13 Sep. 1844, Humboldt, *Briefe an Varnhagen*, p. 169.

39. Volume Three was published in 1851, even though, in the book, the year of publication appears as 1850; see Borch (ed.), *Alexander von Humboldt*, p. 352.

40. The writer Friedrich Althaus, quoted in Borch, p. 355; letter to Cotta, 7 June 1853, Humboldt, *Alexander von Humboldt und Cotta: Briefwechsel*, p. 500.

41. Borch, p. 350.

42. Borch, p. 352; Letter to Varnhagen, 23 Mar. 1852, Humboldt, *Briefe an Varnhagen*. p. 263.

43. Reported by Prince Kraft zu Hohenlohe-Ingelfingen, and quoted in Borch, p. 369.

44. Ibid., pp. 355–6.

45. Letter to Varnhagen, 21 Nov. 1856, Humboldt, *Briefe an Varnhagen*, p. 332.

46. Letter to Varnhagen, 17 Dec. 1856, ibid., p. 344.

47. Letter to Ludmilla Assing (Varnhagen's niece), 12 Oct. 1858, ibid., p. 400.

48. Borch (ed.), *Alexander von Humboldt*, p. 382.

49. Note by Varnhagen from his diaries, 24 Apr. 1858, reproduced in Humboldt, *Briefe an Varnhagen*, p. 394.

25. 'LOVE AND CHEERFULNESS'

1. This was not a typical arrangement. By contrast, Wilhelm von Humboldt's servant at Tegel was housed in very basic accommodation, away from the main household; see Hanno Beck,

Alexander von Humboldt, vol. 2: Vom Reisewerk zum 'Kosmos', Wiesbaden: Franz Steiner Verlag, 1961, p. 192.

2. All existing evidence was comprehensively and authoritatively compiled by Andreas Graf in his biography of Balduin Möllhausen, *Der Tod der Wölfe*, Berlin: Duncker and Humblot, 1991. A further source is Friedrich Schegk's chapter 'Alexander von Humboldt und die Seinen,' in Schegk (ed.), *Lexikon der Reise- und Abenteuerliteratur*, Meitingen: Corian, 1995. Rumours, Hanno Beck reports, existed as early as 1859, and were openly mooted in Mario Krammer's biography *Alexander von Humboldt* (1954). Beck himself states that 'it is probable that Humboldt, when he favoured Seifert in his will so conspicuously and unilaterally, wanted to provide financial security for a child, or children, of his own,' but confines his discussion to a lengthy endnote (Beck, *Alexander von Humboldt, vol. 2*, p. 328, footnote 205). Humboldt's paternity of Caroline Möllhausen is assumed to be highly probable in the entry on Möllhausen by Fabian Lampert in *Killy Literaturlexikon, Volume 8 (Marq–Or)*, Berlin: De Gruyter, 2010, p. 274. There have been dissenting views, of course. Kurt-R. Biermann thinks that Humboldt, who would have been over sixty years old, fathering children is 'unlikely in the highest degree' (cited in Schegk, 'Alexander von Humboldt und die Seinen,' p. 6).

3. See Beck, *Alexander von Humboldt, vol. 2*, p. 328.

4. The letter, to pastor Orth, from 28 July 1927, is cited in Graf, *Der Tod der Wölfe*, p. 114. Unfortunately, the power of the letter as a piece of evidence is somewhat weakened by the fact that only an excerpt of it is extant, which Graf however asserts that he has seen.

5. Friedrich Schegk, who visited Gerd Möllhausen on numerous occasions, records (in 'Alexander von Humboldt und die Seinen') that a signet ring, a clock in the shape of a bronze bell, and a tapestry are still in the possession of the family; Graf also documents the tapestry as well as a silver service and a christening spoon; Stefan Pfafferodt, a grandson of Gerd Möllhausen, confirmed the existence of the christening spoon to the author.

6. Letter to J. G. Cotta, 31 Oct. 1852, Alexander von Humboldt, *Alexander von Humboldt und Cotta: Briefwechsel*, Ulrike Leitner (ed.), Berlin: Akademie Verlag, 2009, p. 487.

7. Letter to Karl August Varnhagen von Ense, Alexander von Humboldt, *Briefe von Alexander von Humboldt an Varnhagen von Ense aus den Jahren 1827 bis 1858*, Leipzig: Brockhaus, 1860, p. 312.

8. Balduin Möllhausen Jr., 'Erinnerungen einer alten Berlinerin an Alexander von Humboldt,' Berlin: *Vossische Zeitung*, 18 Nov. 1920, morning edition, p. 2; my translation. Möllhausen Jr., the grandson of Balduin Möllhausen, here writes about his grandmother's (Caroline Möllhausen) relationship to Humboldt, on the occasion of Caroline Möllhausen's ninetieth birthday.

9. Letter to Cotta, 13 May 1841, Humboldt, *Alexander von Humboldt und Cotta*, p. 241.

10. This was done on 20 September 1853. Karl Bruhns, *Life of Alexander von Humboldt, vol. 2*, Jane and Caroline Lassell (trans.), London: Longmans, 1873, p. 405.

11. Letter to King Friedrich Wilhelm IV, 25 Sept. 1853, ibid., p. 404. The petition was drawn up in 1853, but apparently not sent until 1857, after Humboldt had suffered a mild stroke, which is likely to have brought a new urgency to the matter.

12. Humboldt was right about this. Gabriele von Bülow, Wilhelm's daughter, certainly felt that her own family had been slighted, and was quick to blame Seifert for Humboldt's decision, clearly incomprehensible to her. In a letter to her children just after Humboldt's death (12 May 1859), she wrote 'And with all of this there is Seifert's unworthiness, which makes the incredible decisions by the poor, good uncle so very humiliating and hurtful. [. . .] So then we had to listen to the deed of gift being read out, which the uncle really did make to him [. . .] regrettably, it is clear enough that we—the brothers and I—are the heirs, but that Seifert, through the deed of gift, will get everything.' In Anna von Sydow (ed.), *Gabriele von Bülow: Tochter Wilhelm von Humboldts*, Berlin, 1919, p. 531.

13. Letter to Cotta, 15 March 1841, Humboldt, *Alexander von Humboldt und Cotta*, p. 238.

14. All quoted in Graf, *Der Tod der Wölfe*, p. 236.

15. Letter to Cotta, 31 Dec. 1854, in Humboldt, *Alexander von Humboldt und Cotta*, p. 556.

16. Bruhns, *Life of Alexander von Humboldt, vol. 2*, p. 407; also Beck, *Alexander von Humboldt, vol. 2*, p. 327.

17. Both claims are from the 'Erinnerungen einer alten Berlinerin.' The latter contradicts the official version, adhered to in most biographies of Humboldt, according to which it was Wilhelm's daughter Gabriele von Bülow who fulfilled this role.

18. Preston Albert Barba, *Balduin Möllhausen, the German Cooper*, Philadelphia: University of Pennsylvania, 1914, p. 51.

Index